Transforming Scholarship

"Direct, clear, and compelling, this volume could not be more articulate in exploding every myth associated with this transformative field. This volume is a must for an introductory women's studies course through to a capstone for WS majors; it both orients those new to the field, and provides excellent concrete advice for how to move from the college campus into the world."

—Judith A. Howard, Sociology, University of Washington and Editor Emerita for *SIGNS: Journal of Women in Culture and Society*

"*Transforming Scholarship* will help students to think through the history and significance of the field of women's and gender studies, guide them in answering challenging questions about themselves and their major or minor, and provide support and information about the job search and the ways they want to change the world. Rest assured that all women's and gender studies majors at my school will be given a copy of this text."

—Alison Piepmeier, Women's and Gender Studies, The College of Charleston

"'What can you do with a major in women's studies?' How many times have I heard that question from students and parents! Thank goodness Michele Berger and Cheryl Radeloff have given us a thoroughly researched, accessible answer to that question. I'd highly recommend this book as required reading for first-year college students or as a great graduation gift for high school seniors interested in gender issues."

—Susan M. Shaw, Women's Studies, Oregon State University

"If you have ever wondered what someone can do with a women's and gender studies degree, *Transforming Scholarship* is the book for you. Michele Berger and Cheryl Radeloff have assembled an invaluable resource for both teachers and students that provides practical and theoretical insights into this evolving and dynamic field."

—Anne Lacsamana, Women's Studies, Hamilton College

Intended for use in an introductory course on the subject, or as a practical guide for curious students, this book—with data and inspiration—firmly answers the important question, "What can I do with my interest in women's and gender studies?" This innovative book draws its answers from the largest global database of women's and gender studies graduates ever assembled, and its chapters are filled with impressive empirical data as to how and why these programs are growing rapidly worldwide, and why their students find meaningful employment.

Michele Tracy Berger is associate professor in the Department of Women's Studies at the University of North Carolina–Chapel Hill. She holds adjunct appointments in the Department of Political Science and the Department of City and Regional Planning.

Cheryl Radeloff is a Disease Investigation and Intervention Specialist II with the Southern Nevada Health District. She is also an adjunct professor of Women's Studies at the College of Southern Nevada.

Contemporary Sociological Perspectives

Edited by **Valerie Jenness**, University of California, Irvine, and **Jodi O'Brien**, Seattle University

This innovative series is for all readers interested in books that provide frameworks for making sense of the complexities of contemporary social life. Each of the books in this series uses a sociological lens to provide current critical and analytical perspectives on significant social issues, patterns, and trends. The series consists of books that integrate the best ideas in sociological thought with an aim toward public education and engagement. These books are designed for use in the classroom, as well as for scholars and socially curious general readers.

Books in the Series

Published:

Political Justice and Religious Values by Charles F. Andrain

GIS and Spatial Analysis for the Social Sciences by Robert Nash Parker and Emily K. Asencio

Hoop Dreams on Wheels: Disability and the Competitive Wheelchair Athlete by Ronald J. Berger

The Internet and Social Inequalities by James C. Witte and Susan E. Mannon

Media and Middle Class Mom: Images and Realities of Work and Family by Lara Descartes and Conrad Kottak

Watching T.V. Is Not Required: Thinking about Media and Thinking about Thinking by Bernard McGrane and John Gunderson

Violence Against Women: Vulnerable Populations by Douglas Brownridge

State of Sex: Tourism, Sex and Sin in the New American Heartland by Barbara G. Brents, Crystal A. Jackson, and Kate Hausbeck

Social Statistics: The Basics and Beyond by Thomas J. Linneman

Sociologists Backstage: Answers to 10 Questions About What They Do by Sarah Fenstermaker and Nikki Jones

Gender Circuits by Eve Shapiro

Stargazing: Celebrity, Fame, and Social Interaction by Kerry O. Ferris and Scott R. Harris

Forthcoming:

Surviving Dictatorship: Visual and Social Representations by Jacqueline Adams

Social Theory: Classical and Contemporary Perspectives by Wesley Longhofer

Sociology Looks at the Arts by Julia Rothenberg

The Womanist Idea by Layli Phillips Maparyan

Transforming Scholarship

Why Women's and Gender Studies Students are Changing Themselves and the World

Michele Tracy Berger
University of North Carolina, Chapel Hill

Cheryl Radeloff
College of Southern Nevada

Routledge
Taylor & Francis Group

NEW YORK AND LONDON

First published 2011
by Routledge
711 Third Ave, New York, NY 10017

Simultaneously published in the UK
by Routledge
2 Park Square, Milton Park, Abingdon, Oxon OX14 4RN

Routledge is an imprint of the Taylor & Francis Group, an informa business

© 2011 Taylor & Francis

Typeset in Adobe Caslon, Trade Gothic, and Copperplate Gothic
by Florence Production Ltd, Stoodleigh, Devon
Printed and bound in the United States of America on acid-free paper
by Walsworth Publishing Company, Marceline, MO

Library of Congress Cataloging in Publication Data
Berger, Michele Tracy, 1968–
    Transforming scholarship: why women's and gender studies students
are changing themselves and the world/Michele Tracey Berger,
Cheryl Radeloff.
        p. cm.—(Contemporary sociological perspectives)
    1. Women's studies—United States.   2. Feminism—United States.
3. Women college graduates—United States.   4. Vocational
guidance—United States.   I. Radeloff, Cheryl.   II. Title.
    HQ1181.U5B47 2011
    305.4023—dc22   201003632

ISBN13: 978-0-415-87327-7 (hbk)
ISBN13: 978-0-415-87328-4 (pbk)
ISBN13: 978-0-203-82996-7 (ebk)

TABLE OF CONTENTS

DETAILED TABLE OF CONTENTS

solving, and worldview. That intellectual tradition, as with others, has produced a distinct set of ideas and concepts that students learn through coursework and other learning experiences.

Chapter 2: Claiming Your Education

How is women's and gender studies curricula organized at the undergraduate level in the US and globally? What classes would a student expect to take if he or she were interested in women's and gender studies? What does it mean to major, minor, or concentrate in women's and gender studies? This chapter provides those answers. This chapter explores the basic curricular elements students might encounter in their major, minor, or concentration in women's and gender studies. We cover a variety of types of curricula so that students at different types of institutions can evaluate and make choices about the kinds of training they might receive.

SECTION TWO: YOU'VE COMMITTED TO LEARNING IN WOMEN'S AND GENDER STUDIES: GREAT! NOW WHAT?

Chapter 3: How *You* Can Talk About Women's and Gender Studies Anytime, Anywhere, and to Anyone

The ability to communicate complex ideas to others is heralded as a skill women's and gender graduates possess, yet seldom are beginning students prepared to deal succinctly and powerfully with the stereotypes and misconceptions surrounding women's and gender studies. Not only will we directly address common misconceptions of women's studies, but this chapter will provide models or guides for students to use in developing their own "scripts" of what women's and gender studies is and why it is a useful, desirable, and marketable area of study.

Chapter 4: Discovering and Claiming Your Internal Strengths and External Skills

What are the tangible and intangible skills that one develops through women's and gender studies training? In this chapter, we begin with a discussion of the top concepts that graduates identified in our survey as important to their professional work. These concepts emerge from the feminist classroom and also through applied learning opportunities. We also show you how these concepts are used in their professional lives.

This chapter focuses on supporting the student in assessing what he or she has done thus far in their academic career. We suggest how a student might begin to organize what he or she learns in women's and gender studies (e.g. concepts, theories, frameworks, etc.) through the framework of "internal strengths" and "external skills." Skills and strengths grow out of the work that is done both inside and outside the classroom.

SECTION THREE: YOU'RE GRADUATING: GREAT! NOW WHAT?

Chapter 5: Women's and Gender Studies Graduates as Change Agents: Six Profiles

In this chapter the reader is introduced to the survey data that shows the multitude of employment paths that participants have taken. We present the idea of women's and gender studies students as *change agents*. We have developed three categories of "change agent" types in relation to future career pathways: sustainers, evolvers, and synthesizers. We then explore the experiences of six people who are exemplars of the three categories. Students can use this typology to initially identify themselves, provide possible career options, and investigate options for further skill development.

Chapter 6: Transform Your World: Preparing to Graduate and Living Your Feminist Life

This chapter attends to two issues—helping the students who are poised to graduate think about the transition from college to professional life and also cultivating a vision of social change and transformation.

This chapter contains the nuts and bolts essentials for helping the student understand the preparation that it will take to leave the college environment and engage the world in a new role. The chapter gives suggestions on developing or expanding one's feminist community outside the safe environs of the college campus.

SERIES FOREWORD

This innovative series is for all readers interested in books that provide frameworks for making sense of the complexities of contemporary social life. Each of the books in this series uses a sociological lens to provide current critical and analytical perspectives on significant social issues, patterns, and trends. The series consists of books that integrate the best ideas in sociological thought with an aim toward public education and engagement. These books are designed for use in the classroom as well as for scholars and socially curious general readers.

How do you take a major in Women's and Gender Studies home for the holidays? Students majoring in these areas have expressed the ongoing tension between pursuing a major course of study that enlightens their way and enlivens their lives but elicits disparaging comments from friends and family. In *Transforming Scholarship*, Berger and Radeloff take on the familiar refrain of "what are you going to do with that degree?" and transform it into an opportunity for reflective engagement and response. Based on years of personal experience as faculty members in women's and gender studies programs and an international survey of graduates, the authors offer thoughtful and critically informed information about the practicalities of a degree in Women's and Gender Studies. Their observations also provide insight into why women's and gender studies is one of the fastest-growing areas of study and academic majors in United States universities and globally.

Valerie Jenness
Jodi O'Brien
Series Editors

PREFACE

It was a hot, sweaty day when the idea for this book was first conceived. We sat near a pool at the 23rd National Women's Studies Association meeting, in 2007, being held in Pheasant Run, Chicago. We were meeting to catch up about work and life; as always, we were zooming through ideas, our collective enjoyment of each other's company reaching its usual frenetic pitch. A recent article in *Ms.* about women's studies graduates still having a bit of trouble being understood, published just a few months early, had stirred up an ocean of feelings for both of us. We were pleased that the article focused on all the amazingly cool projects and careers that women's studies graduates were pursuing. But, we lamented that they were still having to grapple with what felt like old questions (the proverbial "So, what can you do with a women's studies degree?"), cynicism and sometimes overt hostility about why they choose that major. That seemed downright depressing to us and didn't mirror all the amazing experiences we saw our students pursuing. We were talking about the ways in which women's studies students still feel underserved in their lives. Michele had just finished running for office, which had been exciting, and Cheryl was becoming deeply embedded in leadership issues in Minnesota. We were feeling our oats and thought that students shouldn't have to reinvent the wheel when it comes to talking about women's and gender studies. After knowing each other almost eight years at that point, we had walked a path together as teacher, student and co-teachers of a class. We felt something forceful and scary pass through us during our conversation—"they need a book," we proclaimed. Once the idea was spoken aloud it felt both powerful and daunting. We knew what we had to do—we wanted to create a book that spoke to the progress and aspirations of women's and gender students, and provided strategies for how to communicate that interest effectively. We wanted to create a book that grappled with the messiness of living one's women's and gender studies values after leaving college. We also wanted to create persuasive data about the experiences of women's and gender studies students. Little did we know that speaking our book idea aloud would compel us to create the largest global database of women's and gender studies graduates ever, or lead us to the inspiring people we have been privileged to interview.

We want this book to help students, but also to encourage women's and gender studies faculty to reprioritize their focus on the women's studies undergraduate experience. For the past decade women's studies has been involved in debates about graduate training and the "state of the field" (see Scott 2008). While these conversations have been useful and interesting, this emphasis has left a significant gap in thinking about the next generation of graduating students' needs. There has been little prioritization in the field of grappling with the unique challenges facing women's studies undergraduates while obtaining the degree or after graduation. In part, this is an empirical challenge as well as a theoretical one. Women's studies has only recently started to produce long-range data about how women's and gender studies students have utilized their training (see Luebke and Reilly 1995; Dever 2004). Only more recently have programs and departments created structures to gather data about graduates. The National Women's Studies Association has recently begun to address this issue through taskforces, reports, and the implementation of a Ford Foundation grant that supports the tracking of both undergraduate and graduate students of Women's Studies. Although this situation is in the process of changing, students are still are caught in the middle when they or practitioners try to find data about outcomes of the degree.

Transforming Scholarship firmly acknowledges and celebrates the ways in which, globally, women's and gender studies curricula has produced a new type of student. It is the research and theory being produced by scholars and activists in women's studies that creates the framework for student interest and engagement. We highlight to student readers the importance of women's and gender studies research, theory building, and pedagogical practices. This is the bedrock that forms the foundation for student transformation that is clearly evident within these pages. For professors, we hope that this book will become the one that you reach for when you are asked by a student: "What can I do with my interest in women's and gender studies?"

We give thanks here to the many people who helped us along the way.

Michele would like to thank: As always to my partner, Timothy Dane Keim who makes me laugh and keeps me sane when my eyes begin to cross during another round of edits. My moods, during periods of sustained book writing, also have the tendency to be cross, too. Thank you for your love, support, and always good cheer.

I would also like to thank my writing group, composed of two dedicated sociologists: Lisa Pearce and Karolyn Tyson. That first round of feedback on early chapters was crucial to having it develop into the work here and I am very grateful that you gave it.

And, lastly, to a brilliant conspirator of all things women's studies related and to my cherished collaborator—Cheryl. You make me remember why I decided to get a Ph.D.! I'm always moving between two states when we're together. One is rolling around on the floor because I'm laughing so hard and the other is deep amazement at the way you have just pulled two different ideas together and intertwined them into a new pattern. I hope to always call you friend and collaborator.

Cheryl would like to thank: During the course of transforming oneself in order to transform the world, I met many folks who not only inspired the book, but gave me support as well. I will always be indebted to all the gender and women's studies students, who I wo/mentored or tormented as students at University of Nevada, Las Vegas, Minnesota State University, Mankato, and College of Southern Nevada, who participated in our survey, but also those who took the time to be interviewed and also gave their insight into the chapters of the book. I am in awe of Judi

Brown, Caryn Lindsay, Jennifer Pritchett, and Diana Rhodes for their contributions to the world.

I also want to thank my fellow graduates from the Elizabeth Kearney Women's Leadership Program, my colleagues from the Mankato American Association of University Women (AAUW), the FIRS (faculty-in-residence) and participant of New Leadership Nevada and Tri-State, as well as my mentors Avra Johnson and Anne Ganey for giving me the encouragement and strength to follow my vision for leadership as well as reviving my belief in sisterhood when I was questioning it. I also want to thank John Alesio, the Department of Gender and Women's Studies at Minnesota State, Mankato, and Provost Scott Olsen for approving my leave of absence in order to explore different career and research opportunities. I also want to thank my peer mentors, in particular Jaime Phillips, Becky Bates, Anne Lascamana, Gina Winger, Sarah Sifers, Caryn Lindsay, Laura Yavitz, Lori Andrews, Crystal Jackson, Nicole Rogers, DeAnna Beachley, Lois Helmbold, my colleagues, past and present, at the Southern Nevada's Health District, and everyone else at UNLV and MSU who helped make me the feminist I am today. I would be remiss for neglecting to thank Mark Rauls and Troy McGinnis for their continued support either through listening to my endless questions, giving advice on survey question construction, or lending their perspectives on academia and women's studies. I always thank my mother Betty and my brother Carl for their unwavering love and support and, of course, to my colleague Michele—from the minute we met, we knew it was the beginning of a beautiful, long, personal and professional friendship. Finally I want to thank my father Robert for his love and support. My father's influence on my feminism is immeasurable.

We both would like to thank: Sarah Tucker Jenkins, our research assistant. She was our rock and her skills conducting research, as well as maintaining and directing correspondence with women's and studies graduates, program directors, as well as interested parties, was incredible. Christal Lustig was always willing to share her keen eye for editing along with her experiences as a women's studies graduate in order to assist our project. The production of this book was helped by the supportive group of readers and informal editors including Christal Lustig, Jamie Phillips, and Kaaren Haldeman.

We also would like to thank many of our current and former students who generously gave their impressions and feedback in informal and formal ways throughout the development of this idea to book. Your collective enthusiasm and sense that you would have used this book spurred us on. We'd like to acknowledge Celeste Allen and Kimmie Garner for their insights on drafts of chapters.

Our sincere thanks also go to the many program and curriculum directors, and department chairs and administrative staff of women's and genders studies worldwide who forwarded our request about our survey to their alumni lists. If the program director didn't have an easily accessible list of alumni, they often created one in support of this project. They also forwarded emails to development officers and their colleagues, as well as posted in their unit's Facebook page. They sent us information about their units when asked and also suggested the names of people we might want to interview. We were greeted with prompt emails and encouraging words that helped us through the long winter months of data collection. We also have to thank the hundreds of participants who took our survey and the many people whom we had the pleasure of interviewing for this book. We would also like to thank the online community on Facebook, called 'Women's Studies: Students and Career', we created as the survey and book idea developed.

We are appreciative of the people who wrote brief pieces for several of the 'sidebars' that we use in the book including: Jill M. Adams, Dr. Nalini Shiv Kumar, Patti Duncan, Dr. Catherine M. Orr, and Dr. Robert Pleasants.

Thanks are also due to the reviewers of this manuscript: Alison Piepmeier, College of Charleston; Jayne Schuiteman, Michigan State University; Lorraine Dowler, Penn State University; Wendy Kolmar, Drew University; Jennifer Fish, Old Dominion University; Kimala Price, San Diego State University; Suzanne Scott, George Mason University; Susan Shaw, Oregon State University. We found your suggestions thoughtful, imaginative, and useful. We wish to thank the production team at Routledge for the careful care the manuscript received from beginning to end. And finally, our editors at Routledge were outstanding to work with during the past two years. Our series editors, Jodi O'Brien and Valerie Jenness, made this a fun, rewarding, and learning experience for us. Jodi's feedback at critical times during revising was also clarifying and helpful. And Steven Rutter is a model editor in every sense of the word. His many years in the field have provided him with wisdom and ability to know how to elicit the best work from authors.

INTRODUCTION
TRANSFORM YOURSELF: AN INVITATION TO EXPLORE YOUR INTEREST IN WOMEN'S AND GENDER STUDIES

Kendra is a first-year student, attending a large, public, four-year university, and is taking "Introduction to Women's Studies"—her first women's studies course and her favorite class of the semester. She's talking on the phone with her mother.

> *Kendra* Mom, I am loving my women's studies course! We just finished a section on women and work. It was fascinating! Did you know that on average women who work full time earn 77 cents for every dollar that men earn?
>
> *Kendra's mother* What? No I didn't, honey. I would have thought things were more equal now with so many women in the workplace.
>
> *Kendra* Yeah, you'd think that, but it's definitely not. African American and Latina women earn even less than the 77 cents. Can you believe it? I was so upset when I read that statistic. My recitation group really dove into the material. Anyway, I just talked with my academic advisor, and I think I want to major in women's studies.
>
> *Kendra's mother* Whoa, wait a minute. What exactly *is* women's studies? I've never heard of that major . . . Aren't you interested in political science anymore?

1

Kendra   Women's studies puts women's concerns and experiences at the center of academic study. And, Mom, that's the great thing about this major, I can take all sorts of courses that are cross-listed between the women's studies department and the political science department. For example, I can study women's political participation in Latin America or in the US. Or I could take a political theory class that focuses on what women have considered important about democracy and citizenship.

Kendra's mother   And you can major in that? Can you get a job in that? What kinds of work do people with a women's studies major actually do? We're not paying all that money for you to come and live with us after graduation. And why is it, as you say, "putting women at the center" is something that is so important?

Kendra hesitates and is flustered. "Well . . . I don't know about the job part."

Later Kendra thinks to herself, "I don't know why I froze when talking with my mother about women's studies. Of course, I know what women's studies is. But I guess I haven't ever really practiced talking about it with someone other than one of my professors and the other women's studies majors. And I guess I haven't really thought about what I would do with my interest in women's studies. I know it's the right choice for me, but how do I reassure my mother and the rest of my family?"

Delia is a double major in women's and gender studies and journalism and is beginning her senior year at a private college. She is talking to a career counselor at the Career Services Office about her future goals.

Delia   I just don't know how I'm going to combine all of my interests when I leave school. I've never really thought about what I would do after I graduate. I've just been enjoying learning so much.

Career counselor   Tell me a little about what you've done so far and how you think it's preparing you for the next step.

Delia   My internship last spring with the local rape crisis center was great, but I don't think I want to pursue nonprofit work. And I think I'd like to keep volunteering at a rape crisis center, but I'm not interested in pursuing more training in the area of sexual assault.

Career counselor   [*nodding*] What else in your coursework has been of interest to you that might give us a clue about directions you can pursue after graduation?

Delia [*pauses for a moment and says*] For my feminist praxis class, I ended up creating a project in which I designed an informational, women's resource website from scratch. I worked long hours on it. That was a great experience. I got to use my technical skills from journalism, and I focused on the importance of positive body image for women, which grew out of what I learned in some of my classes. I think maybe I want to create feminist content for the web.

Career counselor Do you mean as a freelance writer?

Delia No, not exactly. I think I'd like to build something from scratch and run it.

Career counselor [*shaking his head*] Well, that seems a bit ambitious. What about counseling—you could counsel people either who were victims of domestic violence or even eating disorders?

Delia shook her head. That suggestion didn't feel right at all. "I'm really not interested in counseling. Do you have any contacts with magazines like *Bust* or *Bitch*?"

The career counselor replies, "No, I don't."

The career counselor comes up with some additional ideas, but none of them seem to fit Delia's interdisciplinary interests. She leaves feeling unsure about what she wants to do. She visits her department's website and rereads some of the interesting pathways women's studies alumnae have taken. She asks herself, *How do I get from here to there?*

Miguel is on a plane back to his home in Argentina for spring break. He is a junior and a Spanish major with a minor in Gender and Sexuality Studies at a research intensive university. He has great news for his family and is practicing what he wants to say in his mind:

I can't believe my independent study project "Masculine Textualities: The Discursive Practice of Gender in Hispanic Writings," has been nominated by my advisor for the best undergraduate research project on gender and sexuality in the department. I so enjoyed the research of focusing on the ways in which masculinity has been produced through popular Spanish texts in the last forty years. If I win, not only do I receive $250.00 (US), but this paper could help me get into graduate school. I know that you worry about me and what I want to do with my life, but continuing my education in gender and sexuality studies can open doors for me that would not have been opened if I had stayed at home or in a traditional college major. So you want to know what I can do with my degree? And, am I gay?

Miguel's internal scripting has come to a screeching halt.

Added to Miguel's internal dialogue are some issues that he knows he has to deal with. Although he is eager about sharing the news with his family, he knows that he will face difficult questions from his grandparents and his maternal aunt and uncle. They don't understand why studying sexuality is intellectually worthwhile or a legitimate subject. Last year, his uncle accused him outright of being gay, which he had to deny strenuously. He loves them and wants them to understand how important this work is to him. He knows he needs to come up with a different way of framing the importance of this work to them.

Between the positive script Miguel is composing in his head and the negative responses he fears he will get from some of his family members, Miguel thinks to himself:

> I wish I had a book or some other sort of reference that would help me. While my classes have taught me how to think critically and analyze texts, I wish I had a class that would help me deal with my family and my decision to get a minor in gender and sexuality studies. We have talked about homophobia and sexism on systemic levels, and I've talked to my friends about how to deal with gay and lesbian baiting on campus, but it's tough telling my family about my studies at school and having constantly to tell them that I am not gay. Every time I discuss my minor I am troubled . . . not only by the homophobia in my family, but that I feel like I am dishonoring my friends who are queer.

You may be reading this book in your first women's and gender studies class. Or you may be majoring in women's and gender studies and have been given this book by your mentor. Or you may have taken a women's studies class in high school and now find yourself in college and curious about the options on your campus to study issues of race, gender, class, nationality, and sexuality in a gender studies class. Or you may be an activist working on women and poverty in a global context and are considering minoring in women's studies. Are the above scenarios familiar to you? While you were reading them, did you find yourself imagining how you might respond? These scenarios come from real-life experiences that students pursuing an interest in women's and gender studies encounter. We'll return to these scenarios soon.

Whether you have had these experiences or not, you have landed in a place where you can explore all the dimensions of developing and deepening your interest in women's and gender studies. This book is about helping you fulfill your potential as a student in women's and gender studies. We are committed to developing students' capacities to learn, lead, and thrive during and after their major, minor, or concentration in women's and gender studies, or one of the many related fields that have formed in association with this area of study.[1] It is a user-friendly handbook of practical guidance and inspiration for your interest in pursuing a degree in women's and gender studies.

This book will help you to think critically about what you know, how to demonstrate what you know, and how to prepare for life personally and professionally after graduation.

Why *This* Book?

We wrote *Transforming Scholarship* to offer students a useful guide to navigating one of the most richly rewarding, yet often underappreciated and frequently misunderstood, academic majors—women's and gender studies. Women's and gender studies is a vibrant interdisciplinary field of study. Scholars work on a wide variety of subjects including lesbian, gay, bisexual, and transgender (LGBT) and sexuality studies, marriage and the family, the state and politics, the environment, science and technology, sports, religion, gendered violence, international relations, education, art, theater, literature, and urban planning. To get an idea of some of the exciting scholarship women's and gender studies scholars produce, either check out an academic press website, such as Routledge's, and type in "women" or "gender studies," or search your library's catalog or your favorite bookstore's website for one of the subject areas just listed.

This is the first book of its kind—one geared for women's and gender studies students. By writing this book we affirm that students pursuing questions in women's and gender studies are part of an emerging vanguard of knowledge producers in the US and globally. Students in women's and gender studies are trained to consider how their efforts in the classroom can be translated to affect the status of women and men (and anyone outside the gender binary) beyond the borders of their college or university.

Women's and gender studies is a leading stand-alone major and minor on many college and university campuses, or exists on a programmatic level (i.e., as a concentration) in concert with other fields of study. In the United States there are women's and gender studies programs in over 700 academic institutions: including two- and four-year colleges, public and private universities, women's colleges, historically black colleges and universities (HBCUs), and community colleges. According to Beverly Guy-Sheftall, a leading scholar in women's studies, globally more than forty countries offer women's and gender studies curricula or research opportunities (Guy-Sheftall 2009). At the undergraduate level, students taking women's and gender studies classes are able to study subjects that span the arts and humanities, social sciences, education, the natural and hard sciences, engineering, and business. Women's and gender studies programs offer students training in how to think critically and recognize the importance of how interlinked oppressions and privileges shape both women's and men's experiences.

In increasing numbers, students are graduating with degrees that have a concentration in women's and gender studies, and they naturally seek

ACADEMIC BORDER CROSSING: FRAMING WOMEN'S AND GENDER STUDIES APPROACHES

In a college and university setting, you will often hear the words "discipline," "interdisciplinary," and perhaps "multidisciplinary." Areas of study are organized and thought of as belonging to a "discipline" (e.g. history). This reflects historical ways of framing learning that date back to the eighteenth century. Some people will use the term "discipline" in a general way to mean any academic study. In this book we refer to women's and gender studies as an interdisciplinary field of study. This means that scholars, students, and activists grapple with questions about women and men that are informed by a wide variety of perspectives and approaches and "fields of study," including literature, political science, ethnic studies, history, film, etc. And, moreover, an interdisciplinary approach means that the new ideas created from the borrowing, shaping, and exploring of two or more disciplines becomes greater than the sum of its parts. An interdisciplinary approach provides a dynamic set of analytical tools to think about gender. You will find out more about how women's and gender studies is organized in higher education in Chapter One.

to apply what they have learned to the outside world (Levin 2007). During 2006–2007 there were 1,195 women's studies degrees awarded. Moreover, 461 degrees were awarded under the term "Ethnic, cultural minority, and gender studies, other" and 506 degrees awarded under "Area, ethnic, cultural, and gender studies, other." Student demand for these classes and training has increased every year (Digest of Education Statistics).

The continued success of women's and gender studies has been forty years in the making, with the first program in women's studies, specifically, established in 1970 at San Diego State University (Guy-Sheftall 2009: 57). Although women's and gender studies is a well-established and thriving academic interdisciplinary field of study, students in women's and gender studies still face unique challenges, as we read in the opening scenarios.

In the first scenario, Kendra was excited about the possibilities of women's studies and was trying to find support for her interest in continuing as a major. But she was unprepared for the leap her mother made from declaring a major to thinking about future employment. The first scenario also indicates, surprisingly, that many people in the general public don't realize that women's and gender studies is an academic pursuit and that you can major in women's and gender studies. Nor do many people know that you *can* find employment using your women's and gender studies training!

The second scenario demonstrates the kinds of questions you may face when you are at the end of your academic journey: How do you take what you know out into the marketplace? Delia was trying to figure out how

DATA SUPPORTS ECONOMIC VALUE OF A WOMEN'S AND GENDER STUDIES DEGREE

Our global research study suggests that a women's and gender studies degree can help you in *any* job. Whether you share your knowledge of the politics of gender, race, sexuality, and class with clients when you are filling out demographic questions for official forms, or you subtly challenge the gendered descriptions of Halloween costumes through your job as a copy editor for a corporation, a women's and gender studies education makes you a valuable asset to any organization.

to take what she had already learned in women's and gender studies classes and use it professionally. Unfortunately, her career counselor was not as helpful as she had hoped in showing her how she could fulfill her desire to create feminist web content. Although it would have helped Delia to come to the meeting with a stronger sense of what her interests were, the career counselor should be expected to do better, given that women's and gender studies is no longer a brand new major. Nor did the career counselor help her assess her strengths and skills developed through her coursework and internship.

Although women's and gender studies remains one of the fastest-growing majors and minors on campuses and universities, students cannot always envision or articulate the real-world benefits of their degree (Luebke and Reilly 1995, Dever 2004, Stewart 2007). Thus, like Delia, students can be bogged down by the persistent question of "What does one do with an interest and/or a degree in women's and gender studies?"

A 2007 article in *Ms.* magazine, "Transform the World: What Can You Do with a Degree in Women's Studies?", beautifully captured the tension between the lingering popular ignorance of women's and gender studies as a field and the dynamism and enthusiasm of the undergraduate women's studies experience. The truth is that women's and gender studies graduates go on to become professionals in many areas, including politics, medicine, and higher education administration, and secure employment in the private, public, and government sectors. They also become practitioners in the trades and independent business owners. Many women's and gender studies graduates also remain committed to the pursuit of gender equality as lifelong advocates and activists. However, there is no single employment path for women's and gender studies graduates, nor is there an easily recognizable cookie-cutter model to emulate.

In the third scenario, Miguel is clearly feeling elated at being chosen as a finalist for a prestigious award, but he's also worrying about how to talk with his extended family about his strong interest in gender and sexuality. If you express an interest in women's and gender studies, you may find yourself faced with personal questions and assumptions about your political beliefs and sexual identity. This might seem daunting, but it comes with the territory, and once you are prepared for it and have responses for when and if it comes up, you will be prepared to engage in a confident and straightforward way.

Given the range of educational choices available and the expansion of women's and gender studies globally, we believe there is no better time to be an undergraduate doing work in women's and gender studies than now. A central aim of this book is to help students take advantage of the opportunities and challenges in pursuing intellectual work in women's and gender studies.

Transforming Scholarship is ambitious in scope and goes further than the few short articles or previous books about women's and gender studies students (Luebke and Reilly 1995; Magezis 1997; Garrett and Rodgers 2002; Dever 2004). Our goal is to give you concrete information so you can confidently answer the question: What can you do with a women's studies degree? To do so, we did extensive research for this book. We have surveyed over 900 women's and gender studies graduates (1995–2010) from around the globe about their experiences as students and their career paths. In the survey we have graduates from Georgia State University to the University of Ghana. This is currently the *largest global dataset* about contemporary women's and gender studies graduates! Over 125 institutions are represented in this survey. We also conducted interviews with a small sample of men and women who responded to our

WHAT WE AIM TO GIVE YOU IN THIS BOOK

- We encourage you to be proactive in thinking about your education from beginning to end. We encourage you to consider how your undergraduate education prepares you for life after college, beyond how to write a resume and apply for a job.
- We help you make connections between the rich, intellectual tradition that women's and gender studies offers you as a student and why that might be of value to you.
- We help you apply the critical thinking skills that you are developing in your women's and gender studies classes to your academic and professional career.
- We affirm your desire to translate what you do in the classroom to a lifestyle of praxis, theory, and learning after you graduate.
- We affirm your desire to make a living doing what you believe in and love.
- We bring together information and up-to-date research in one easy-to-read guide.

survey. We have gathered information from employers and directors and chairs of women's and gender studies programs to provide you with the best resources available to guide you through women's and gender studies.

The book you hold in your hands begins by acknowledging the opportunities and challenges that face the typical women's and gender studies student. We address why choosing to focus on women's and gender studies in an academic environment is a unique experience. We also provide a contemporary framework for students to understand themselves as a type of "change agent." This framework allows you to think in a new way about the benefits of pursuing work in women's and gender studies and what you have to offer employers once you graduate. We prepare students with skills for the "emotional management" that many will face in pursuit of their concentration or degree.[2] This book will provide you with the skills and tools to navigate any resistance that you may face while pursuing your coursework or career goals. From the scenarios presented in the beginning of this section, if you face any similar circumstances to those experienced by Kendra, Delia, and Miguel, after reading this book, you should have more resources in your toolkit for responding to tough questions and situations. Another goal of this book is to enhance your ability to integrate what you learn in your women's and gender studies classes into your life (before and) after you graduate. Thus, we take a holistic approach to the women's and gender studies student.

We have witnessed many students (and professors) struggle with some of the challenges that we identify in this book. We hope this book will help people explore the many work and career options available for women's and gender studies graduates and realize their potential. Given the transformative potential of women's and gender studies at the undergraduate level, we would like to see students find more encouragement and support for this interdisciplinary field of study.

Ultimately, we believe this book will also be useful to parents, college advisors, career counselors, and fellow faculty colleagues. But most of all, this book is for you—the college student interested in women's and gender studies.

You may have found us while taking your first women's and gender studies class, or you may be graduating soon and suddenly find yourself terrified of the prospect of life after college. *Transforming Scholarship* will support you in any stage of your academic career.

Who We Are

We come to this book as scholars, teachers, workers, life coaches, and leadership trainers. As a team, we bring strong and unique skills to writing the pages that follow. We have a long, combined history of learning, teaching, and mentoring in women's studies at various institutions as graduate students and professors. We also have disciplinary ties to other academic fields (Michele is a political scientist by training with a Ph.D. from the University of Michigan, and Cheryl is a sociologist with a Ph.D. from the University of Nevada, Las Vegas). Our collaboration on this book is the result of a longstanding professional relationship. Not only did we have the privilege of co-teaching a course together, but we have been able to encourage and support each other in a variety of roles ranging from mentor and colleague to friend. We believe that a women's and gender studies degree not only provides the intellectual tools to succeed in life, but is also an area of study that fosters an environment of community, leadership, and empowerment. You will hear more about us as we move through the book, but below we share snapshot profiles.

Michele

I attended Bard College, a small, private liberal arts college that in the late 1980s did not have a well-publicized women's studies major, minor, or concentration. Early on I began taking cross-listed classes that had either "women" or "feminist" in the course description (e.g. "Women and Contemporary Anthropology" and "Feminist Political Theory"). My mother was a civil rights advocate and influenced me enormously to believe that women can and should be equal stakeholders in the world. I was a dual major in creative writing and political studies. I was deeply influenced by feminist literary theory and contemporary women authors. On my own, I practically inhaled the works of other women writers that I read, including Toni Cade Bambara, Alice Walker, Isabel Allende, and Ursula Le Guin. Maybe you, too, through your women's and gender studies classes, have found incredible authors whose works you cannot put down.

Through political studies I was exposed to feminist political theory and feminist legal theory. Although formal women's studies classes were not regularly offered, there were several faculty members willing to commit themselves to teaching about women's lives. What I could not get in the classroom, I tried to fill in on my own. I read *Ms.*, *off our backs*, *On the Issues*, and other feminist magazines and journals. Maybe you're reading magazines such as *Bitch*, *Bust*, or *Ms.* I took full advantage of the amazing feminist speakers who came to campus, including bell hooks, Amber Hollibaugh, and Jo Freeman.

FEMINIST SCHOLARS AND ACTIVISTS YOU SHOULD KNOW: BELL HOOKS AND AMBER HOLLIBAUGH

bell hooks' influence on women's and gender studies is profound. Born Gloria Watkins, bell hooks chose her name (the lower case letters are intentional) based on the accounts she heard growing up about her grandmother, a strong female relative who was not afraid to speak out in a culture that too often silenced women. hooks is not only a feminist scholar who graduated with her Ph.D. from the University of California, Santa Cruz, but a public intellectual and social activist whose commentary on social, racial, sexual, and cultural issues is evident not only in her numerous publications (articles and books), but her media appearances as well. hooks is also a passionate educator, influenced by the work of Brazilian educator Paulo Freire, and she sees the classroom as emancipatory rather than disciplining.

Amber Hollibaugh describes herself as a "lesbian sex radical, ex-hooker, incest survivor, Gypsy child, poor-white-trash, high femme dyke." Her powerful voice, as evidenced in her book *My Dangerous Desires: A Queer Girl Dreaming Herself Home*, explores the often contradictory and controversial states she has occupied as a social activist, critic, filmmaker, and, at times, social outcast regarding feminist debates over sexuality. Amber Hollibaugh is also instrumental in raising awareness about gender issues in the AIDS/HIV community through her work as the founding director of the Gay Men's Health Crisis Lesbian AIDS Project and her documentary film *The Heart of the Matter*, which focuses on sexuality and the denial of women's risks for HIV/AIDS. In 2008, she joined the staff at the Howard Brown Health Center in Chicago, Illinois, where she acts as the Chief Officer of Elder and LBTI Women's Services (www.howardbrown.org/hb_news.asp?id=747). For more information about Amber Hollibaugh, you may want to listen to her story in the "Voices of Feminism" oral history project in the Sophia Smith Collection at the Smith College Libraries website (www.smith.edu/library/libs/ssc/vof/vof-intro.html).

FOR YOUR LIBRARY

Amber Hollibaugh. (2000). *My Dangerous Desires: A Queer Girl Dreaming Herself Home*. Durham, NC: Duke University Press.

bell hooks. (1981). *Ain't I a Woman: Black Women and Feminism*. Boston: South End Press.

———. (1984). *Feminist Theory from Margin to Center*. Boston: South End Press.

———. (1984). *Teaching to Transgress: Education as the Practice of Freedom*. New York: Routledge.

———. (1994). *Outlaw Culture: Resisting Representations*. New York: Routledge.

The tools and theory-building skills I acquired in my classes prepared me to write a senior project (required of all Bard students)[3] on rape law reform of the late 1970s and 1980s, relying heavily on the work of legal scholar Catherine MacKinnon. Although I did not specifically tell any of my professors that I had almost been sexually assaulted when I was sixteen, I think I was drawn to the topic because of personal experience. I found it intellectually stimulating to study feminists who were interested in rape law reform. I came to understand both the opportunities and the barriers they faced as they confronted laws that differentially positioned women and men in relation to sexual assault. I can still remember how outraged I felt when I discovered that many state laws condoned "marital rape."

The laws of the 1960s and 1970s claimed the sexist view that wives had no right to refuse a husband's sexual advances and therefore no legal recourse after being sexually assaulted (or battered). For me, being able to read theoretical works by feminist legal scholars and political theorists and discuss the thorny issues of rape and sexual assault from both personal and academic vantage points distinguished my classes focusing on feminism and women's advancement from my other classes.

One of the reasons I went to graduate school right after college was because I felt a deep urgency to bring new voices and new ways of knowing into the academy, especially those from historically "marginalized communities" (e.g. women of color from impoverished backgrounds). I was eager to continue studying how feminist theory challenged typical assumptions about everyday social patterns that seemed "natural." I had already begun to apply some concepts that stemmed from my classes in feminist theory through my activism on campus on a variety of issues

UNDERSTANDING VIOLENCE AGAINST WOMEN

The United Nations defines violence against women as any act of gender-based violence that results in, or is likely to result in, physical, sexual, or mental harm or suffering to women, including threats of such acts, coercion, or arbitrary deprivation of liberty, whether occurring in public or in private life. There are many forms of violence against women, including sexual, physical, or emotional abuse by an intimate partner; physical or sexual abuse by family members or others; sexual harassment and abuse by authority figures (such as teachers, police officers, or employers); trafficking for forced labor or sex; and such traditional practices as forced or child marriages, dowry-related violence, and honor killings, when women are murdered in the name of family honor. Systematic sexual abuse in conflict situations is another form of violence against women.

In a ten-country study on women's health and domestic violence conducted by the World Health Organization:

- Between 15 percent and 71 percent of women reported physical or sexual violence by a husband or partner.
- Many women said that their first sexual experience was not consensual (24 percent in rural Peru, 28 percent in Tanzania, 30 percent in rural Bangladesh, and 40 percent in South Africa).
- Trafficking of women and girls for forced labor and sex is widespread and often affects the most vulnerable.
- Forced marriages and child marriages violate the human rights of women and girls, yet they are widely practiced in many countries in Asia, the Middle East, and sub-Saharan Africa.
- Worldwide, up to one in five women and one in ten men report experiencing sexual abuse as children. Children subjected to sexual abuse are much more likely to encounter other forms of abuse later in life.

You may encounter in your women's and gender studies classes facts and statistics about the global gendered nature of sexual violence that may be shocking to you and propel you to learn more and even to become active on your campus. For more information see World Health Organization: www.who.int/mediacentre/factsheets/fs239/en/.

(e.g. reproductive rights). In my graduate school applications, I quoted Audre Lorde, the self-defined Black, lesbian feminist warrior poet and author who inspired me throughout my studies. She said, "In our world, divide and conquer must become define and empower" (Lorde 1984: 112). Those words resonated deeply with me because I felt that coalition-

AUDRE LORDE: POET, THEORIST, AND VISIONARY

Audre Lorde's worked has shaped and inspired two generations of writers, scholars, and activists. Lorde produced several volumes of poetry and created new directions in non-fiction with her untraditional memoir (*Zami, a New Spelling of My Name*), but she was not only a famous poet, she was also one of the most compelling black feminists of the past century. The topics she chose to write about broke open taboos on race, class, the role and notion of "difference," health disparities, sexuality, eroticism, marginality, and the role of community building among feminists. The body of her work has left a legacy for all those concerned with social justice

building and self-definition were the building blocks of feminist theory and could be applied to many situations.

 FOR YOUR LIBRARY

Rudolph P. Byrd, Johnnetta Betsch Cole, and Beverly Guy-Sheftall (Eds.). (2009). *I Am Your Sister: Collected and Unpublished Writings of Audre Lorde.* Oxford: Oxford University Press.

Audre Lorde. (1978). *The Black Unicorn.* (poetry) New York: Norton.

———. (1982). *Zami: A New Spelling of My Name.* (nonfiction) Trumansburg, NY: Crossing Press.

———. (1984). *Sister Outsider.* (nonfiction) Trumansburg, NY: Crossing Press.

I chose to attend the University of Michigan because of the dynamic work on gender and sexuality taking place there. They had an established women's studies program that offered a graduate certificate in the field of women's studies. I deepened my knowledge base in gender and criminology and in scholarship by women of color, and I learned how to ask new questions about women's lives.

I never thought that much of my academic career would focus on women and HIV/AIDS. As an undergraduate, I researched feminist legal reform in the area of rape and sexual assault. In graduate school I found my way into feminist criminology courses offered in the department of sociology. I became fascinated with female lawbreakers and how the criminal justice system responds to women. This led me to conduct ethnographic research in Detroit with women who were actively using crack cocaine and engaging in street-level sex work. At the time, there were very few cultural or academic spaces that critically examined how women (especially women of color) were coping with the rapid deterioration of urban environments. Over a four-year period, I met women who had been in the "life" and were now HIV-positive and creating and conducting grassroots activism on behalf of themselves and other stigmatized women. I conducted in-depth interviews with sixteen women who were transforming the political landscape through their community activism. Their political participation challenged many assumptions political scientists typically make about women's activism.

By the time I finished my graduate training, I felt compelled to study marginalized women with HIV/AIDS who had become politically active and to talk with a wide variety of scholars across disciplinary lines. After the dissertation, this work resulted in my book, *Workable Sisterhood: The Political Journey of Stigmatized Women with HIV/AIDS*. Although my doctorate is in political science, I actively choose to define myself as an interdisciplinary scholar. This choice reflects my training and deep commitments to creating interdisciplinary conversations in which women's lives are researched with increasing complexity and rigor—a legacy reflecting my core interest in women's studies.

As a faculty member in women's studies at the University of North Carolina (UNC) at Chapel Hill, I teach students from a wide variety of backgrounds. As the Director of Undergraduate Studies in my department, I counsel students on course selection, internship opportunities, and career options. I also see this role as an important opportunity to help students tackle what at first feels like the daunting question, "What do I do with this degree?" I definitely consider myself an "ambassador" for women's studies. And, as I often meet people who have no idea what a "women's studies professor" is or what makes women's studies unique, or how vital and needed our voices are in the academy, I have to practice some of the very same skills that are presented in this book—so I view these encounters as useful opportunities to frame a message about women's studies research and training that feels inviting and perhaps connects to issues women and men might struggle with or have heard about in the news: pay equity, the number and visibility of female elected officials, ongoing high rates of sexual assault, violence and assault against the LGBT community, representations of women athletes, and the number of women globally living with HIV/AIDS.

"TO BE OR NOT TO BE A FEMINIST: THAT IS THE QUESTION"

In *No Turning Back: The History of Feminism and the Future of Women*, Estelle Freedman unpacks the term "feminism" and traces its roots. Feminism was coined in France in 1880s. The term "feminisme" combined the French terms for woman (*femme*) and social movement or political ideology (*isme*). Feminism, as with other social movements, implies the need for social change. Therefore, those who adopted ideas of social change for women were called feminists. Currently, many people claim a feminist identity, ranging from individuals who actively work for social change and gender equality to those who utilize one of many theoretical frameworks to analyze the world through the cultural products of our society (i.e. music, film, art, literature, new social media), social institutions (e.g. military, education, the state, economy, religion), or internalized and socialized into our very ways of thinking (i.e. gender roles). The label of "feminist" has also been rejected by some women, due to critiques of the claiming of a feminist identity as being to limited to a particular group of women, especially women who belong to dominant groups (an example of this would be Alice Walker's preference for the term "womanist" to capture some African American women's distinctive expressions of gender identity); questions surrounding biology and identity ("men cannot be feminists, only allies"); as well as stereotypes about the behavior and attitude of "feminists" that are uncomfortable to those who may be less vocal in their work for social justice. There is no one model of feminist identity or expression of feminism. The practice of feminism and struggles for gender equality globally offer an umbrella to a dazzling array of concerns, demands, and interests. Feminism as a manifestation of political and social expression keeps women's studies accountable, and although the two are intertwined, they are not synonymous. Women's studies is an academic endeavor that has its priorities within higher education and is accountable to a wide variety of constituencies . . . including feminist activists.

During your women's and gender studies class discussions, you may have been asked about your perspectives on feminism as well as whether you identify with this label. You may still be in the process of deciding your personal position on whether you claim a feminist identity. Hopefully this book will clarify some ideas you have about this label and help you make a decision that best fits your needs.

FOR YOUR LIBRARY

Rory Dicker and Alison Piepmeier (Eds.). (2003). *Catching a Wave: Reclaiming Feminism for the 21st Century.* Northeastern, MA: Northeastern University Press.

bell hooks. (2000). *Feminism is for Everybody: Passionate Politics.* Boston: South End Press.

Courtney E. Martin and J. Courtney Sullivan (Eds.). (2010). *Click: When We Knew We Were Feminists.* Berkeley: Seal Press.

Ruth Rosen. (2006).*The World Split Open: How the Modern Women's Movement Changed America.* New York: Penguin Press.

Cheryl

I attended Bowling Green State University (BGSU), a mid-sized public university in northwestern Ohio, in the mid-1980s. When I entered college, I really had no idea what I wanted to declare as a major. I was "undecided" my first two years and then chose interpersonal and public communications as my major. You might also find yourself at the same crossroads in trying to decide on a major. Eventually I discovered popular culture. I was excited (and a little scared) to declare a major in a subject that many considered non-traditional and limited in future career opportunities. Yet I was encouraged by the professor of my popular music course to choose this area for my degree, and I have never regretted the decision. During my first year, as I was fulfilling my core requirements, I happened upon a women's studies course. This course challenged me and made me question my world as I had known it growing up in Beavercreek, Ohio—a middle-class suburb of Dayton. Eventually I found myself taking more courses in women's studies and discovered that I could minor in it fairly easily with the number of credits I had accrued in this area during my five years at BGSU (they were cross-listed with my other core and major requirements).

It was also during my time at BGSU that I became an activist. The late 1980s and early 1990s was a period in which the pro-choice/pro-life debates about abortion had burst into the public arena.[4] Operation Life (a pro-life grassroots organization) was staging rescues at abortion clinics. While researching the history of abortion in Bowling Green, I had the opportunity to interview the founder of the Center for Life—a feminist abortion clinic in Toledo, Ohio—and take a tour of the establishment. This encounter was significant in that it enabled me to assist and support a friend who wanted to terminate her pregnancy. It also motivated me to put my pro-choice beliefs into practice by not only standing in solidarity with the clinic when the Center was targeted for a rescue, but also by taking part in two pro-choice marches on Washington, DC.

My initial goal to continue my reproductive health activism after college was fulfilled when I had the fortune to volunteer and eventually become employed with Planned Parenthood of Miami Valley as an HIV educator and counselor in the early 1990s. Not only was I educated about contraceptives and sexually transmitted infections (especially HIV and AIDS), but I was able to interact with and hear the everyday lived experiences of women and men who were trying to negotiate issues of sexuality, power, family, gender roles, economics, social class, race/ethnicity, and stigma. In addition, Planned Parenthood emphasizes education and knowledge, and my job there fostered my interest in further learning. My work involved comprehensive sexual education presentations in local community, public-school classrooms on sexually transmitted diseases (STDs) and birth control.

While I loved my position as an HIV educator and counselor, I found that I was limited in my ability to assist clients who were survivors of sexual assault. Agency and public health funding can only do so much, and I began questioning larger issues about the connection between reproductive health and public resources. My concerns eventually led me to pursue further education. Beginning at the University of Toledo, I pursued graduate work in Sociology and completed my journey at the University of Nevada, Las Vegas (UNLV). I was influenced by my experience working at Planned Parenthood, and my graduate work largely addressed issues of gender, sexuality, and stigma.

My dissertation, "Vectors, Polluters, and Murderers: HIV Testing toward Prostitutes and the State of Nevada," was a qualitative case study examining the role of the state in regulating gender and sexuality. The overall aim of my study was to investigate how public policy is influenced by existing attitudes and beliefs about the association of disease with prostitution. Through textual analysis of legislative and legal records, interviews with policymakers, and observations of legal and criminal justice procedures, I analyzed the process by which policymakers integrate and disseminate sources of information for decision-making purposes. This research is important not only in raising questions about the state in relation to gender and sexuality, but also because it focuses these questions locally on the state of Nevada.

While completing my dissertation, I gained valuable work experience through teaching introductory level and upper division women's studies courses and serving as the Graduate and Professional Student Association president. I have taught in several women's studies departments over the past several years, both at four-year state institutions and community colleges. Currently, I am re-exploring issues of reproductive and public health at the Southern Nevada Health District where I am employed as a disease investigator with the Office of HIV/AIDS/STDs. I feel that my previous research on HIV testing of prostitutes in the state of Nevada, my experience with a local HIV prevention Community Planning Group (CPG-SoN), and my background in women's reproductive and sexual health have brought me full circle.

Women's and Gender Studies Students Change Their Communities While Still in School

Our shared undergraduate histories of an interest in women's and gender studies and exploring co-curricular opportunities and activist interests— on and off campus—is mirrored by the graduates in our research. Our study finds that a whopping 72 percent of all graduates in women's and gender studies were active in campus organizations, local organizations, national organizations, and global organizations or *created* new organizations while pursuing their undergraduate degree. In many of their organizations, graduates often noted that they took on leadership positions.

Several of the organizations that students created were self-described "feminist clubs" that created space for like-minded women and men to come together. They also created feminist-inspired literary publications. Students participated in student chapters of national organizations (such as NOW, the National Organization for Women) or participated directly through the local or state chapters of these organizations. The organizations themselves span a wide variety of topics, though many of them are focused on women, gender, and sexuality issues. Graduates were also active in honor societies, forums, and organizations that promoted cross-cultural dialogue, student newspapers and magazines, radio and television programs, arts programs, sororities and fraternities, small feminist-oriented clubs, women's leadership programs, religious organizations, intramural sports, and programs mentoring at-risk youth. And, if some students interned or took advantage of a service learning opportunity, they often joined that organization as a member. It was also not uncommon for students to list that they were active in organizations that spanned campus, local, state, national, and international concerns.

This very high rate of participation suggests to us that there is an incredible drive for many students to connect the theory they learn in the women's and gender studies classroom to the world. They begin the path of being a change agent early on and then strengthen their civic engagement skills. We'll explore this link between theory and action in women's and gender studies training further in Chapters One and Two. Moreover, the valuable experience that undergraduates receive by participating in community and campus groups can create strengths and skills that can be used later on in employment situations.

Below are representative examples of the types of international, national, state, local, and campus organizations that graduates were members of and actively participated in:

- Voices for Planned Parenthood (VOX)
- Macalester College Peace and Justice Committee (Macalester College)
- Young Democrats of America
- College Partnership for Kids
- National Organization for Women (NOW)
- Women for Choice
- Liberal Party of Canada
- Feminist Students United (University of North Carolina, Chapel Hill)
- National Association for the Advancement of Colored People (NAACP)
- Bangladesh Association for Young Researchers (University of Dhaka, Bangladesh)
- Bedford/Sackville Literacy Network (Canada)
- Canadian Federation of University Women

- Halifax Women's Network
- American Association of University Women (AAUW)
- OUTloud (LGBT organization) (Hollins University)
- Charleston Women's Collective
- NARAL Pro-Choice America
- Golden Key Society
- National Society of Collegiate Scholars
- College Republicans
- Queer Insurgency (University of Southern Maine)
- Toni Cade Bambara Collective (Spelman College)
- Campus Girl Scouts
- Caribbean Student Alliance (University of Delaware)
- Amnesty International
- Campus Anti-Sexism Society (Instituto Universitário de Lisboa, Portugal)
- Center for Women and Transgender People; American Indian Counsel and Sexual Assault Support Team (Oberlin College)
- Campus Coalition Against Trafficking (Montclair State University)
- Queer Issues Committee (Minnesota State, Morris)
- March of Dimes
- Vagina Monologues—V-Day Project
- Student Association of Vegan and Vegetarian Youth (University of Rochester)
- Alternative Spring Break
- Michigan Italian-American Association, Do Random Acts of Kindness (University of Michigan)
- Critical Resistance (a national organization dedicated to opposing the expansion of the prison industrial complex)
- Arizona State Women's Coalition
- Radical Cheerleaders and Inside-Out Writing Project (a crafts/writing workshop space for incarcerated women) (University of California, Santa Cruz)
- Men Against Sexual Violence (MASV)
- Swarthmore Asian Organization (Swarthmore College)
- Pomona College Women's Union (Pomona College)
- Tufts Student Sexual Assault Response Assistance (SSARA) (Tufts University)

- Take Back the Night
- Actiongirls (feminist activist group) and CJAM Radio (feminist talk show) (University of Windsor, Canada)
- Michigan Women's Justice & Clemency Project
- Working Advocates to End Racism (University of California, Santa Cruz)
- Single Parents on Campus (University of British Columbia, Vancouver, Canada)
- American Civil Liberties Union (ACLU)
- Women's Health Collective (University of Massachusetts, Amherst)
- Religious Coalition for Reproductive Choice (University of Washington)
- Gay and Lesbians of Notre Dame (Saint Mary's College)
- Habitat for Humanity
- Dance Marathon
- Student Global AIDS Campaign and Advocacy for Adult Male Survivors of Sexual Assault (University of Michigan, Ann Arbor)
- The Finnish Association for Women's Studies
- United Nations Development Fund for Women (UNIFEM)
- Hillel
- ReelOut Queer Film Festival (Queen's University, Kingston, Ontario, Canada)

Structure of the Book

Transforming Scholarship uses the format of "you're doing x" and "so now what?" It focuses on the action steps you'll need to take along each stretch of your journey as a women's and gender studies student and graduate. In each chapter you will find important information to help you become an active participant in shaping your learning experiences. We have developed creative exercises at the end of each chapter that will allow you to ask smart questions of yourself and your program.

This book is organized around three major sections, each with a core theme. We explore the meaning and value of women's and gender studies in academic life in our first section: "You've Discovered Women's and Gender Studies and Want to Know More: Great! Now What?"

Chapter One introduces the history of the birth of women's and gender studies as an interdisciplinary area of study. It orients you to the intellectual landscape that you will explore in your academic setting. You'll find out why you are part of an educational vanguard that will contribute specific ideas, skills, and talents to the global marketplace. You will also learn some demographic information about women's and gender studies professors and students.

Chapter Two provides a basic overview of the kind of curriculum you will most likely encounter in the women's and gender studies program at your school. As you will discover in Chapter One, women's and gender studies programs are configured differently at many institutions. This chapter includes information about the multiple learning components and options available for many students and how to decide between internship, honors thesis, or study abroad options. Chapter Two will allow you to assess what options you have available to you in your academic context and how you may want to choose among those options or supplement them.

Making the most of your women's studies training by becoming an advocate and partner in your education is the core theme of the second section: "You've Committed to Learning in Women's and Gender Studies: Great! Now What?"

Chapter Three provides you with some tools to think about how to communicate with others, why you chose women's studies in the first place, and what you think the benefits are. We want to equip you with the ability to communicate well with others—good communication skills are a necessity for any college student, but they are strategically important for students in women's and gender studies. Although you are most likely to find affirmation about women's and gender studies from professors and peers, you may find that others (such as friends, parents, co-workers, the general public) may need more information from you about what women's and gender studies is all about before they express any enthusiasm.

Chapter Four asks you to think about your inner strengths and the external skills and knowledge your women's and gender studies training has provided you with. We encourage you to spend time assessing the work that you have done in women's and gender studies during the course of your academic career. We build on and extend the work of pioneering researchers Barbara Luebke and Mary Ellen Reilly, who conducted research on early women's studies graduates (Luebke and Reilly 1995). They posit that women's studies majors develop a unique set of skills including: empowerment, self-confidence, critical thinking, community building, and understanding differences and intersections among racism, homophobia, sexism, classism, ableism, anti-Semitism, and other types of oppression. We update and extend this critical work and provide a new set of lenses to help students evaluate themselves on these and other inner strengths and external skills. At the end of the chapter, we ask you to try out a few exercises to explore understandings of your own inner strengths and external skills.

The theme of using your women's and gender studies education to transform your world comprises the next section: "You're Graduating: Great! Now What?" The section prepares you for the process of transitioning from academe to your professional life.

Chapter Five provides critical information about women and men in the world using what they learn in women's and gender studies. We draw from interviews with employers, directors, and chairs of women's and gender studies programs, as well as students, to help capture the diversity of career options for students. We present and develop the idea of women's and gender studies students as *change agents*. Briefly, a change agent is an undergraduate who has strong experiential learning capabilities and a commitment to public engagement beyond the borders of the academic classroom. A change agent may be someone who organizes a collective action, begins their own feminist organization, or even works within an existing system and organization and radicalizes it in their own way. The size of the change is not as important as the motivation and vision behind it.

Through our research, we have identified three categories of change agents and how they relate to career pathways in women's studies: sustainers, evolvers, and synthesizers. You can use these terms initially to identify yourself and investigate options for further skills development in pursuing your dream career or whatever your next step may be. You'll enjoy learning about the diversity and variety of occupations available to you, and this should help put to rest the idea that women's and gender studies students do not have marketable skills. You will hear the stories of graduates who have been change agents in their own right and are professionally successful. You will learn of successful graduates who are often invited back to their educational institutions for "career day." You will hear of their triumphs and challenges in the process of finding one's way in the professional world. These very human stories will keep the process "real." While six former students will be profiled in depth, these profiles are augmented by a variety of data gained through research using online surveys and interviews.

Finally, Chapter Six provides strategies for ways to make a graceful and seamless transition from college to the professional world. One of the hardest experiences that students have shared with us over the years regarding their post-graduation transition is that they sometimes find themselves as the only "feminist" or person committed to gender equity in their office, graduate program, or new circle of friends. We help you explore the expectations that you may have as you move into new situations (such as work, graduate school, or travel) after graduation. Invariably, graduating women's and gender studies students feel the tension of leaving the ethos and praxis of women's studies, the secure college environment, and the inevitable adult contradictions of living in an unpredictable world that is fraught with inequality. We suggest that building feminist-friendly allies and networks can be seen as an extension of some of the skill-building you developed as an undergraduate. We highlight some resources and organizations that will help you during this critical time.

We have included several features in this book that will help you move through the material more easily. The sidebars contain facts or short examples related to our comments or definitions of terms used along the way. They will also contain quotes from our survey or our interviewees. We identify our interviewees using first name, the year graduated, and the institution attended. We leave our survey responses anonymous.[5] Several chapters feature an extended discussion on a theme or topic, called a "Spotlight." Spotlights allow student voices to emerge to show how they have lived the goals and principles that underlie women's and gender studies throughout their undergraduate careers and beyond. You will also see "For Your Library"—these sections will suggest books, articles, and other materials for you. We have also included a detailed description of the research methods we used in gathering the stories and experiences of women's and gender studies graduates in the Appendix.

This book is an important first step on your path to exploring your interest in women's and gender studies and pursuing your degree and your career. We are excited about the many possibilities that you will discover along the way. We also hope that this book will inspire you to mentor others who may express an interest in women's and gender issues and/or women's and gender studies. We know how daunting it can be to think about all the challenges that await you as part of your journey— from taking classes to declaring a major to finding employment as a women's and gender studies graduate. But you are not alone, nor set adrift in uncharted waters. Throughout this book, think of both of us as your de facto "womentors" or "fementors," here to guide you on your journey and help you to realize what strengths you have developed as part of your degree, how those talents can best be marketed and utilized in the workforce, and how you can continue your women's studies education and activism outside of the classroom and into the community.

CASE IN POINT: ONE STUDENT, ONE COURSE

Dr. Robert Pleasants shares his experience about the difference that just one class in women's and gender studies made in his life. He is the Interpersonal Violence Coordinator at University of North Carolina, Chapel Hill.

> I took my one and only women's studies course my last semester at the University of North Carolina at Chapel Hill. I'd like to say I enrolled because I was passionate about social justice and eager to learn feminism, but those weren't exactly my motivations. In truth, a good friend and on-and-mostly-off-again girlfriend was a women's studies major, so I enrolled hoping to better understand and maybe impress her as well. To my surprise, the experience far surpassed my self-serving expectations.
>
> Maybe you had a similar experience in your first women's studies course: the novelty of a course that encouraged reflection and personalization of knowledge; the realization that a professor might actually care what you and other students do outside of the classroom; those moments of striking clarity that simultaneously enlighten you and turn your world upside down. Instead of being a class that simply helped me understand women, the course provided a theory and a language that made sense of the inequalities I always saw but did not really fully understand. It also helped me understand myself and the world around me, encouraging me to think about the relationship between the two.
>
> So imagine my frustration at the end of the semester: I felt inspired in a way I had never experienced in my four years of college, I wanted more, and . . . I

was graduating. As things turned out, my plan to understand and impress my ex worked, and so I gained a new partner who shared my interest. Together, we continued to seek new knowledge of feminism, continuing conversations with friends about gender issues, seeking feminist media and books, and holding each other accountable. Simultaneously, we asked ourselves what we could actually *do* with this new knowledge. So we volunteered, first as community educators teaching middle- and high-school kids about relationships, harassment, and sexual assault. Then, when my partner started law school, we began volunteering together as crisis line volunteers at an agency for survivors of relationship abuse, and also meeting great new feminist friends. When I started graduate school in the field of education, I began working part-time at the agency. Because my dissertation was on men learning feminism, I once again took classes in women's studies and read even more. I was also fortunate enough to teach a class on gender and violence, working with amazing feminist undergraduates. Two of them realized the university did not have any staff members solely devoted to violence prevention, so in collaboration with two other graduate students and me, they painstakingly amassed research and support across campus, successfully lobbying for a new position on campus.

A year after finishing my Ph.D., I realized the job we created was the perfect fit for me. I applied for the job and got it, and since then I've been lucky enough to get paid to spend my time fulfilling my passions for teaching and feminism. Needless to say, I'm glad I decided to take that one class.

SECTION ONE

YOU'VE DISCOVERED WOMEN'S AND GENDER STUDIES AND WANT TO KNOW MORE: GREAT! NOW WHAT?

1

THE BIRTH OF WOMEN'S AND GENDER STUDIES AND WHO WE ARE NOW: YOUR INHERITANCE AS A STUDENT OF WOMEN'S AND GENDER STUDIES

Right now, your women's and gender studies classroom probably feels like the center of the universe. You may either physically sit in a women's and gender studies classroom or perhaps you access it as an online course. No matter how you interface with women's and gender studies, you are likely to discover that the type of experience it provides—due to coursework, how you engage in the classes, and the material you cover—is different from your other courses. This chapter takes you behind the scenes to help you understand that what happens in a women's and gender studies classroom is an outgrowth of activism, debate, and rich intellectual tradition.

This chapter highlights the history of women's and gender studies, providing some background about why the program is interdisciplinary in nature, who your professors are, and who is likely to be sitting next to you in the classroom.

The Women's and Gender Studies Classroom

You have probably heard of or read about the social unrest of the late twentieth century. During the 1960s and 1970s, student activists in the US protested not only the war and government policy, but also the very knowledge that was being taught and produced in establishments of higher learning or post-secondary educational institutions. Students and faculty alike were experimenting with the structure and style of teaching, ranging from consciousness-raising sessions in the classroom to changing the physical structure of the classroom itself—such as seating, moving the space from inside to outdoors, or emphasizing student participation rather than the passive learning model of the "banking concept of education" (see Friere 2001). People experimented with class design to provide a better format for engaging students. This time of transition had a profound effect on the development of the women's studies classroom and teaching practices. You might have noticed that you are often seated in a circle

THE WOMEN'S AND GENDER STUDIES CLASSROOM: STUDENT REFLECTIONS

I think the fact that I felt included and accepted in a classroom discussion about my own gender was important. This way people feel more open to discuss things in a "round-robin" forum. What better of a time to talk about issues affecting women, than with OTHER women, in a WOMEN friendly environment! THAT is why I loved this as my minor!

(Libby, 2007, North Dakota State University)

Being immersed in women's and gender studies classes has heightened my ability to critically reflect upon myself, others, and the world around me. While I have always valued time to reflect, these courses have enhanced the quality and depth of my reflections in many areas of my life, from dynamics at family gatherings and uses of gendered language, to service involvement in the community and a different perspective on history. My degree has shown me how I can pursue my passions for incarcerated women's rights, affordable, accessible reproductive healthcare, creating non-judgmental, inviting spaces for immigrant communities, and women's empowerment during the pregnancy and birthing processes in direct and indirect ways and encourages me to connect and devote myself to these interests as my life and career progress.

(Kimmie, 2011, University of North Carolina, Chapel Hill)

One of the very first concepts introduced during the WOST 101 Intro to Women's Studies Course is the "invisible knapsack." Peggy McIntosh wrote the "White Privilege: Unpacking the Invisible Knapsack" in 1988 and it resonates just as loudly twenty-two years later as it did then. Often I look back to that document and repeat it as one would a prayer, or a vow, or a mantra.

(Stacy, 2008, Minnesota State University, Mankato)

that creates a space where everyone faces everyone. It might seem strange to you that a simple change like this—seating students in a circle where they can see and hear one another—was unique and transformative. But it was! This new arrangement allowed for a greater accountability for each student, the possibility for rapport to form more deeply between students and faculty, and a more level playing field in which the distance between professor "knowers" and student "learners" was decreased. This arrangement also served as a type of "container" when strong emotions got fired up.

Faculty members in the 1960s and 1970s drew upon a new pedagogy that was more participatory and personal, which later became known as "feminist pedagogy."[6] They helped to develop the concept of "student-centered learning." The new courses offered faculty and students the opportunity to conduct in-depth scholarly work on subjects that had previously not been a part of the college curriculum, or were at the margins of more traditional disciplines, such as domestic violence, women's roles in historical periods, and women's literature. By listening to and valuing the experiences of students, topics that may have been largely ignored rose to prominence as they reflected the everyday concerns and interests of students. Rather than being the objects of study (such as wife and mother in nuclear family structures as challenged by Betty Friedan in *The Feminine Mystique*; deviant career woman; and/or over-sexualized prostitute or woman of color), women's studies was able to do more than just "add women" superficially to traditional curricula. Women's studies courses allowed students to choose what subjects to study, to question how subjects would be studied, to challenge ideas of objectivity and power within research, and to create knowledge that would support the changes occurring on local, state, and national levels due to feminist organizing (including rape laws, domestic violence, women's health advocacy, women entering non-traditional occupations, wages for housework).

Time Travel: What You Might Have Learned in an Early Women's Studies Class

We are transporting you back in time to an early women's studies class to explore the overlapping connections students made in the classroom and in their lives during the 1970s, one phase of the second wave women's movement. The fight for women's healthcare provides a useful example.

Let's imagine that you took a class on "Women and Health: History, Tensions and New Beginnings" offered for the first time in 1977. If you were enrolled in this early women's studies course, you might have found yourself investigating and discussing why there were so few women doctors in practice. In the 1970s fewer than 10 percent of all doctors were women. You and your classmates would have focused on the many ways that women faced widespread discrimination both as consumers and providers of healthcare (Baxandall and Gordon 2001). You might have heard from your female classmates powerful anecdotes about feeling ignored, infantilized, dismissed, or ridiculed in an everyday encounter with a male physician. You would have spent time reading new feminist scholarship that critically examined the ways that childbirth had become an increasingly medicalized procedure that benefited the schedule of physicians and hospital staff but left many women feeling alienated from their bodies. You might have been amazed to read historical accounts of the role of midwifery in the US and Britain during the sixteenth and seventeenth centuries. Feeling motivated from discussions in class, you might have joined or even created a "women's health group." These informal groups sprang up around the country and "provided direct services, promoted health education, and agitated to change the mainstream health movement" (Baxandall and Gordon 2001: 117). Your professor might have stressed how important it was to gather narratives from women's lived experiences and bring them into the classroom. So, one of your options for a short assignment might have been to interview a woman in your family who was older than you about her experiences accessing and receiving medical treatment.

Toward the end of the semester, one of your longer assignments may have asked you to research and reflect on the ways that current treatment of minority women in the healthcare system were connected to a history of US colonialization. In order to do this you would have to draw on concepts of marginality, the interplay of racism and sexism, and economic discrimination that you had learned from other women's studies classes. The professor would have suggested scholarly articles and books from the established fields of economics, history, and sociology and perhaps new scholarship emerging in ethnic studies and African American studies. Your professor might have also directed you to feminist periodicals, including *Ms.*, but also to smaller magazines and journals that proliferated during the 1970s. In completing this assignment and as you read widely, you would have seen that there were gaps in the way most disciplines treated the subject of "minority women and health" and, indeed, women's studies, though an interdisciplinary analysis was trying to create new knowledge about women and health, not just by closing the gaps, but by creating new areas of inquiry and novel ways of defining the problems. You would have put into practice the interdisciplinary process of creating an original way of gathering data, incorporating new voices, and generating knowledge that tries to highlight the "why and how" that women experience unequal treatment in the area of health. Toward the end of the semester, your professor might have suggested that for women's needs and concerns to be fully addressed in the healthcare system, it would not be enough just to create more women doctors (the "add and stir approach"), but would require a rethinking of the roles of health, wellbeing, and the healthcare system.

Finally, if you had read the newly published *Our Bodies, Ourselves* for class—devoted to explicit discussion and photos of sexual and reproductive issues and stressing that women were experts on their bodies—you might have rushed out and purchased this book for your female friends and relatives. You might have said that this book altered everything that you knew about understanding your body, and, moreover, that it provided valuable information to support your active role in making important health decisions. This class could have even triggered a re-evaluation of your emerging goals for employment and spurred an interest in becoming a doula, doctor, midwife, or nurse!

We hope this brief example gives you a sense of the energy and enthusiasm that was generated in those early women's studies classes and how students often found ways to connect their experiences directly to the social movement happening outside the classroom.

 FOR YOUR LIBRARY

Boston Women's Health Collective. (2005). *Our Bodies, Ourselves: A New Edition for a New Era,* 4th edition. New York: Touchstone Press.

Rosalyn Baxandall and Linda Gordon (Eds.). (2000). *Dear Sisters: Dispatches from the Women's Liberation Movements.* New York: Basic Books.

Sandra Morgen. (2002). *Into Our Own Hands: The Women's Health Movement in the United States, 1969–1990.* Rutgers, NJ: Rutgers University Press.

Your Women's and Gender Studies Professor

If we were to rely solely on media images of a category called "women's and gender studies professors," it would be slim pickings. In the past fifty years it was unusual to even see a woman *portrayed* as a college professor. Typically, stereotyped images of college professors included rumpled, white, older befuddled men (i.e., the absent-minded professor) who pontificated to a classroom (often of other men), or lecherous, leather-patch-and-tweed white men who used their position and influence to seduce naïve co-eds (have you ever seen *Animal House*?). If female students of women's studies were represented at all in the movies, they were portrayed as ethnic print-wearing, Birkenstock-shoed, vegetarian, cheer-less, angry, man-hating women in films such as *PCU* (1994). These characters were one-dimensional misrepresentations of women who often "only needed a man" in order to become happy.

Recently, however, media representations have begun to challenge these stereotypes of students and professors. In films such as *Nutty Professor II: The Klumps* (2000) and *Something's Gotta Give* (2003), Janet Jackson and Frances McDormand are portrayed as smart, witty women who challenge the main male character's ideas about love and life. In fact, at the end of this decade, HBO (a major cable network in the US) made news by initiating conversations about developing a comedy series entitled *Women's Studies*, which would follow the day-to-day life issues experienced by a women's studies professor (Andreeva 2009). While the impact of this character on popular culture and societal ideas about women's studies professors has not yet been evaluated, evidence of changing attitudes about this field shows that we have definitely "come a long way, baby."[7]

If you are already taking women's and gender studies courses, then you have met your professor or professors. Women's and gender studies professors come from a diversity of intellectual backgrounds and training. Historically, people who were known as women's studies professors were activists and academics from other fields who were interested in women's lives. Many of the faculty members we trained with in college, for example, might have claimed the title of feminist or women's studies academic, but were not formally trained in women's studies. They typically advocated and fought to have women's studies on their campuses, supported the advancement of female faculty, and took on equity issues. But their main intellectual work continued to be in their home discipline and department.

In their disciplines, they put questions about gender front and center and published research in discipline-specific journals. Many women and men who pioneered women's and gender studies are considered Baby Boomers (that is, people who were born between 1945 and 1964). Soon this group will be retiring from the discipline, and those of us who will inherit their legacy are women and men who have advanced degrees (such as MAs and Ph.D.s) or graduate certificates in women's and gender studies.

The next wave of women's studies professors are women (like us) and men who have trained in some formal way at either the undergraduate or graduate level in women's studies. Your women's studies professor most likely possesses a Ph.D. (Doctor of Philosophy), a JD (Juris Doctorate, or law degree), or another advanced professional degree (e.g. MPH, a master's in public health; MSW, a master's in social work, etc.). It is also common to find scholars who have trained in one of the traditional disciplines including anthropology, English, history, political science, or sociology, and who also possess a graduate certificate or master's degree specifically in women's studies. Scholars who have pursued Ph.D.s in women's and gender studies at one of the handful of doctoral-granting programs are also increasing. According to a recent report by the National Science Foundation (NSF), "Doctoral Recipients from US Universities Summary Report 2007–2008," in 2008 approximately 114 Ph.D.s were awarded in the Social Sciences category of "area/ethnic/cultural/gender studies." Of these, thirty were male and eighty-four were female (www. nsf.gov/statistics/nsf10309/pdf/tab36.pdf). This number is quite impressive when you compare the number of degrees awarded under this category in 1998 (fourteen) (www.nsf.gov/statistics/nsf10309/pdf/tab47.pdf). Unfortunately, this information may be misleading because of the lack of a specific reference to women's studies as well as the number of Ph.D. candidates who receive women's and gender studies degrees, but may be part of a joint program within another discipline or some other institutional issue. Current trends indicate that the number of faculty who teach in women's and gender studies who hold a Ph.D. in women's and gender studies will continue to increase as demand for women's and gender studies curricula continues to grow in higher education.

Women's and gender studies, as an interdisciplinary field, has paid attention to issues of underrepresentation of groups and is committed to promoting a diverse faculty, particularly promoting the visibility and advancement of women of color. So how are we doing in the US? A recent National Women's Studies Association (NWSA) report, "Mapping Women's and Gender Studies," which partnered with the Ford Foundation and the National Opinion Research Center, found that 30.4 percent of women's studies faculty are faculty of color, compared with 19 percent of faculty nationally in other disciplines (NWSA 2007).[8] This is a good trend for women's and gender studies, but it still requires institutional commitment and effort to maintain and/or improve these numbers. There is, however, less data available to critically assess how women's and gender studies as a field is faring in hiring individuals from other marginalized

THE GROWTH OF THE WOMEN'S AND GENDER STUDIES PH.D.

Over the past three decades, doctoral programs in women's and gender studies have been evolving. There are currently thirteen doctoral programs in women's and gender studies. Some are dual-degree programs—for example, the University of Michigan offers a dual degree in women's studies and psychology. The continued growth of these programs suggests a community of scholars and students engaged in ongoing questions that matter.

- Arizona State University
- California Institute of Integral Studies
- Claremont Graduate University
- Emory University
- Indiana University, Bloomington
- Ohio State University
- Rutgers, the State University of New Jersey
- Texas Women's University
- University of Arizona
- University of California, Los Angeles
- University of Iowa
- University of Maryland, College Park
- University of Minnesota, Twin Cities
- University of Washington

For more detailed information, see the NWSA "Guide to Women's & Gender Studies" webpage (www.nwsa.org/research/theguide/phd.php).

groups, including lesbians and other members from the LGBT community, physically challenged individuals, or men.

Establishing "Women's Studies"

In this section we briefly discuss the historical roots of the founding of "women's studies."

"Back in the day" or the Birth of Women's and Gender Studies

Today you stand as some of the latest in a long line of students who paved the way for women's and gender studies on campuses across the US and now the world. Women's studies has its roots and origins in the social movements of the 1960s and 1970s, specifically the civil rights and women's movements. Women's studies courses and other interdisciplinary studies (e.g. American Studies) were born largely due to student activism and demand. This was a time when more women in the United States were attending colleges and universities than ever before!

While many students attending college during the late 1960s and early 1970s were "traditional" in age and pre-college education, many others were non-traditional (e.g. veterans, married or divorced women, those of different socio-economic strata, racial/ethnic backgrounds, and sexual orientations). This generation of new students (and new professors) created a unique culture in higher education that challenged the status quo as we describe below. Feminist activism spilled onto college campuses, forcing new questions about academic study. The earliest integrated women's studies programs at major universities were founded around 1970, although there were a few courses in women's studies and other related disciplines that were offered at a number of colleges and universities before this time. While acknowledging the importance of individual- and group-level change in the classroom, the first women's studies educators knew they had to change the very structure and curriculum of higher education. At many of the newly coeducational colleges and universities of the 1970s, women's studies developed as part of the process of incorporating and integrating women into their campus communities. Often the first women's studies professors taught women's studies courses as an unpaid teaching overload— out of their absolute commitment to this academic endeavor!

While there were programs in existence that assisted women in going back to school (such as displaced homemaker programs), they did not

EXCERPT FROM "WHY OWL?"

In general, the Women's Liberation Movement is a young movement. Statistics on age are not available but observation indicates the average age of women participating in the movement to be around 25. Older women in the movement are exceedingly rare. OWL (women 30 and above), unlike the younger women's liberation groups, was consciously created by women who:

1. Felt different from the main body of the movement because of age, life experiences, family commitments and goal orientations.
2. Felt that we had experienced long years of personal oppression and participated in the events of life (child birth, child rearing, marriage, divorce, homemaking and careers) that many of the younger groups theorized about . . .

challenge the status quo of the institution per se. Women who were either entering or returning to higher education in the 1960s and 1970s were questioning larger social structures (such as the state, family, military) in relation to their own lives, and education was one of the arenas where palpable change could be achieved. A great example of the tone of this era (which still resonates today) is the Older Women's League (OWL) manifesto "Why OWL?" Written in 1970, it captures the sentiment of women who fought to challenge traditional gender roles that often left women as widows or divorced, unprepared for the workplace, and discriminated against when they were able to obtain employment. OWL also took up the sexist ways in which society viewed women as they aged. They fought for job training, employment services, better childcare options, and a housewives' bill of rights.[9]

Creating Change and the Importance of Research, Theory, and Praxis

The first women's studies faculty were innovative pioneers in creating this new academic endeavor. They wrote their own textbooks, compiled and shared reading lists, developed new curricula, organized conferences, and established academic journals. Their courses provided the first opportunity for women's lives and experiences to be studied seriously in higher education from a gender-inclusive perspective. Yet the advances made by these innovators were in concert with the skills and knowledge they had gained as members of civil rights, liberal, and radical women's groups and organizations. The early twin goals of women's studies as an academic enterprise were to (1) document and redress the exclusion of women's experiences from the traditional male-defined curriculum and (2) pose interdisciplinary questions and analyses across the social sciences, arts, humanities, and sciences. Early on, scholars realized that no single discipline could answer or address women's experiences. Therefore, early on a commitment to multiple approaches and perspectives from a variety of disciplinary communities in addressing women's lives took root. Faculty also emphasized acknowledging and studying women's lives through women's own diverse experiences. Early founders believed that women's studies needed to stay connected and relevant to the everyday issues that women faced and to work on challenging the myriad persisting inequalities.

From the beginning of the institutionalization of women's studies in the academy, the concept of integrating research, theory, and praxis became central. This "triad" of research, theory, and praxis as being equally valued is a unique feature of women's studies in higher education. We will explore this concept more in this section. As you move through your women's studies classes, you will often hear this triad mentioned. In Chapter Two you will see how women's and gender studies curricula are organized around and reflect this triad.

Research

In the academy, one of the primary ways that knowledge is advanced is through the publication of scholarly articles and books based on original research. In the early phases of the movement, women's studies faculty contributed to the academic knowledge base that had been primarily androcentric, or male-centered, in nature. Scholars during the 1970s and 1980s spent much of their time documenting the ways women's experiences were left out of various types of research projects and priorities, and one aspect of this inquiry was to question the stereotypes about women that were pervasive in research (Hesse-Biber and Leavy 2007). These stereotypes were prevalent in science and other seemingly "neutral" forms of empirical research. Hesse-Biber and Leavy discuss a well-known example by anthropologist Emily Martin, who pioneered a critique of gendered bias in the sciences:

She examined textbooks that dealt with human reproduction and found that these texts tended to construct a story where romance and gendered stereotypes about the egg and sperm were created, re-created, and enforced. She found that typically the egg was spoken about with the terms that depicted its passivity, where it "is transported," is "swept," or even "drifts." The sperms, in contrast, were typically spoken about in active, aggressive, and energetic terms, such as "velocity" and "propelling," where they can "burrow through the egg coat" and "penetrate" it (p. 17). Martin shows that so-called truthful and objective medical textbooks were infused with nonobjective stereotypes, shaping both the medical and cultural understanding of natural events ... She argues that medical textbooks were depicting gender stereotypes through scientific language that had little basis in reality.

(p. 37)

Researchers began to ask new questions when women were included in the center of analysis. This meant rejecting the idea that women could simply be "stirred" into disciplines without a serious rethinking of research and theoretical approaches. Scholars looked everywhere for answers in the social sciences and humanities. They examined the study of culture, systems of representation, the analysis of literary texts, and creative expression and the ways in which these systems are shaped by and reflect ideas about gender and society.

Research was conducted through multiple methods: experiments, oral histories, historical analysis, surveys, textual analysis, ethnographies and other qualitative data gathering.

WHAT'S IN A NAME?—WOMEN'S STUDIES, GENDER STUDIES, OR SOMETHING ELSE?

You may be in a program that does not use the moniker "women's studies." Programs and departments are in an intense period of redefining women's studies, gender studies, and sexuality studies. You may be studying these tensions in some of your classes. In this book, we use the term "women's and gender studies" inclusively, noting both the historical formation of "women's studies" and its transformation over time.

The act of naming is powerful. Not only does it have an impact on how we think of ourselves, but also on how others perceive us. In the 1990s, discussions about the use of "women's" versus "gender" studies began to emerge in electronic list serve forums such as WMST-L (an online community of women's and gender studies scholars). Those who advocate for retaining "women's studies" (WMST) point out the historical roots of the discipline as a response to the lack of scholarship and curriculum regarding women. In other words, "women's studies" was the academic response to the women's rights movement. Women's studies put *women* at the center of analysis. Some people are worried that "gender studies" will depoliticize both feminist scholarship and contribute to women's subordination. The use of gender as a category is not a "neutral" concept, but in fact has the potential to re-establish privilege to those group members who society constructs as normative—men of a certain heritage or class. Similar arguments have been made regarding the terms "gay" versus "sexuality" studies as well as African American/Native American/Chicano versus ethnic studies. Another concern of "women's studies" advocates is that this name change has been encouraged by institutional actors outside of the discipline for financial and economic reasons (e.g. enrollment numbers, resource sharing) rather than as a response to changing theoretical and political identities.

Conversely, those who support "gender studies" see the name change as reflecting the shift away from binary identity politics in which a single category (women) can represent the complexity of experiences of individuals and groups who experience gender differently based on their race, ethnicity, sexuality, age, ability, or social class. Some see gender studies as inclusive and less likely to make assumptions about "all women" (also known as "essentialist"). As the very concept of "women" has been questioned by post-modern and post-structuralist theory, as well as by the transgender and intersex community, many question "women's studies" as being too reductionist, limiting, exclusive, and normative.

A recent development in naming has been the combination of women's studies and gender studies in the single name, women's and gender studies. For many advocates, not only does this acknowledge the historical roots of the discipline, but it also attempts to incorporate critiques in order to describe the field's current theoretical canon accurately. For some, this is yet another example of accommodation or an "add and stir" approach in which prevailing structural issues are not challenged. For others, women's and gender studies has a history of acknowledging limitations and responding to them. As we see it, the fact that women's/gender/feminist/sexuality studies exists and continues to explore the very names by which we identify shows the continued application of theory into practice, as well as an intimate engagement with politics that re-affirms the very roots of our existence as an academic and intellectual endeavor.

For more information see:

http://userpages.umbc.edu/~korenman/wmst/womvsgen.html#TopOfPage

Theory

Theory, the second component of the conceptual triad, is an important component in women's studies. It's grounded in experience, critical reflection, and interaction with the larger world. In many disciplines, ideas, concepts, frameworks, and perspectives that had been defined as normal, universal, and centrally important were revealed to focus on a small number of people—usually upper middle-class, heterosexual, able-bodied white men. The development of theory as a vital tool with which to challenge oppression and domination has become central in women's studies. Early women's studies scholars sought new theoretical concepts to explore the features of women's lives (e.g. sexual violence, prostitution, motherhood) that had yet to be fully understood. Scholars in philosophy and political science took up central concepts of citizenship, political participation, and democratic rights, and rethought them by looking at women's experiences. Scholars in theology began questioning the interpretation of seminal works of organized religion and questioned the very language that is used in religion and faith-based communities to marginalize women (see Daly 1993; Christ 1992).[10]

We think it is important to stress that many women's studies scholars were also making changes in their own disciplines and creating organizations within their professional groups that would make scholarship on women a priority. For example, in sociology the foremothers of Sociologists for Women in Society (SWS, an organization within sociology dedicated to supporting and promoting gender scholars and research through conferences and the publication) were making changes within sociology as well as in women's studies. Thus women's studies emerged in concert with changes going on in established disciplines by the very women (and men) who were also shaping women's studies.

Praxis

Finally, we turn to praxis in women's and gender studies. Praxis is about the integration of learning with social justice. As a term, it means that seeking knowledge for knowledge's sake will not change structures of domination and oppression in women's lives.[11] Praxis is about applying one's knowledge to challenge oppressive systems and unequal traditions. It is related to the well-known phrase "the personal is political" espoused by many advocates of the second-wave women's movement. Over time, for those in women's studies, it has meant training students to think and learn about inequalities beyond the borders of the classroom. This integrated triad of concepts helps to distinguish women's studies' intellectual goals from other disciplines.[12] Women's studies as an academic endeavor seeks to weight all three of these concepts equally in teaching, research, and engagement outside of the academy.

NWSA—Professional Outcome of an Academic Movement

Every academic discipline has its own professional organization, and the field of women's studies is no different. The National Women's Studies Association (NWSA) was formed in 1977 and signaled an important moment for women's studies—it was emerging as a key player in the academic landscape, and it had members to prove it. It suggested to the larger academic community that there was enough interest in teaching and research among people who considered themselves committed to women's studies to form an official association. NWSA continues to be the premier organization for scholars and students of women's studies. It holds an annual conference with over 1,600 attendees in past years, including K–12 teachers, college professors, undergraduate students,

STUDENTS AND THE NWSA CONFERENCE

The annual conference of the NWSA encourages undergraduate and graduate representation through participation in roundtables, poster sessions, and paper presentations. Between 2006 and 2009 between 39 percent and 46 percent of the NWSA membership was students (undergraduates and graduates), and between 41 percent and 46 percent of the conference registrants were students. These are significant numbers. You may find yourself working with a professor and being asked to present your work there. Or you can take the initiative and find out about presenting your own work there. If your institution is a member of NWSA, they receive three student memberships for free. If you are interested in attending, this could lower the cost. NWSA also has regional representatives across the country. Some of the regions also host conferences that students can attend as well as present at. (Data gathered by NWSA staff.)

graduate students, higher education administrators (such as deans, etc.), and women's center directors.

Women's studies practitioners also find support through a variety of professional organizations, ranging from those tied to their "home discipline" to caucuses, sections, or organizations that promote the advancement of women, women in academia, workplace issues, and research and scholarship on women and gender, such as the Association for Feminist Anthropology, the Association for Women in Computing (AWC), the Association for Women Geologists (AWG), the Association for Women in Science (AWIS), the International Association for Feminist Economics (IAFFE), the Modern Language Association's (MLA) Division on Women's Studies in Language and Literature, the Western Association of Women Historians (WAWH), Sociologists for Women in Society (SWS), Society for Women in Philosophy (SWIP), Society of Women Engineers (SWE), and the Women's Classical Caucus (WCC) (for more information see: www.socwomen.org/acad_orgs.pdf).

There are also organizations that were formed in the nineteenth century to support female co-eds and utilize the resources of women who had achieved a college degree. The AAUW is an exemplary organization devoted to researching issues that affect women in academia (as well as providing generous support for gender scholars through fellowships).[13]

Congratulations! You've just breezed through a brief sketch of the legacy that you have inherited as a women's and gender studies student. As you can see, women's studies as a distinct academic interdisciplinary field would not have been possible without the social movements that preceded its founding. Moreover, given its origins in social movements, women's studies was from its beginnings activist in orientation. Professors and students saw women's studies as committed to transforming women's roles in the world and not simply understanding such stratified roles. Its goal was not "disinterested" academic inquiry—rather women's studies focused on ending gender oppression and challenging traditional paradigms. Indeed, the relationship of women's studies to the women's movement was crucial in establishing and developing the field. The women's movement, in particular, helped pressure colleges and universities to establish women's studies programs and helped establish the study of women as a worthy endeavor.

FOR YOUR LIBRARY

We encourage you to do further reading about the history, debates, and development of women's and gender studies. You will feel more informed when you talk to your professors (always a plus!), and it will help you understand the larger patterns that have shaped the knowledge that you are learning.

Jane Aaron and Sylvia Walby (Eds.). (1991). *Out of the Margins: Women's Studies in the Nineties*. Bristol, PA: Falmer Press.

Marilyn Jacoby Boxer and Catherine R. Stimpson. (2001). *When Women Ask the Questions: Creating Women's Studies in America*. Baltimore: The Johns Hopkins University Press.

Ann Braithwaite, Susan Heald, Susanne Luhmann, and Sharon Rosenberg (Eds.). (2005). *Troubling Women's Studies: Pasts, Presents, and Possibilities*. Toronto: Sumach Press.

Florence Howe (Ed.). (2000). *The Politics of Women's Studies: Testimony from the Thirty Founding Mothers*. New York: The Feminist Press.

Ellen Messer-Davidow. (2002). *Disciplining Feminism: From Social Activism to Academic Discourse*. Durham, NC: Duke University Press.

Joan Wallach Scott (Ed.). (2008). *Women's Studies on the Edge*. Durham, NC: Duke University Press.

Robyn Weigman (Ed.). (2002). *Women's Studies on Its Own. A Next Wave Reader in Institutional Change*. Durham, NC: Duke University Press.

These activist and political roots are part of women's studies history, which it shares with Chicano studies, American studies, peace and justice studies, Native American studies, environmental studies, and African and African American studies. Not surprisingly, these interdisciplinary fields are sometimes attacked as less scholarly because of their political origins. Traditional disciplines, without seemingly overt activist beginnings, by comparison look neutral and unbiased. I (Michele) was surprised to find when I did my dissertation field research, the discipline of political science (often exclusively focused on quantitative analysis) emerged as a field through philosophy and civics. One hundred years ago, a person studying the field of politics was just as likely to read literature and study languages as he (or she) was to learn statistics. Political science as a discipline went through major shifts post World War II and then again in the early 1980s. The truth is that the boundaries of what a discipline encompasses are ones of constant change and development. Knowledge and what is perceived as important in the make-up of a discipline shifts and changes. In a hundred years, we can assume that women's studies will be configured very differently than it is now. We will return to this point about women's studies origins and the ways in which it is sometimes viewed by others in Chapter Three.

Programs, Departments, Research Centers, Curricula: What Does it Mean for You?

As stated in the introduction, women's studies programs and departments have proliferated across US higher education and globally. There is amazing diversity in how these academic programs are organized. Learning about how your program is organized can help you understand options and choices that may be available to you.

As with many interdisciplinary fields, academic programs such as women's and gender studies can have a variety of organizational features. There are typically two models of women's and gender studies programs and departments and how they are organized. In the first model there are self-governing academic departments with faculty. The second model pertains to small and mid-sized academic programs where faculty are shared across departments and programs. The organization of women's and gender studies into programs and departments tends to reflect a particular US perspective. Across the globe, women's and gender studies at the undergraduate level might be organized as well into "programmes" or research centers.

In the first model, the department is self-contained and has autonomy in how (and who) it hires and tenures, how it develops and delivers curricula, and how resources are allocated to faculty and students. The second model usually includes a program with shared faculty lines. This means that there is usually a director of the program, but he or she is housed in another department (e.g. anthropology). The director coordinates other faculty members who have shared lines across the university to teach and do service for the women's studies program. In this model, faculty "homes" are (usually) within the traditional disciplines where department chairs have the authority to choose the amount of support they give their faculty in teaching women's studies courses. Women's studies has developed over the past three decades through these different models, and there is no model that is inherently better than another—all are institutionally specific. Each model has different implications for students, but, more importantly, both of these models have been successful in the establishment of training women's and gender studies students.

At the end of the chapter, we suggest some ways to find out how women's and gender studies is organized in your institution. Here, however, we touch on a few basic things to keep in mind about how departments and programs are organized and how this relates to you:

- *Resources, or the Money*: How long the program or department has existed can determine how the resources are allocated to support its goals. Most programs and departments typically have budgets that may cover funding for outside speakers, undergraduate travel to conferences, and social events for their students.

- *The People*: Programs and departments employ administrative staff to help support students and faculty with tasks such as registration, classroom scheduling, event planning, travel requests, etc. You may interact with a project manager to handle a technical issue or a student services manager who will help you set up your internship.

  In larger programs or departments, there may also be a faculty advisor whose designated responsibility is to assist students in course selection and plan of study, internships, and other extracurricular activities (for example, this might be Director of Undergraduate Study).

  Some programs and departments are organized in such a way that faculty teach the coursework and do not have to worry about having their time being re-allocated to another "home" discipline's needs.

  As a student in a department, you may have access to many faculty teaching core courses regularly. There may be additional opportunities for research with a professor or other opportunities as well.

- *Courses*: In some programs or curriculum models, affiliate faculty come from a variety of disciplines. Faculty members not only teach a "core curriculum" course, but also offer other courses that are "cross-listed" in their home department. The faculty service in a program or curriculum is seen by the home departments as voluntary or donated, but all parties work together in a collaborative way. Affiliate faculty members do not reside in a single unit of women's studies and have their responsibilities elsewhere. The faculty may meet with the director of the program once or several times a year. This model might allow you the opportunity to work with a diverse array of faculty and to sample cross-listed courses in the faculty member's home department or program.

- *Institutional Culture*: Programs and departments are always interested in student culture. Being part of a department can also contribute to your sense of legitimacy when talking about women's studies to peers and people outside of the college or university. Most people tend to have a general sense that "majors" are in "departments."

The potential challenges for students in a large department or program include size and faculty accessibility.[14] Bigger departments, especially those at research-intensive universities, may not always feel as welcoming as smaller units or programs. Yet students often find their niche in this model through the development of close working ties with a specific professor or a group of fellow students. We have found that when students (and professors) go through coursework together, they bond. The result is a cohort effect. These relationships extend outside the classroom and often result in spontaneous meetings after class for coffee, informal support groups, and even consciousness-raising experiences. In this model, students may seek out opportunities to work with a specific professor on independent research or for teaching assistant opportunities. Not only will you gain insight into the world of academia, but if graduate school is something you are considering, your professor will be able to craft a letter detailing the work you have done with them.

In discussing how women's and gender studies fits into higher education, we would be remiss if we did not acknowledge the important role that community colleges play in training students. Community colleges are an integral component of higher education, and women's studies classes are flourishing within them (Roy 2009). Judith Roy notes that in 2009 ". . . community colleges educated 46 percent of all US undergraduates" (Roy 2009: 62). Faculty members in community colleges make a significant commitment when teaching women's and gender studies because they already have high teaching responsibilities and usually do not have an appointment in a program or department (Roy 2009). Many professors at community colleges, however, are committed to helping students both fulfill their potential and "overcome daunting obstacles to meet their goals" (Roy 2009: 62). They are also excited about meeting the growing demand for women's and gender studies classes at the community college level. Jill M. Adams, Assistant Professor of English and Women's Studies at Jefferson Community & Technical College, explores below what makes teaching at the community college level so important:

> "This is the most exciting—if intense and overwhelming—course I've taken in college," wrote a student during a mid-semester check-in for an Introduction to Women's Studies course I was teaching. In reaction to an activism project, another student wrote that he had never taken the time nor felt the inclination to *do* something when hearing about an issue that upset him: "Now I know I *can* do something and that it makes a difference." These students and countless others are the reasons I teach—and why women's and gender studies is so powerful.
>
> Teaching college students can be exciting in and of itself, but teaching in a community college setting makes it the amazing experience it is. As is typical of community college enrollments nationally, the engaged, insightful, passionate students in my classes vary in age (ranging from 18–60+), ethnicities, social and familial backgrounds, and gender identities.
>
> The students are overwhelmingly first-generation college attendees, hold down full-time jobs while taking courses (often full-time), and come to the college with unique life experiences and academic goals. As in a university-setting, many students just out of high school are discovering themselves and spreading their wings; but at the community college there are students in the same classrooms who are raising (or [have] already raised) a family, and/or people who have been laid off from a job they've worked for twenty years. Three generations of folks may be in the same class.
>
> The disparate backgrounds of the students create a scaffolding of "real life" on which to layer the course material and makes the

exploration of women's and gender studies poignant and profound. When we discuss intersectionality, feminism, privilege, and oppression the students have experiences with which to contextualize the academic discussion. It's a riveting moment to discuss second-wave feminism and have students recount experiences of marching on/in Washington, DC or being fired from a job because of pregnancy. Similarly, the unique element of W&GS [women's and gender studies] within a community college setting is that these students are collectively *living* marginalization and power inequalities both in their personal lives—as do students at all academic institutions—but additionally in their perception of and access to education itself.

Although change is underway, community colleges have been perceived/stereotyped as somehow "less than" four-year universities: less than academically, less than socially. It's not uncommon to hear someone say that attending a community college means you weren't good enough (read: smart enough) to get into a "real" college. Consequently, students may lack confidence in their abilities, in the college, and in the education possible at the institution. However, a surprising impact of these doubts is often a keen and deep affinity for women's and gender studies concepts and issues. The W&GS discipline offers students a credible, respectful, authentic, and authoritative means of acknowledging—and perhaps validating—their experiences and choices. They see themselves in the course material; indeed, they *are* the course.

But the college doesn't end at the classroom door. A significant aspect of the community college philosophy and mission is to be part of the community. Most community colleges are non-residential so students commute in, take classes, and commute out, thus leaving limited time for, and access to, extracurricular engagements. W&GS as a field of study provides targeted opportunities for students to engage with community-based partners through activism, service learning, and internships which in turn support their learning and create tangible avenues to value themselves and life choices. When those outlets aren't necessarily typical via extracurricular activities, then fostering them academically is even more critical.

The community college setting is a living testament to the values, concepts, needs, and impact of women's and gender studies; and the field is vital to supporting student voices that can be marginalized even within higher education. And students do find their voices: about self, identity, and activism. Watching the metamorphosis from uncertainty to knowledge and confidence is a gift. I love my job. It's exhilarating, intellectually-stimulating, challenging, frustrating, and ultimately personally and profession- ally rewarding.

Women's and Gender Studies Students—Who Are They?

Who's that sitting next to me?

There are lots of reasons why students come to women's and gender studies. Think, for example, about your own learning path. What made you switch from, say, a business major to women's and gender studies? What identities do you have as a women's and gender studies student and why? Although there is no existing comprehensive international database about women's and gender studies students, we wanted to touch on who might be in the classroom with you over the next several years. You may have been exposed to some of the ideas discussed in your women's studies class through one of your parents' involvement in women's and gender equality movements, your own experience with activism, or from classes in middle or high school. We are seeing more and more students who have had some positive contact with women's and gender studies prior to taking our courses. Some students enter women's studies already familiar with the key perspectives of the field. We think this trend is the fruition of the hard work of activists, educators, and many in the nonprofit sector who are committed to gender equity and the promotion of women's studies. Still, for many students, finding women's studies is an unanticipated discovery and an area of study with which they had not previously been familiar (unlike English, history, education, business, communication, etc.).

The graduates in our survey comprise a good picture of women's and gender studies students.

Your Women's and Gender Studies Classroom:
Data from Graduates

During the course of your undergraduate studies in women's and gender studies, you may have become close with the other students in your classes. You may have shared some intimate information about your experiences growing up, your thoughts and beliefs about controversial topics, and your hopes and fears about your life after graduation—yet what are some of the overall characteristics of women's and gender studies graduates?

Women's studies majors and minors at the undergraduate level are predominantly composed of female students.[15] Female students make up the majority of women's studies majors and minors, although not all students identify as either "women" or "men." As gender and transgender politics have become more visible on college campuses, the gendered composition of our students has reflected this. Ideally, biological determinism should not play a role in who can major in women's studies, but as evidenced in the works of feminist scholars such as Emi Koyama (2003) debates still erupt in feminist academic and activist communities about whether men can be feminists and the role of trans-men and trans-women in "female-centered" spaces.[16]

Yet the preponderance of females in women's studies should not be surprising given the history of the field. Women's and gender studies offers the opportunity to study issues of power and gender dynamics in a way that supports many young women's learning trajectories. However, in the past several years there has been rising male participation in women's and gender studies programs. We think that several factors are responsible for this. Due to the women's movement, more men have been raised in egalitarian households over the past three decades and are generally interested in women's lives. Some male students come to view classes in women's studies as an extension of their interests shaped by family dynamics. Women, men, and transgendered students take women's and gender studies courses and enjoy them enormously, and see that they can study in this interdisciplinary field. Additionally, male, female, and intersex students often take an introduction to women's studies course as part of fulfilling general educational requirements and decide that they wish to take more. They also may find classes on masculinity and gender that are of interest.

According to our study, the overwhelming majority of women's and gender studies students identify as biologically "female" (95 percent), followed by "male" (4 percent), with the rest identifying as "intersex" or "other." Even though many of our respondents did identify with traditional classifications of sex in the survey, the nature and placement of the question was raised as an issue by several participants:

> I'm a trans man, and I know you want me to say "female," but really, this question is worded awfully. And it sucks that the sex I was assigned at birth is regarded as more important than how

I identify (which I assume you consider it to be, based on this being the second question in the survey).

Contemporary women's and gender studies scholars have sought to question and challenge binary sex classifications, therefore, it is not surprising that some respondents do not identify with ascribed or "traditional" sex or gender categories.

The majority of the graduates who answered our survey were born in the United States (82 percent) with about 9 percent born in Canada. Other graduates hail from a variety of countries including Germany, South Korea, Brazil, Australia, Kenya, Russia, Scandinavia, Japan, and China. After graduating with their degree in women's and gender studies, the majority of those surveyed now live in the United States (83 percent) with about 2 percent residing in either the UK or Canada. Other places your fellow classmates may reside after graduation include Germany, Scandinavia, the Netherlands, South Korea, Spain, Italy, Trinidad and Tobago, or Ghana.

As for race and ethnic identities, the majority of women's and gender studies graduates marked "white" (82 percent). About 5 percent of the graduates marked "black/African American," 3 percent identified as Hispanic/Latino, 4 percent claimed an Asian or Pacific Islander heritage, 1.5 percent claimed a Native American or Alaska Native ancestry, and less than 1 percent claimed a Middle Eastern identity. About 6 percent of those surveyed claimed a multiracial/ethnic heritage along with a few respondents who identified as Roma and Jewish. Survey respondents were given the opportunity to claim as many ethnic identities as they felt appropriate, as well as describing their racial/ethnic heritage in the "other" category. However, the classification system used also reflects the traditional "big five" categories commonly used in the United States by survey researchers and government entities. As the majority of women's and gender studies graduates either were born or raised in the United States, these racial/ethnic categories may be familiar; yet, as recent debates over the census—and as raised in women's and gender studies classrooms— have shown, these classifications do not capture the complex heritage of our graduates in the United States or Canada, nor in the world.

In addition to the mix of students in the women's and gender studies classroom in terms of biological sex, racial/ethnic classifications, and countries of origin, age of graduates varies as well. The majority of those in our survey (who all graduated between 1995 and 2010) were 23–26 years of age (31 percent) at the time of their graduation. Another 29 percent were 27–31 years of age, with 18 percent being 32–36 years of age at graduation. By comparison, the most prevalent range in which our graduates started their women's and gender studies degree program is 18–22 years of age (84 percent). Therefore, more "traditional" aged under-graduate students are actively choosing women's and gender studies as part of their degree selection process.[17]

While there has been a lot of debate about the institution of marriage, not only in the women's and gender studies classroom, but also in the realm of politics, law, media, as well as in families in the United States and abroad, only 29 percent of the graduates surveyed identified as "married." Another 2.1 percent identified as being in a formal, legal domestic partnership. The majority of those surveyed identified as either being "single, never married" (42 percent), being in an "informal" domestic arrangement, or "living together" (19 percent). Only about 10 percent of those surveyed identified as either being divorced or in a dissolved civil union. As legal marriage or formal legal domestic partnerships are not uniformly available to everyone who participated in our survey, the "single, never married" majority may reflect this issue. Yet many of those surveyed described their relationship status in other ways. It seems we currently lack a good term for those who are in long-term, long-distance relationships.

As the number of women's and gender studies departments and programs have increased since its inception, we found that the majority of graduates surveyed were majors (61 percent), with minors comprising almost a quarter (24 percent) of the sample. About 7.2 percent of the respondents indicated that they had a concentration in women's and gender studies. We also acknowledge that internationally a major or minor may not have an equivalent.

Many women's and gender studies programs emphasize a global or multicultural perspective, and this is reflected in the fact that a third of our respondents participated in an international studies or study abroad experience. Of those who participated in undergraduate study abroad, 36.7 percent had some women's or gender studies courses as part of their overseas curriculum.

While about a third of women's and gender studies graduates experienced an international studies program, 45 percent of graduates completed an internship during the course of the undergraduate experience. Of those who completed an internship, 58.5 percent received college credit for their internship.

After completing a degree in women's and gender studies, there are a variety of ways that graduates stay in contact with their colleagues from their classes and degree programs. Email (58.8 percent) and social networking sites, particularly Facebook, (53 percent) were the primary methods of communication. Yet a fairly high number of graduates have face-to-face meetings (39.2 percent). Unfortunately, 27.4 percent of those surveyed have not stayed in contact with anyone since they graduated with their degree.

Many of our graduates had a variety of experiences in terms of getting prepared for their professional lives and careers. The majority of those who responded to the survey (40.1 percent) utilized campus career services. Another source of information on careers for our graduates was guest speakers (38.6 percent). About a quarter of those surveyed (25.6 percent) received information from seminars. "Books/pamphlets" and "websites" each accounted for 15.5 percent of our samples as a source of information about careers and professions. Sadly, 32.2 percent our respondents indicated that their department or program did not offer career services. It seems that women's and gender studies undergraduate departments and programs need to assess how they prepare students for life after their degree and develop resources to assist them in this endeavor.

After completing an undergraduate degree in women's or gender studies, a notably high 57 percent of those who responded to the survey completed some graduate or professional degree courses.

During the past two decades, many women's and gender studies departments and programs have been instrumental in supporting the development of queer and sexuality studies (or allies of new interdisciplinary perspectives). Many biologically identified or transgendered men find women's and gender studies to be compatible with their sexual identities and interests. For example, many men participate in campus organizations and events directed by LGBT centers and/or Women's Centers.[18] On many campuses, these entities have long-standing cooperative working relationships in which students gain internship or

SPOTLIGHT: MATT EZZELL

Matt is an activist and professor and was a women's studies major who graduated in 1995 from UNC Chapel Hill. Women's studies was not entirely foreign to him because he had a sister who graduated with a women's studies minor, and when he was in high school his mother went back for an MA in literature, specializing in contemporary African American women's novels: "I saw how rewarding it was for them. I thought I'd take a class . . . to see what it was about." He also was interested in understanding his sister's lifelong struggle with eating disorders, which began as a young girl. By high school Matt had an awareness that the way that he and his sister were treated was different, based on their gender identities. This was a formative experience for him as a young man, "I really highlighted the modeling industry as the problem. I saw women who looked like my sister . . . I knew there was something wrong with the media and modeling industry. That was the start . . . the seed."

Soon after arriving at college he took a sociology class cross-listed with women's studies, "Introduction to Sex and Gender in Society":

> I went in thinking, this class is going to help me learn more about my sister's experience and it's going to help me be a better brother to her and help me make sense [and] understand what she is going through. And I definitely got pieces of that . . . But what I did not anticipate is that I learned more about myself as a man in this culture than I did about women. And that was transformative. It gave me a more informed critical lens to see the social world, it gave me more language to make sense of my experiences as a man and my sister. I never identified with the norms of dominant masculinity and did not know what to do with that. I tried to fit in and was uncomfortable with doing that. I grew up in a small town in North Carolina where football was king, and I did not play football and I had no desire to and that was not easy and that marked me as different within the community of boys in that town, and finding women's studies was something that gave me [an understanding of] the social construction of gender [which] was transformative. It showed me what it could mean to be a feminist and identify as a feminist.

We'll return to Matt's story throughout this book.

volunteer experience while simultaneously receiving credit in their women's studies units.

Ultimately, the women's and gender studies classroom is a global classroom. In our experience, we have seen that our classes have become increasingly diverse in terms of social-class status, nationality, ethnicity, and sexual orientation. Over the course of your academic career, you are likely to be taking classes with students who have been shaped by a variety of experiences and social contexts.

Why You Are Part of an Educational Vanguard

The work that you will be committing to in women's and gender studies has a rich intellectual and social history. For the past four decades, the university has been producing a new type of student in higher education. We believe women's and gender studies students are emerging as a type of educational vanguard (Luebke and Reilly 1995; Boxer 2001). What do we mean by this? Women's studies' early twin goals of reaching across the disciplines to answer questions about gender and challenging the status of women were innovative in higher education. Since that time, women's and gender studies has developed classroom practices and pedagogical styles that have been adopted by many other disciplines. It has broadened the traditional liberal arts education to encompass a specific focus on inequality, power, and advocacy that continues to be distinctive. The student–professor relationship has also been rethought—moving from an expert-to-student relationship to a relationship of co-collaborators. Women's and gender studies has pushed for curricula transformation and that translates into students who have been trained to learn multiple perspectives and to demonstrate the application of knowledge in pursuit of a more equitable society. It encourages students to evaluate their goals and values, as well as synthesize knowledge. The emphasis on synthesizing knowledge and applying it in new contexts is exciting to students and encourages them to become involved in issues they care deeply about. A number of women's and gender studies graduates discuss this as one of the primary components of their training that they value highly. As Celeste, a double major in psychology and women's studies explains:

> I find that women's studies training broadens your thinking—you start to see opportunities to improve the institutions/groups/etc. you are a part of; you begin to incorporate programs, etc. that are inspired by lessons you learn in women's studies.
>
> For example, in my sorority, KD [Kappa Delta], we have a Girl Scout troop that we do various activities with and at the same time, we have been donating to the Dove foundation in

support of their campaign for "real beauty." After a class about
the social construction of women's bodies and learning a great
deal about eating disorders and distorted body images among
young girls, I spoke with our leaders, and we began to have
"workshops" with our Girl Scout troop during which we discussed
"beauty" (kinds of beauty, what it means to a be a "beautiful
person," etc., etc.). My knowledge gained from this women's
studies class as well as the passion it excited in me surrounding
this issue sparked a cross-pollination of awareness in activism that
hopefully encouraged healthy lifestyles and positive body images
among young, active girls, who will soon (or are already) "at risk"
for succumbing to the many pressures regarding appearance that
are faced by girls today.

                         (Celeste, 2010, UNC, Chapel Hill)

Our research and framing about the unique role of women's and gender
studies students in higher education is complemented by discussions of
how women's and gender studies students view themselves. Narratives
and vignettes can be found in the scholarly articles, magazines, online
discussions, and several introductory textbooks in women's studies that
have emerged over the past two decades.[19] One women's studies graduate,
reflecting on applying her women's studies training now as an obstetrician
and gynecologist, says that de-masking "unspoken assumptions" was an
important lesson that she now uses in her work environment:

Being realistic and intelligent about power relationships and
inequities is another lesson of women's studies. Being a student
of women's studies did not influence my career choice, [but] it
helped shape my values, how I see the world, and what I see as
my role in it as an African American woman. I value women as
full members of society in whatever roles they choose. However,
I recognize the world as gendered and unequal. I feel that I have
a responsibility to change that status quo wherever possible . . .
These values are neither objective nor neutral. But the fallacy of
objectivity is another lesson of women's studies.

                      (Thompson 2002, in Kesselman, McNair, and
                                Schniedewind, Eds., 2008: 634)

Another women's studies graduate has found that the training to examine
how assumptions about gender shape the world has been useful after
college: "I left the Women's Studies program at SUNY [State University
of New York] New Paltz with energy and enthusiasm to go out into the

world and make a difference in the lives of women." She joined the Peace Corps and discusses how her women's studies training led her to think critically about the challenges of working with women and children on health literacy given many of the structural dimensions of their lives:

> My women's studies education gave me an understanding of the problems that women living in the third world face. It also gave me insights into how grassroots level initiatives work. It was with these things in mind that I was able to reach as well as be taught by the women of The Gambia. I learned in Women's Studies the importance of listening and learning from women of different cultures. I knew that what I needed to do was to join the women in their work.
>
> (Rivera 2006, in Kesselman, McNair, and Schniedewind, Eds., 2008: 634)

Her women's studies education allowed her to consider working in a participatory way with the women, to begin to understand the complexity of their lives as both distinctive and similar to her own. It also allowed her to re-evaluate what she thought about "women's work" and how underappreciated it was. Her training "enhanced my appreciation for the work women do and enabled me to bring to the world of women's work insights and ideas that will somewhat ease women's burdens" (635).

A core theme of what you are hearing through these vignettes is the role of what is often defined in higher education as "civic" engagement. Women's and gender studies students come from a long tradition of supporting students to understand and contribute to the social world. But how do we think more critically about the relationship between civic engagement and women's and gender studies? To examine this concept further, we talked with Dr. Catherine M. Orr, Associate Professor and Chair of the Department of Women's Studies at Beloit College. She and several women's and gender studies colleagues from around the country have been working on how to document the role of civic engagement in women's studies:

> Whether it's running a mentoring group for girls at a local junior high school, taking a leadership role on a collaborative media project to promote a neighborhood community center, or staffing a rape crisis center hotline, Women's Studies students bring a unique set of perspectives to their civic engagement work.

But first, what is civic engagement?

Civic engagement is a catchall term that describes learning that happens outside of the college or university classroom and benefits both the student (by expanding her/his abilities to apply knowledge across multiple contexts) and the community beyond the campus (by providing volunteer labor and cultivating the next generation of community-minded individuals). And whether it's called "service learning," "experiential education," "community-based learning," or "mentored internships" in nonprofit organizations, civic engagement has become central to the mission of most US colleges and universities. In fact, over 90 percent of students, administrators, faculty, and student affairs professionals agree that "preparing students to contribute to the community should be an essential goal of a college education" (Schneider, in Dey et al. 2009: ix).

What's different about civic engagement in women's studies? Women's studies situates civic engagement in a unique curricular context. With the discipline's historical roots in activist movements, its social justice mandate, and its reflective approach to its own knowledge production, women's studies offers students a distinctive method for learning how to grapple with the tensions between theory and practice in civic engagement contexts. By encouraging critical reflection on, say, the values of "the community" or "the good citizen," a women's studies approach to civic engagement demands that students *analyze the historical and cultural foundations that create the need for their service in the first place*, as well as *interrogate their own motivations* to "help others."

For example, Tobi Walker, former program director of projects at Rutgers' Center for American Women and Politics, notes that in her service learning courses, she tells students that "community can be a problematic concept . . . [in that it] necessarily excludes, defining some individuals as 'inside' and some as 'outside'" (2000: 28). In this manner, Walker is asking her students to rethink the very concept of community as an inherent "good."

Analyzing the foundations of what so often goes unquestioned is at the heart of civic engagement in women's studies. Following this principle, a women's studies professor might ask her student who is doing a service-learning project at a community center in a poor neighborhood, "How is the need for a community center in this particular neighborhood a product of prior exclusions? And how does knowing about the historical and cultural legacies of this particular community inform how you do your work there?"

In addition to bringing analytical concepts to bear on what the student encounters in any community-based context, civic engagement in women's studies requires some amount of personal reflection in which the student is asked to consider how their own historical and cultural location (e.g. gender expression, racialized identity, regional bias, class interests, sexual orientation, professional experience, level of education, age, etc.) has an impact on what they are able to learn from and do for others in any given context. Without such self-awareness on the part of students, differences of race, culture, class, etc., can too often disrupt their best efforts to "do good." In this way, women's studies teaches students entering communities that are not their own that (1) they are products of historical and cultural forces, (2) these forces form both their sense of selves and differences among individuals but are neither neutral nor simply chosen, and (3) the students themselves are responsible for attempting to negotiate as best they can the impacts of these differences in that community-based context.

Ultimately, the goal of a women's studies approach to civic engagement is to prepare students to make their classroom learning relevant, worthwhile, and, in the best cases, truly transformational for themselves and others.

Graduates Speak to You

So far in this chapter you have learned some of the historical context that contributed to the development of women's and gender studies in higher education, time-traveled back to an early women's studies class, and discovered the role that women's and gender studies has played in shaping a new kind of student. You may have just begun exploring the possibility of doing more work in women's and gender studies, and so we thought this might be a good time for you to hear how graduates from our survey reflect on that same choice that you'll face (or are facing right now): What do I major, minor, or concentrate in? On our survey, we asked graduates: "What advice would (or do) you tell other students or friends considering a course of study or degree in gender and/or women's studies?" While we received many emphatic responses that said "Do it!" and "Go for it!" below we highlight some of our longer and more detailed answers:

It's a fantastic interdisciplinary degree that gives you the communication skills employers need. You'll use these skills the rest of your life. Put it together with a foreign language, internships and study abroad and you can't be beat. Do what you love. Follow your bliss . . . A women's studies degree is a fabulous, well-rounded liberal arts course of study and I would do it again in a heartbeat.

(2003, WMST major, Hollins University)

Please study Women's and Gender Studies because it applies to the threads of our making as humans. I do not for one minute regret doing a minor in Women's and Gender Studies; it changed my perspective on the world for the better. Women's and Gender Studies impacts every part of our lives and expands one's views and intelligence regarding such areas as the workforce, education, domesticity, violence, poverty, and love. Women's and Gender Studies is not only about human rights for females but also about how humans interact with one another in every sense. It teaches the history of nations and can help you to better understand how, for instance, racism, sexism, and heterosexism affect our everyday lives.

(2009, WMST minor, St. Norbert College)

Major in what you believe in. Job markets are always changing. You will have many jobs. And if you study something you are passionate about, the chances are at least some of those jobs you will have will be deeply fulfilling.

(2003, Gender Studies major, University of
Southern California)

. . . your undergraduate degree is more about who you are than what you'll do. If you think an organization would really say "OMG you are a women's studies major" and not hire you for that reason, then you don't want to work for that organization in the first place. Women hold up half the world!

(2007, WMST major, Wellesley College)

Try one class—see if you like it. Try a second class—they can vary widely based on topic and professor. If you find you like it, stick with it. Gender and Women's studies can be applied to any field, whether that be psychology, math, engineering, community health—it all involves people and people are shaped by their identities.

(2009, Gender & WMST and psychology, double
major, University of Illinois, Urbana-Champaign)

I have told people, and would continue to say, that to choose a course of study or degree in gender and/or women's studies is probably the best foundation one can have from which to grow as a critical thinker and life-long learner. Choosing to do a degree in women's and gender studies takes confidence and a willingness to be challenged academically, politically, and personally. I consider it a tremendous privilege to have earned this degree, and with it comes the responsibility to make a contribution to your piece of the world, whether in the field of women's and gender studies, in law, health, arts, community activism and beyond, or in my field, education.

> (2007, WMST major, Queen's University, Ontario, Canada)

I would encourage more men to participate because Gender Studies isn't just about women, nor should it be only the focus of women. If some men knew that feminism was really just about equality then I think we'd have a happier world.

> (2005, Gender Studies major, University of Notre Dame)

I wouldn't hesitate to recommend it. It has certainly added a dimension to my life that I wouldn't have anticipated. I didn't get into this until I was in my 40s. I can't imagine how my life would have been different if I had been able to do this degree right out of high school.

> (1996, WMST major, University of British Columbia)

... I found it personally interesting, but I also knew I was going to law school after I completed my undergraduate degree. Thus for me it was a good forum for learning critical analysis, researching and writing, as well as developing an understanding of multiple perspectives of an issue or topic. No doubt there are more opportunities to do interesting work or further studies in this space now than there were 15 years ago.

From a more personal perspective, my mother was Chinese, and came from an arranged marriage in which my grandmother was an object and who could only speak when spoken to. My father was from a very traditional patriarchal Scandinavian household who favored sons over daughters. It was eye opening for me to realize I could do and be so much more than what I had grown up to believe. I loved challenging traditional ideas, rules and norms! The women's studies curriculum was great for me—it was in my undergraduate studies that I began what has been a lifelong journey of self-discovery, trying to understand who I am, what I have been told is me, what and who society expects me to be, and what and who I'd like to be going forward. I would probably have undergone a similar journey of exploration in any case, but a women's studies degree gave me the space and frame of reference in which to structure my thinking in more meaningful ways.

In addition to changing the way I view myself as a woman, it has changed the way I view other women in all walks of life. I do a lot of international travel for my work, with a focus on environmental and social issues in emerging markets. I am particularly sensitive to the role of women in their communities and thinking about how women are a vastly under-served segment of the population in terms of access to capital and banking. They are also the most likely segment of the population, along with children, to be negatively impacted by the development of major projects or by poor health and safety standards of employers in their local communities. Further, they are less likely to be able to be heard in the absence of appropriate grievance mechanisms. I am always thinking about how we can include these types of considerations at the top levels of business decision making in banking institutions that finance the companies and projects in these communities, or provide the financial products to serve and provide access to capital to the individuals in these communities.

I would further add, that by challenging traditional notions of what it means to be a woman, and what we understand about sexuality, my women's studies courses opened my mind to alternative approaches to gender roles and sexuality. This has made me generally a more open and accepting person over the years. Coming from a small, very close-minded, conservative, provincial town in Michigan, this was an important step for me in recognizing, being more sympathetic to, and accepting "non-traditional" lifestyles. I am so much richer for opening my world to different people with different views, value systems and lifestyles. I take this into my personal and professional life and, given the international nature of my work and extensive travel I have done on a personal level, I have found that I am intellectually interested in and curious about people everywhere and what makes them who they are—nature/nurture, cultural norms and influences, geography, race, creed, origins, sexuality, etc. This makes me a better person, a better professional, a better advocate.

(1995, WMST major, University of Michigan)

Women's health is a fascinating, empowering area to be in and nursing is a profession with great potential for intellectual growth, career advancement, and flexibility. I would not have arrived at women's health nursing if I had not studied women's studies first.

(2005, WMST and French, double major,
Dickinson College)

For students who are interested in pursuing women's studies, I strongly encourage it. I have talked to a few undergraduate students who worry about the employability of women's studies graduates (or whose parents worry about this). I tell people that from my own experience and perspective, employers (and grad school admissions committees) in many arenas are less interested in what someone's undergrad major was, and more interested in skills like critical thinking, writing, communicating with people of diverse backgrounds and perspectives, etc. Women's studies courses provide a lot of opportunities to develop these kinds of skills, and can prepare students for a range of future career paths.

(2003, Gender and WMST double major,
Oberlin College)

TAKE IT! It will probably change your worldview . . . it did for me. I always took gender roles and rules as law until that world was flipped on its head in my Intro to WMST class. Seriously, it made me go "Wait, I was TAUGHT how to act like a girl?" and it really changed how I did things. It also made me more free to act how I am, not what I'm supposed to be. It opened up new possibilities for me in terms of what it meant to be a woman.

(2009, WMST and Psychology, double major,
College of William and Mary)

Women's and Gender Studies: Contributing and Fulfilling the Academic Mission

Women and gender studies, through its focus on what voices have been excluded from knowledge, has consistently posed valuable questions to higher education. Women's studies courses also tend to meet other university-wide requirements that colleges and universities collectively consider to be important. In fact, the expectations that universities and colleges have for their students are often reflected in the front pages of your college curriculum under the description of the core curriculum courses you must satisfy in order to graduate. While the specific courses offered at your particular institution may be unique, the curriculum for your college and university has largely been influenced by a growing interest of educators and state officials alike to produce a well-rounded student who has been exposed to a variety of perspectives. These concerns get codified into standards that are encouraged by accrediting boards, state legislatures, state and university systems, and boards of regents and trustees. Women's and gender studies has played an important role in shaping what a civically engaged, globally competent student looks like with liberal arts training.

Women's and gender studies majors and minors receive instruction and coursework that satisfies both global and diversity requirements for outside review boards, and institutional demands as well. For example, by the end of Cheryl's introductory women's studies course, students will have learned:

1. to gain knowledge of the history of women's studies and its contemporary state
2. to be able to read, analyze, and critically examine theoretical perspectives on sex/gender, race/ethnicity, social class, and sexuality; this is done through participation in class discussions, interactions with classmates and written discourse
3. to promote awareness and personal reflection on the significance of how sex/gender, class, sexuality, and race/ethnicity are viewed in themselves and in others
4. to understand the relationships between the social constructs of sex/gender, race/ethnicity, sexuality, and social class
5. to be open and increase awareness and respect for individuals, groups, perspectives, and experiences that may differ from their own.

These learning outcomes correspond to larger curricular goals that colleges and universities have developed to enhance the knowledge and interpersonal skills of contemporary students. Often students acquire this information through a variety of different classes in different disciplines. As women's and gender studies is interdisciplinary in nature, our curricula not only requires students to become proficient in the many disciplines pertaining to women's and gender studies, but also to understand that our field was founded by the absence of women in these other disciplines. In Chapter Two, you'll see how that plays out in the kinds of courses that may be offered at your college or university.

LINKING WOMEN'S AND GENDER STUDIES TO CORE UNIVERSITY PRINCIPLES

At Cheryl's former institution, Minnesota State University, Mankato—and this is similar to other institutions—her "Introduction to Women's Studies" courses, as well as other introductory-level women's and gender studies courses, often satisfy core requirements for students defined as important by the college or university. A summary of the other areas that are satisfied through taking introductory women's studies courses includes:

- History and the Social and Behavioral Sciences: To increase students' knowledge of how historians and social and behavioral scientists discover, describe, and explain the behaviors and interactions among individuals, groups, institutions, events, and ideas. To challenge students to examine the implications of this knowledge and its interconnection with action and living an informed life.[20]
- Human Diversity: To enhance students' understandings of individual and group differences, the contributions of pluralism to United States society and culture, and the historical and contemporary responses of the United States to group differences.
- Global Perspective: To increase student understanding of the growing interdependence of nations, traditions, and peoples and develop their ability to apply a comparative perspective to cross-cultural social, economic, and political experiences.
- Ethical and Civic Responsibility: To develop students' abilities to identify, discuss, and reflect upon ethical perspectives and use these perspectives to engage in civic responsibilities.

(from Minnesota State University, Mankato, 2008,
"Advising, General Education & Cultural Diversity")

While it is unclear the degree to which these core requirements were influenced by the goals and activism of the women's studies department at Cheryl's university, their presence indicates that women's and gender studies curricular ideas are integral to undergraduate education. Yet, as much progress as has been made in higher education, we believe there is still more to accomplish.

YOUR TURN: EXERCISES

Who Are You in this New Learning Community?

Don't be shy! Go now and investigate your women's and gender studies program if you have not done so already. Find out if there is an undergraduate advisor in the program. Usually, there is an assigned faculty member who has the responsibility of orienting students to the program. Arrange to speak with that person. Visit the department or program's website. Gather the available literature on your program. You can even request to meet with the chair or director of the program. Students are often hesitant to do this, but directors and chairs truly enjoy talking with students about their programs and how they can serve your interests. You can also talk with a professor whose class you are taking.

If you happen to be a person who shrinks into the back seat of a classroom and hopes like heck you don't get called on, we've put together some starting points for one-on-one conversations with professors. Begin by asking *them* about their own academic experiences: What did you major in as an undergraduate? What did you study as a graduate student? What is your research about? How does it connect to women's lives, gender, or sexuality? How did you come to teach in women's and gender studies? What professional conferences do you typically attend to present your research? Do you attend the National Women's Studies Association conference? If so, what do you find useful about attending? Does the department offer credit or other support to undergraduate students to attend academic conferences? How does the women's studies curriculum fit within the college or university's mission and general education requirements? Can you direct me to some informative blogs, listserves, or websites for women's studies students? . . . Obviously, we don't wish for you to slam your instructors with 120 questions about their journey to professordom, but take some of these as guides to begin a truly personal and insightful conversation with someone who has been in your proverbial shoes. If you are still unsure about women's studies as a major or minor, a faculty member in the program or department can help you.

Make it a practice to try to meet with all your professors at least once during the semester. Attending your professor's assigned office hours can go a long way in building rapport. Chatting with your professor about the program and your interests allows the professor to get to know you, too. This is a good practice for students to take up. After all, in the spirit of Adrienne Rich and the next chapter, women's and gender studies students should not just get an education, but claim one.[21] You may find that a year or two later, you would like to ask your professor for a letter of recommendation for a job application or for graduate school. It would be best to do so after having established a relationship. That professor will remember you and be able to craft a more personal and effective letter in support of you.

2

CLAIMING YOUR EDUCATION

Have you ever read the well-known and anthologized essay by poet, essayist, and feminist Adrienne Rich that discusses "claiming an education"? In this inspiring essay, Rich highlights the importance of being an active participant in the process of "becoming educated." This piece stirred an entire generation of women (and men) students to apply themselves to their interests, to take ownership of their education, to question what they were taught and how it was relevant to them. In this chapter, we want to share with you several key components of women's and gender studies curricula that you will most likely encounter. We hope that this will be your first step on the path of "claiming your education" in women's and gender studies.

Given the plethora of women's studies programs and departments, there is no way we can comprehensively discuss the enormous diversity and creativity that exists in the curricula offerings across the US and the globe. You are in luck, however, because despite this diversity, most women's and gender studies curricula are organized around several key components. Here, we feature the most basic components of these programs. At the end of the last chapter we asked you to speak with your professors and gather some literature about your department or program. You can use the information that you have obtained as a way to compare

ADRIENNE RICH, FROM "CLAIMING AN EDUCATION"

I have said that the contract on the student's part involves that you demand to be taken seriously so that you can also go on taking yourself seriously. This means seeking out criticism, recognizing that the most affirming thing anyone can do for you is demand that you push yourself further, show you the range of what you can do. It means rejecting attitudes of "take-it-easy," "why-be-so-serious," "why-worry-you'll-probably-get-married-anyway." It means assuming your share of responsibility for what happens in the classroom, because that affects the quality of your daily life here. It means that the student sees herself engaged *with* her teachers in active, ongoing struggle for a real education.

(Rich 1979: 27)

notes with the topics we discuss below. We want you to use these insights as guideposts on your journey. If there's a component below that is *not* being offered at your institution, there is no reason why you cannot ask the appropriate person (department or program chair or undergraduate advisor) to see if your request can be accommodated either through that office or in conjunction with other departments. We begin with how women's and gender studies curricula are typically organized.

Majors, Minors, Concentrations, Certificates, Double Majors

Majors

An academic major offered either through existing departments and programs or through self-designed study is a standard feature of organizing one's interests. A major provides a particular focus throughout the academic career. You will most likely have to declare or apply for a major by the end of your sophomore year. Committing to a major could mean that you have a strong sense of the types of courses you want to take and the concepts and ideas you will learn that reflect this specialized area of education. Generally, upon deciding on a major, a student is introduced to a list of required classes that either fulfills what the department or program considers "core" curriculum (that is, the classes that introduce and reinforce the prevailing ideas, concepts, and skills that a student should encounter and be aware of through their educational experience) as well as "elective" courses. Electives also introduce and reinforce the subject area of the major, but may be more diverse in topic, may introduce new and emerging areas in the field, and may or may not reflect the "canon" (that is, ideas that are considered to be standards) of the discipline. Often in American universities and colleges, courses are assigned numerical "credit hours" that reflect the amount of physical time in the classroom, as well as the amount of hours doing work in preparation for fulfilling course objectives (e.g. reading, writing essays, conducting research, constructing projects). As a student progresses in their degree, the number of credit hours completed increases and eventually the student will "do the math," add up the courses they have successfully completed, and hopefully achieve the correct number of credit hours for their major, as well as for university requirements. As a word to the wise, many of us have found ourselves in the situation in which we may be either lacking the correct amount of credit hours to complete our degrees, or may have gotten a "passing grade" in a class, but did not fulfill the grade point average (GPA) needed for the major. We suggest that you speak to your academic advisors (as well as your professors) early and often in your college career in order to avoid walking into a graduation ceremony to find out that you do not have your degree due to these circumstances.

While getting a women's and gender studies degree will be one of the best decisions of your life, it is not always easy. From introductory to upper division courses, you will be expected to engage in some difficult tasks, such as reading (and synthesizing) conceptually sophisticated texts (often written for a specific audience that is familiar with certain terms and ideas), writing essays that are expected not only to be grammatically correct, but intellectually provocative, as well as developing strong speaking and presentation skills. But by the time you have finished your undergraduate degree, the very challenges you have been able to master will become the skills desired by employers.

Minors

Minors are designed to augment and complement major fields of study. As with a major, women's and gender studies minors must complete a certain amount of classes that have been specified by the program or department, but the number of credit hours may be considerably less than that of the major. Often, minors do not have to complete the same core requirements as majors, such as research or theory classes, and may only have to complete one of the introductory-level classes offered at their institution (e.g. either an "Introduction to Women's Studies" or a "Gender, Race, and Class" course). At many institutions, minoring in women's studies is the only option available for gender and women's studies students. At some institutions, you can take classes that are "cross-listed" or that fulfill more than one major/minor.

Concentrations

Some colleges and universities use the terms "major" and "concentration" interchangeably. For other women's and gender studies degree programs, a concentration is an area within the degree on which you may be asked to focus. For example, at Smith College, students are expected to have at least three areas of concentration in order to complete their degree. The courses in the concentration must be upper division (that is, junior or senior level or 300 and up) and focus on the methodologies that shape the area. The areas of concentration at Smith for completing a degree in the Program of the Study of Women and Gender include: Queer Studies; Women, Race, and Culture; Forms of Literary and Artistic Expression; Historical Perspectives, Forms of Political/Social/Economic Thought/Action/Organization; and Scientific Inquiry (see www.smith.edu/swg/concentration.html for more details). Other programs offer students the option to do a concentration in women's and gender studies. This is organized as if it were a second minor and usually involves three to five classes.

Certificates

Another option to take women's and gender studies is to pursue a certificate in this course of study. At some institutions, a certificate is similar to a minor and/or a concentration in terms of course requirements and with a focus of specialization on the intersections of gender, race, sexuality, class, and diversity. For example, according to Ohio University's "Women and Gender Studies" website:

> The certificate is comparable to a minor in that it requires about the same number of credit hours. The advantage of the certificate is that it is interdisciplinary, allowing students to study issues

relating to gender from a variety of perspectives. As such, it provides an excellent complement to the wide variety of undergraduate majors available at Ohio University.
(www.ohio.edu/womenstudies/undergradcert.html)

Interestingly, many online programs offer women's and gender studies certificates (e.g. University of Massachusetts Online, Florida International University Online). A benefit of having a women's and gender studies certificate is that it can be awarded to students who are seeking a degree, who have already completed a degree, or who simply want to focus on women's and gender studies without obtaining a degree. Completion of a women's and gender studies certificate is included in your university or college transcripts. Therefore, certificate holders may have an advantage over non-certificate holders for employment opportunities, specifically if they call for proof of a specialization in women's and gender studies.

Double Majors

This is a very popular choice for those interested in women's and gender studies. They find themselves equally excited about, say, art history and women's studies and are willing to do the additional work to complete both majors. Some students choose to double major because they think it helps to support their interest in women's studies with a traditional field. A major in women's and gender studies can be combined with another major (such as psychology, law, journalism) so that professional development as a psychologist, lawyer, and media strategist is strengthened by expertise in gender analysis.

In our surveys and interviews we see that students are able to get great jobs either with a stand-alone or a double major.

Common Features of Women's and Gender Studies Curricula

A Required Introductory Class

This often counts for general education, focuses on issues of gender, sexuality, race, and class, and places special emphasis on the works and contributions of women of color, working-class women, and lesbians. The introductory class often fulfills a diversity requirement at the college or university. The titles of this type of course include: "Introduction to Women's Studies: Women, Art and Culture" and "Gender, Race and Class."

At many large universities, the introductory class may include several hundred students with a discussion section taught by graduate students. At other institutions, this class may be taught by one instructor and "capped" at a maximum of thirty-five to forty students in order to allow more interaction and dialogue between students. Often, this may be your formal introduction to women's and gender studies. This is usually the course that many students find fundamentally challenges their perceptions of the way they think the world is, and here they "fall in love" with women's and gender studies. It is also a time when students learn some of the major themes in terms of research and theory: gender and violence, women's economic disadvantage, power and privilege, and how they have an impact on us at an individual level as well as at a societal or macro-level. Danista Hunte reflects on her experience in an introductory class:

> I remember trying to fit Introduction to Women's Studies in my schedule for five semesters and feeling frustrated each time chemistry or some other requirement took precedence. Finally ... I was able to fit [it] into my schedule. After three years at Vassar College, I thought my feminist development was far beyond the introductory level and there would not be much for me to learn from the class. I was wrong. My politics was changing daily. It seemed that everything that was changing and developing could be linked to a reading or discussion in women's studies. I learned life lessons that take some people all of their lives to learn.
> (Hunte 1991: 29)

If you have already taken an introductory class, it might have been the first time that complicated feelings of being "gendered" as a woman or a man came to the surface—something that can elicit strong responses from student learners. Most programs are designed to try to build a "cohort" experience. Thus, it can be ideal to take the introductory class when you are a first- or second-year student. However, given that many women's and gender studies programs are flexible and let students enter at different stages in their academic career, sometimes these courses will also include upper-division students. Usually entrance into upper-division courses is premised upon completing the introductory course. We suggest taking the introductory course early on in the process. In this way you are better able to build peer networks and get to know professors, as well as explore opportunities in your department. By starting here, you will also learn the specific terms and concepts used in women's and gender studies literature.

Below are some examples of course descriptions from introductory courses in women's and gender studies from different institutions:[22]

Introduction to Women's Studies: Women, Art, and Culture

An examination of women's creative powers as expressed in selected examples of music, film, art, drama, poetry, fiction, and other literature. We will explore women's creativity in relation to families, religion, education, ethnicity, class, sexuality, and within a cultural tradition shaped by women.

(University of Maryland, College Park,
The Department of Women's Studies)

Women: Self and Society

WS 223 focuses on the lives and unequal status of women in contemporary US society. Throughout the class, we will examine what it means to be a female today and explore the images and messages we receive from our culture; special attention will be given to issues of gender, race, class, and other differences. A major focus of WS 223 will be to understand our everyday lives in such a way that we can critically understand ourselves in relation to others and social institutions. By taking this course, it is hoped you will learn new information about women in society that will help raise your consciousness of the realities, choices, and strategies for change.

(Oregon State University, Women's Studies Program)

Introduction to Gender and Sexuality Studies

This interdisciplinary core course is an introduction to key concepts, questions, and analytical tools developed by scholars of feminist and queer studies in diverse fields. Students will work in thematically organized reading groups responsible for developing and maintaining a Blackboard information/discussion forum and one in-class presentation.

(Swarthmore College, Gender and
Sexuality Studies Program)

Gender Issues in the Contemporary Context

Gender Issues in the Contemporary Context is a foundational unit that offers an introductory look at Women's Studies and Gender Studies at Macquarie University. Lecturers from departments throughout Macquarie contribute to this interdisciplinary unit: from Asian Languages, Education, Ancient History, Law, Philosophy and Politics, as well as from interdisciplinary women's studies, gender and sexuality itself. Lecturers focus on a particular aspect of the study of gender in their own discipline. Topics covered include differences between first, second and third wave feminists; the politics of "raunch," the body and appearance; the legal regulation and media handling of abortion issues; psychological and philosophical meanings of oppression; the politics of housework; contemporary forms of masculinity; culture-gender analyses of sexual harassment, family violence, misogyny and rape; female genital mutilation; gender relations in ancient Athens and modern Japan, and more.

(Macquarie University, Interdisciplinary Women's
Studies, Gender and Sexuality, Sydney, Australia)

Introduction to Comparative Women's Studies

This course provides an introduction to women's studies, the interdisciplinary nature of this area of study, and the major issues involved in considering gender in intellectual inquiry. An exploration of disciplinary perspectives (especially those of sociology, anthropology, history and literature) on the study of women, as well as interdisciplinary perspectives. Cross-cultural analytic frameworks will be employed.

(Spelman College, Women's Resource and Research Center)

As you move through the program in women's and gender studies—whether you choose to major, minor, or concentrate in it—you will take a variety of courses. Where Michele teaches, for example, the curriculum is organized around three core components: foundations, interdisciplinary perspectives, and theory and practice. After students take the introductory class, they are then able to navigate through other curricular components of their program or department.

Core Courses and Cross-Listed Courses from Across the University

As you learned in the last chapter, one reason why women's and gender studies has developed an interdisciplinary model is that, during its formation, scholars saw that all the disciplines presented either biased knowledge about women or that women were missing from the discipline altogether. No single disciplinary perspective could correct this neglect.

Thus, women's and gender studies argues that the sum of knowledge is greater than its parts. You will usually have a broad array of choices of electives to study. In many undergraduate programs you will find courses on globalization and women, women and health, gender and communication, leadership and women, feminist research methods, and gender in science. Depending on your institution, you may see cross-listed courses on women and business and women and public health. Increasingly, classes in sexuality studies are also offered and administered in women's and gender studies programs and departments.[23]

The nature of interdisciplinary study allows you to deepen your perspective in, for example, gender and politics by taking cross-listed classes in public policy, political science, and communication. Taking elective courses also allows for comparative perspectives such as: What are the driving questions that political science raises about women and gender versus those raised in anthropology?

The Wonderful World of Electives

Here is a sample of the kinds of courses that you may see as electives in your women's and gender studies program.

Family Values in the 21st Century

> Family values are increasingly invoked in Australia and other Western nations as the 21st century unfolds in a global response to the US-led War on Terrorism. The new mood of fear and fundamentalism carries with it shifts in the relations between the sexes, the races, the religions, the classes, the generations—deepening and compounding their effects of division and domination (as in the case of the 2000–2001 ethnic gang rapes in Sydney). Whilst the rhetoric of family values appears to want to return us to an earlier era in our thinking and our social structures, such a transformation of the world is taking place that is impossible to get back to the way things were. It is imperative to explore the changed landscapes of our political life, our popular culture, our experience of home and work, in order to grasp these changes in our Australian context. This unit explores the rhetoric of family values across a range of fields in contemporary Australian culture.
>
> (Macquarie University, Interdisciplinary Women's Studies, Gender and Sexuality, Sydney, Australia)

Courtship and Courtliness from King Arthur to Queen Victoria

Prerequisite: WMST 101 or consent of instructor. Explores the cultural foundations of western romantic love in courtly literature of the French Middle Ages. Songs of troubadour poets and chivalric tales of knights and ladies will be read against amorous compositions by medieval women authors and further compared with contemporary manifestations of love in the modern world (modern song lyrics, greeting cards, the singing telegram, popular fiction, film). Literary texts will be studied in relation to pertinent historical and art historical materials.

(UNC, Chapel Hill, Department of Women's Studies)

Gender, Sexuality and Politics: Debates in Contemporary African Contexts

In the second half of the twentieth century, African countries began to take shape as states formally independent from colonial governance. While there is no uniform narrative to be told about the different circumstances through which this independence was achieved, it is true to say that the past fifty years have witnessed dramatic changes in the shape, cultures and politics dynamic of states as different as Uganda, Sudan, South Africa, and Nigeria. Alongside these changes have come many debates about gender and sexualities, debates which have catalysed discussion and conflict about the meaning of the "democratic" state, the advantages and disadvantages of legal reform, the relationship between the "modern" and the "traditional," and the relationship between African contexts and the political agendas and interests of other contexts. The course explores a number of these debates about gender and sexualities as a way both of deepening knowledges about the politics of gender internationally, and of exploring the complexity of different African contexts' engagement with political change, war and conflict, and cultural challenges.

(University of Cape Town, South Africa,
African Gender Institute)

Women's Spirituality Across Cultures

Prerequisite: WMST 101 or consent of instructor. How women's spirituality interacts with officially-sanctioned religious institutions in a range of cultural contexts and how it forges alternatives to those traditions.

(UNC, Chapel Hill, Department of Women's Studies)

Feminist Pedagogy

The concept of praxis is a core tenet of many feminists' work and women's studies programs. For feminists, the idea of transforming theory into practice is often addressed through the practice of feminist pedagogy (i.e., theories about teaching). This course will focus on both teaching and learning and borrows from Simone de Beauvoir's classic phrase, "one is not born a good teacher/instructor/facilitator, one becomes one." In part, this course is designed to give you the "hands-on" opportunities to actively participate in the creation of a course or other organizational/community-based program. We will work together and discuss the process of selecting texts, designing assignments, writing a syllabus, and preparing a lecture. At the same time, we will reflect on the theory and practice of feminist pedagogy and what feminism means in the classroom. For example, how can we confront issues of oppression in the classroom and potentially use these moments for enlightenment? As instructors, how can we empower students and yet retain authority? How can we bridge service learning with theory and use it to further enrich women's studies as a rigorous, academic discipline? How can we challenge traditional hierarchies in the classroom and still grade students? Ultimately, this course is designed to help prepare students who are planning to do a teaching internship, a graduate teaching assistantship, or participate in community education related to feminism, diversity, or social justice.

(Minnesota State University, Mankato, Department of
Women's Studies)

SIMONE DE BEAUVOIR

Simone de Beauvoir is a name that you may encounter in some of your women's studies texts or through a course on feminist theory. She was an influential twentieth-century French writer (of essays and novels), philosopher, and social theorist. *The Second Sex*, published in 1949, solidified Beauvoir's influence on a generation of scholars and thinkers. *The Second Sex* provides a detailed analysis of modern women's challenges and the ways in which, through sex-role socialization (and prescriptions of "femininity"), women are created as man's "Other." The presumed mystery and aura of femininity that surrounds women, de Beauvoir argues, is one social control mechanism that allows men to stereotype women and supports hierarchy and patriarchy.

A Feminist Theory Class

Theoretical perspectives in women's and gender studies reflect the diversity of training that students receive in a variety of academic disciplines. One major lens used by women's studies scholars to view the world is feminist theory. Yet feminist theory is an umbrella term for a multitude of paradigms or perspectives that view differently the roots (and consequences) of gender inequality. It is increasingly common as a requirement for women's and gender studies majors and minors to take at least one feminist theory course. The course may be an overview of how feminist theorizing has developed over time, or it may be a course that examines how feminist theorizing has shaped a particular discipline (e.g. "Feminist Literary Theory").

A Required Class on "Minority," "Women of Color," "Global," or "Third World Women"

Women's studies is a multiracial, comparative, multiethnic effort that aims to redress issues of power and oppression in relation to race, ethnicity, and nationality. Students are expected to understand the concept of multiple forms of oppression and privilege and how they operate in the lives of women. As women's studies has matured as an academic field, it has attempted to address critiques raised both externally and internally about whose histories, narratives, and lives occupy the center of scholarship and teaching. Most "waves" or generations of feminist scholarship and activism have been critiqued for marginalizing the contributions of various communities of women (e.g. women of color and lesbians) within the women's movement. Many scholars and activists have contributed to pushing women's studies to change its focus in order to look at the intersecting forms of oppression and privilege that shape all women's lives.[24] This requirement has evolved in response to the early challenges of women's studies, which tended to replicate some of the very patterns of exclusivity and privilege along lines of race and ethnicity that they were once trying to dismantle.[25] Below is one example of the sort of class that addresses these issues.

The Struggle Continues: Women of Color in Contemporary US Social Movements

This course will examine the roles of women of color as grassroots activists, leaders and thinkers in the new social and community movements of the post-war period. Starting with the political movements of the 1960s such as the American Indian, Asian American and Black Power Movements, the course will explore the racial and gender dynamics shaping women's participation. We will explore the construction of the political identity "women of color" as a basis for contemporary organizing for social change.

We will look at specific examples of contemporary organizing by women of color in the areas of: spoken word, reproductive rights, HIV/AIDS, and domestic violence, prisoner resistance (among others). Drawing on new theories about community organizing, pathways to consciousness, activism and social movements, we will seek to understand the ways in which women of color organize on behalf of themselves and others for social justice. We will also explore the different models of leadership that emerge from their participation.

(UNC, Chapel Hill, Department of Women's Studies)

The Global Presence of Women's and Gender Studies

Women's and gender studies is flourishing in many places around the world. In the above section, we drew heavily on how majors, minors, etc., are organized in the US system. When we look outside the US, we see some differences in how "undergraduates" are trained globally. In many parts of the world (such as the UK), undergraduate education is post-secondary education up to the level of a Master's degree. Below, we provide a snapshot of both established programs and programs that have emerged more recently.

- Institute for Women's Studies in the Arab World (IWSAW) at the Lebanese American University offers six courses that address the topic of women's and gender studies: "Introduction to Gender Studies," "Representations of Women in the Arts and the Media," "Women and Economic Power," "Women in the Arab World: Sociological Perspectives," "Psychology of Women: A Feminist Perspective," "Issues and Debates in Feminist Theory." They are in the process of preparing a graduate program (MA) in gender studies (see www.lau.edu.lb/centers-institutes/iwsaw/index.html).
- The Center for Gender Studies, at the University of Basel, Switzerland, offers a Bachelor's, Master's and a Ph.D. program in Gender Studies. The Center for Gender Studies was founded in 2001 and is chaired by Prof. Dr. Andrea Maihofer. Prior to 2001,

generally, gender studies was not widely institutionalized in Switzerland. Since then, the Center has become an independent unit in the Department of Social Sciences and Philosophy in the Humanities. In 2005, the Gender Studies Bachelor's, Master's and Ph.D. programs were successfully evaluated by international experts commissioned by the University of Basel. Alumni often send their publications (published doctoral dissertations or research results) to electronic newsletters or platforms (e.g. www.gendercampus.ch) in order to announce their findings to a wide audience. There are former students in government jobs as diversity and/or equity managers and others who informally put their gender expertise to use in their specific job situations—in the Federal Department of Public Health, for example. The center offers the possibility of a graduate degree in Gender Studies (in cooperation with other Swiss Universities, see the homepage http://genderstudies.unibas.ch/en/research/phd-program-gender-studies/). The Ph.D. program at the University of Basel consists of about fourteen members. Many postgraduates find work in the public sector, administration, or communication or find employment as gender equality experts at larger companies. The Master's degree in Gender Studies (always in combination with another major) provides a broad spectrum of possibilities after graduation.

- The University of Auckland's Women's Studies Programme is in the process of being reorganized into a more streamlined Gender Studies Programme. It is run under the auspices of the Anthropology Department and consists mostly of social sciences courses with a few literature courses available on a less-regular basis. It will be available for a Major, Minor, BA Honors (this is a graduate degree in New Zealand), MA, and Ph.D. in 2011. The undergraduate programme will consist of eight courses (see www.arts.auckland.ac.nz).

- Women's and gender studies is offered through the Institute for Gender and Development Studies at the University of the West Indies, St. Augustine Unit. This is an autonomous multidisciplinary and interdisciplinary unit located in the Office of the Vice-Chancellor of the University. Currently, a minor in gender studies or a minor in gender and development are offered. Many of the students enroll in the graduate program and pursue a postgraduate diploma in gender—or do a Master's or a Ph.D., or go to law school. Others find work in the nonprofit sector, work in local and regional non-governmental organizations (NGOs), work for international organizations such as the UN, UNDP, IDRC, UNIFEM, UNICEF, or enter into public service, getting employment in government ministries that deal with gender and gender affairs (see www.sta.uwi.edu/igds).

Institutional collaboration and innovation has been a cornerstone strategy as women's and gender studies has become rooted in colleges and universities. Below, Dr. Nalini Shiv Kumar, Director of the Centre for Women's Studies, St. Ann's College for Women in Hyderabad, India, discusses the history of the Centre and how it collaborates with other academic partners. The Centre for Women's Studies currently offers a certificate in women's studies.

> One small step to sensitize, to create awareness and respond to some perplexing questions of the young impressionable minds paved the way for a centre, to address women's issues way back in 1991. The Centre, christened "Dhruti" (meaning courage) evolved with an all women crew and the Ulyssean motto "To strive, to seek, to find and not to yield." The centre encourages the male faculty to also participate and contribute to the same. Our focus has been to empower women from the cradle to the grave, to help the young women to acquire an expanse of intellectual resources enabling them to organize themselves and become self reliant, help preserve their dignity, protect their rights, fight against gender discrimination and establish an androgynous society. In the academic context, the methodology popularly endorsed is orientation and awareness programmes to facilitate legal literacy, to work for developmental programmes in their interest. In the activities organized by the centre the notable ones are: a foundation course to all the first year undergraduates called "Making of Modern Indian Society," a project on "Women in Advertisement and Media," a seminar titled "21st Century Women," a one day seminar featuring Indian celebrities, Shatrughan Sinha (Film Actor), Mani Shankar Aiyar (Politician), Mohini Giri (Chairwoman—NCW [National Commission for Women]), Ms. Satya Saran (Editor—*Femina*) and other famous dignitaries, [a] campaign against child marriages and female infanticide, anti-arrack [alcohol] movement, a cycle expedition of 20 km in collaboration with NCC [National Cadet Corps] for

spreading the message of Female Literacy, [an] anti-dowry pledge—an annual event on 8th March (Women's Day), a workshop on "Early Marriages and its Impact on Women," a survey on "Early Marriages and its Impact on Women," a survey on "Decision Making as a Tool of Empowering Women," a national level seminar titled "A Multi-Dimensional Perspective of the Role of Women in Nation Building."

Dhruti and Women's Studies Research Centre and Maulana Azad National Urdu University, have entered into collaboration for the conduct of seminars, exhibitions, workshops and sensitization programmes on women's issues. The research centre has some funding from the University Grants Commission. In the first phase, the centre's main objective is documentation and dissemination of women's concerns. The immediate plans ahead include: documentation of women's interests, promote health and fitness and support them to develop entrepreneurial skills. In the pipeline are projects on Women Achievers of Andhra Pradesh, India and a Directory of AP [Andhra Pradesh] Women Politicians in Power and [a] compilation of course material for Women's Studies.

(www.stannscollegehyd.com/index.aspx)

Capstone Course or Honors Thesis

Capstone courses—or honors theses—vary greatly from campus to campus, but you can be sure of one thing: they are designed for you to really explore a subject that fascinates you. At some institutions, a capstone course is a senior seminar that focuses exclusively on a particular theme. On other campuses, the course is used to connect students' learning experiences with projects that are outside the classroom. The honors thesis or senior capstone project usually allows a third- or fourth-year student a focused amount of time on one project of interest. Some departments or programs may incorporate a feminist methods or methodology course in addition to or as part of the capstone course. For example, students may be asked to perform original research as part of a capstone course that addresses how feminist research approaches differ from other disciplinary perspectives. A senior capstone project may be completed alone or in collaboration with other students in your cohort or class.

Nuts and Bolts of Honors Theses—What You Need to Do and When You Need to Do It

Honors theses are usually researched and written by one student. If you were interested in pursuing an honors thesis, you would probably need to apply toward the end of your junior year. A high grade point average and a research class are usually the standard requirements. These are great options for students interested in research or extended creative activity and who want to work intensely with a faculty member, typically over the course of a year. You will form a committee, usually comprising your faculty advisor and main person responsible for helping you with the project and one to two other faculty members.

At the end of the year-long researching and writing process, you meet with your committee to officially defend the central arguments you have made in the honors thesis. Two or more faculty members serve on the committee and ask you questions for an assigned time period. The purpose of the defense or oral presentation at the end of the process is to allow you the opportunity to present your work and critically discuss the research process. This can sometimes be an emotional and powerful experience—conveying to others the passion you have for the subject you chose to study so intensely.

In sum, an honors thesis provides you with an excellent opportunity to work on research, writing, and presentation skills. It also may provide you with opportunities for publishing and or presentation at an academic conference. You may also use a chapter of an honors thesis for a writing sample for graduate school. If you are a junior and think you might want to start an honors thesis project, do not hesitate to talk with your mentor or a faculty member about the requirements.

The Internship or Practicum Experience

Theory is intimately entwined with practice. Theory is elevated through practice. These philosophies have shaped women's and gender studies and helped move students out of the classroom and into the real world. We are also committed to reducing hierarchy and power asymmetries, and to raising awareness about organizations (and organizational forms) that have helped foster and maintain social change. Thus, it is important for students to experience activism firsthand by working with activists/mentors/ potential employers. Students can then compare and contrast their on-the-job experiences with those they may have studied in class. Ultimately, women's and gender studies fosters learning opportunities that support students in their explorations of how to bridge theory and practice.

An internship provides you with valuable work experience in a given field. Internships usually have a faculty mentor or coordinator to act as a liaison between the organization providing the internship and you, the student. You are typically awarded university credits for the semester you work as an intern. When asked about their most valuable school experiences, aside from being in the classroom, many students describe an internship that helped them put into practice what they were learning in class. Maria, a former student of Michele's agrees: "I can honestly say that interning was one of the most rewarding experiences I have had at Carolina." Maria interned for a lawyer who specialized in divorce, custody, and domestic violence cases. She learned how to do formal tasks such as preparing and filing Certificates of Service, the etiquette of a courtroom, and legal terminology. One of the most valuable lessons for Maria was an assignment that was given to her. The main lawyer (and another women's studies intern) had discovered the lack of compiled information available to victims of sexual assault or rape on the UNC campus. Throughout the semester, Maria and the other interns worked on compiling a brochure to help students on campus know their options and how to proceed if ever assaulted. They worked with the Dean of Students office, Campus Counseling and Wellness Services, the Carolina Women's Center, and referenced the Honor Code. She felt that it was an important contribution to gather the plethora of resources into one brochure:

> Hopefully, with the distribution of this brochure around campus, our efforts will help one person take the action that is right for him or her.
>
> (Maria, 2009, UNC, Chapel Hill)

Employers typically look for candidates who have conducted an internship in their professional field of interest. Internships are also a great opportunity for students to find out what they might *not* want to do. Each of us has had conversations with students who came to women's and gender studies after finishing coursework or (yikes!) even graduating in another field only to find that what they once thought was their dream career was, in reality, a nightmare. For example, students who thought their gift was counseling discovered that they had a talent for grant writing and data analysis. Others were able to channel their fears of public speaking into a persona that shone during public presentations.

Nonstandard Curricula Offerings—A World of Possibilities

Praxis or Activism Project

Another element of some women's and gender studies programs is a praxis or activism project. As discussed earlier, praxis is the concept of putting theory into action. Over the course of your degree, certain topics or research questions may continually resonate with you and make you want to spring into action! Praxis, activism, or collective action projects allow students in either an independent study or formalized class structure to pursue original research or to initiate activism on their campus or in the community.

Depending upon the goal of the class, you often have a choice of working independently or as a group on a project. For example, some classes might encourage independent research as a way for students to

---

JO (JOREEN) FREEMAN: SCHOLAR, ACTIVIST, LAWYER, AND JOURNALIST

Jo Freeman describes herself as a "guerrilla scholar" in the essay "We've Come a Long Way." She earned her Ph.D. in Political Science in 1975 from the University of Chicago, but she held her last academic position in the late 1970s. Jo Freeman critically examines important yet sensitive topic areas in feminism such as institutional sexism, social movements, politics, and identity issues, as well as the feminist movement itself. Not only is she the author of an influential text that is still highly regarded in the discipline, *Women: A Feminist Perspective*, but she is also known for both the "BITCH Manifesto" and "TRASHING: The Dark Side of Sisterhood." She has not been afraid to challenge cherished second-wave feminist ideas about the role of consensus in groups.

In her influential essay "The Tyranny of Structurelessness," Freeman provocatively argued that:

> . . . there was no such thing as a structureless group; pretending there was allowed responsibility to be shirked and power to be hidden. In fact, every group had a structure, usually based on friendship networks, and in the absence of formal democracy, these networks would make the important decisions.

> (Freeman 1970: 73–74)

See www.jofreeman.com/aboutjo/longway.htm for more information on Jo Freeman.

develop their own agency and self-direction in the workforce. Other departments recognize that group praxis or collective action projects are characteristic of most organizational structures. Sometimes, decision-making structures are traditionally organized and others seemingly have no organizational form.[26] These courses allow you to set the parameters of your project, determine the rules of group interaction, and ultimately test some of the ideas posed by Jo Freeman on the challenge of feminist principles of consensus in organizations. These projects also demand that you complete the project to the best of your ability over the course of the semester and present your accomplishments for evaluation by your peers and professors.

Study Abroad

An old adage states that travel is one of the best teachers. We live in an interconnected, global world that relies on informed global citizens. Study abroad (also known as education abroad)—another type of applied learning possibility—is increasingly becoming an accessible and affordable option for many students. More students are traveling abroad for a semester or longer than in previous decades. We think studying abroad deserves important consideration from anyone interested in women's and gender studies. Over a third of graduates we surveyed said that their study abroad experience was connected to work in women's and gender studies.

Your college, university, and/or program may offer the option of studying abroad. Given its institutional arrangement, it may have partnered with another organization or university to provide you with a direct experience in that country. The more common way for a student to pursue this option is by visiting the study abroad office (or equivalent) on campus. This office should be able to direct you to gender-specific programs of study at other universities. According to Caryn Lindsay, Director of International Programs of Elizabeth and Wynn Kearney International Center at Minnesota State University, Mankato, if you are considering education abroad you should begin planning your experience early in your college or university career. Besides applying for financial aid and other scholarships, it is important to speak with your academic advisor regarding college credit and how your international courses will satisfy degree requirements. Often, study abroad program courses satisfy general education requirements. Therefore, your upper division and specific degree requirements will be achieved at the university or college from which you will graduate. Organizations your study abroad office may refer you to in your search for international educational opportunities include the Council on International Education (CIEE, www.ciee.org/) and the American Institute for Foreign Study (AIFS). Both of these organizations offer programs that have specific courses in Gender and Women's Studies and LGBT Studies. For example, some of the courses listed for study abroad in fall 2010 and spring 2011 in Stellenbosch, South Africa, include:

- Global Health 214/314 (3) HIV and AIDS: A South African Perspective
- English 344/444 (2) Queer Studies: An Introduction
- English 314/414 (2) Women Writers Interrogating Empire
- courses in political science regarding transition and conflict
- courses in conservation ecology.

All the courses are taught in English, yet students can also pursue language studies in courses ranging from French, German, and Spanish to Mandarin and Xhosa. Besides courses, the Study Abroad Program at Stellenbosch University also offers service learning opportunities as well as a certificate.

Your study abroad office will be able to direct you to an incredible array of options for traveling. Additionally, you may want to talk with a financial aid officer to find if various kinds of financial aid are applicable to potential study abroad opportunities. Here are some important programs that help to pay for student travel:

- Gilman International Scholarship Program: The Gilman Scholarship Program provides assistance of $5,000 to study abroad for students receiving federal Pell Grant funding at the time of application. Award amounts vary depending on the length of study and student need, with the average award being approximately $4,000. Applicants must be US citizens, be undergraduate students in good standing, and be applying to or have been accepted for a program of study abroad eligible for credit by the home institution. Approximately 1,200 scholarships were awarded during the 2008–2009 academic year. Students who apply for and receive the Gilman International Scholarship to study abroad are then eligible to receive an additional $3,000 Critical Need Language Supplement from the Gilman Scholarship Program for a total possible award of up to $8,000. Application materials and instructions must be downloaded from the website at www.iie.org/en/ Programs/Gilman-Scholarship-Program.

- Rotary Foundation Scholarships: Each year Rotary Clubs—seeking to promote understanding between countries with Rotary Clubs— offer graduate and undergraduate scholarships for one academic year. They place about 800 undergraduates in fifty countries and about 4,400 graduate students in a hundred different countries. Undergraduates must be between eighteen and twenty-four, and unmarried. The scholarship includes round-trip airfare, registration, tuition, fees, books, room and board, and limited educational travel. Consult the Rotary website for more information at www.rotary. org/en/StudentsAndYouth/EducationalPrograms/AmbassadorialSc holarships/Pages/ridefault.aspx.
- The Boren Scholarship: This scholarship, as offered by the National Security Education Program, is available for both undergraduate and graduate students who are both willing to learn a language such as Vietnamese, Farsi, or Arabic, and are willing to work for one year for one of a number of US government agencies, such as the Department of State, Department of Agriculture, CIA, or the Department of Justice. For more information on the Boren Scholarship, see www.borenawards.org/.

Besides study abroad opportunities offered by international organizations, some departments offer courses developed by their faculty (usually during winter break, spring break, or summer) on a specific international topic

A RESOURCE FOR STUDY ABROAD

GoAbroad, a website for those exploring scholarships for education abroad, is another resource for the savvy women's and gender studies student. This website allows students not only to search the country where you would like to pursue your education, but the type of award you are interested in (e.g. grant, scholarship), the academic level at which you will be, as well as the field of study you will pursue. For more information on GoAbroad, see http://scholarships.goabroad.com/index.cfm?utm_id=SCH1.

and/or experience. Often, this course may relate to your professor's current area of research, or an area in which they are considered an expert. The benefit of studying abroad can include credit for your experience, which counts as part of your official coursework, familiarity with the professor who is teaching the class, and colleagues with whom you can share your experiences when you come back home. Students may spend their semesters abroad studying comparative feminist movements in places such as the Netherlands, India, or South Africa, for example.

Dr. Patti Duncan, Assistant Professor in the Department of Women's Studies at Oregon State University below discusses her unique experience taking students abroad in a variety of different contexts, and what she and students gained.

Making Critical Connections Abroad and at Home

Study abroad offers a unique opportunity for making critical connections in women's studies. As a former student of study abroad programs, I know just how deep an impact such experiences can have on students. So, as a professor of women's studies who teaches about transnational women's and feminist movements, I have found teaching in study abroad programs particularly effective and often transformative for my students.

In 2007 I developed a travel seminar, "Gender, Migration, and Globalization," in collaboration with the Center for Global Education. With thirteen undergraduate students, I traveled to Mexico, where we were based primarily in Cuernavaca. I felt this seminar would be an opportunity for students to deepen their understanding of the long-term effects of globalization, NAFTA, and US immigration policies. I wanted them to understand how NAFTA affects women and how immigration itself is a gendered and racialized process. I hoped students would have an opportunity to observe firsthand the ways in which theories are put into practice, and I knew this experience would be a way to make critical connections between the work we do in the classroom and the world beyond the borders of the university and the US. Interspersed with visits to local grassroots and non-governmental organizations like CIDHAL, a women's center, were discussions with activists from the Independent Human Rights Commission, and others working on issues of gender, poverty, and globalization. We had the opportunity to visit the State Congress to meet with members of the Gender Equity Commission, and we visited a maquiladora with a local activist working for maquila workers' rights. We heard panel discussions on human rights and the environment, reproductive health, and issues of gender and sexuality for local communities. And in Mexico City, we visited the Frida Kahlo centennial art exhibit at the Palacio de Bella Artes.

Our group also had the opportunity to visit families who had been affected by emigration to the US, both in Cuernavaca and in the nearby indigenous community of Ixtlilco. There, we learned that nearly every family in the community had been fragmented by the need for at least one member to cross the border for economic survival. This experience enabled a powerful discussion about the politics of mobility, travel, and tourism, and the varying degrees of privilege associated with our subject positions as US citizens and/or students. It required students to consider not only the role of migrant labor in the Mexican and US economies and in our own communities, but also the impact of gender, race, and class on migration.

In the fall of 2008, I was able to extend my teaching abroad experience when I was selected to teach for the Semester at Sea program, for which I spent an entire semester traveling by ship through twelve countries. During our time at sea we functioned on a university schedule, but at each port we spent several days learning about the issues most central to local communities. In my classes aboard the ship, I helped students connect the theories in assigned readings to local and national movements in each of the countries we visited. In India, for example, I took the students in my "Gender and the Global Economy" course to the Working Women's Forum, where we participated in a discussion about women, poverty, and micro-credit. In South Africa, I led a group of students in my "Sexualities in a Global Context" course to the Triangle Project, where local activists shared their experiences about working for lesbian, gay, bisexual, and transgender human rights. And in Brazil, my "Global Feminisms" students were able to discuss reproductive justice issues with the staff of a family planning center.

For students of women's studies, I believe study abroad can be simultaneously wonderful, challenging, exhilarating, and sometimes extremely painful. They often develop a much more nuanced understanding not only of women's oppression but also women's multiple forms of resistance within a global context. Students may seek experience in different ways—some through books and classes, others through encounters with people in the countries visited, or through the friendships developed within study abroad programs. Central to their experiences is often encountering the "other." What does it mean to encounter the other, and to truly see them? For all of us who travel, there may be multiple encounters. These encounters are not always easy. Many students in my study abroad classes have been challenged to stretch their ideas, their values, their belief systems. But this, too, is part of the education. In South Africa, my students encountered children in the townships who they'll remember forever. In both Ho Chi Minh City and Hiroshima, some of them were pushed to think through histories of war that their own government was directly involved in, and to try to see the effects of those wars from different perspectives. In Mexico, they witnessed firsthand the devastating impact of US trade policies and globalization.

When I teach women's studies outside of the US, I often reflect on the multiple meanings of "home," particularly in relation to issues of gender, race, class, and sexuality. What is home? Where is home, for all of us and for those we encounter? My mother left her home in South Korea when she was pregnant with me, determined to give me a better life in the US, convinced that being born here would make a difference, would make me feel at home here. But her own sense of home remained elusive, and this affected me. Home became some mysterious "other" place. We live in a world today marked by conflict and displacement; loss of home is an everyday occurrence for hundreds of thousands of people. Of course the meanings of home are profoundly political, and we must also consider the politics of travel and tourism, of migration, both forced and voluntary. Who gets to travel, and how, and why? Refugees, migrant workers, victims of trafficking, students, those on luxury vacations? US privilege and the privilege to travel lie at the heart of the study abroad experience, and we shouldn't turn away from this fact. I've often seen students stumble up against these politics as they struggle to be responsible travelers, critical of exploitative forms of capitalist tourism, sometimes critical of one another. And returning home, they often struggle with their knowledge that the home they return to is necessarily very different from the one they left. They may struggle with their newfound sense of responsibility, and their desire to continue to make critical connections and to effect change. I see this as one of the most significant—and potentially transformative—effects of study abroad.

Before committing to a study abroad experience, there are some issues you may want to consider. One anticipated outcome of a study abroad experience may be culture shock. Even if we have lived in different parts of our country of origin or traveled, we are not always aware of our cultural privilege, comfort, or ethnocentricism. Understanding of language, etiquette, or even the ability to negotiate complex organizations or systems (such as healthcare) are often taken for granted. According to Caryn Lindsay, most students who participate in education abroad programs will participate in a pre-departure orientation process. Culture shock is an anticipated aspect of this experience. Because "culture shock" has been researched as well as acknowledged in this field, students are able to address their cultural adaptation through several types of orientations including online, face to face, on-site in-country, and re-entry orientations. All in all, there are more support services available for students pursuing an international experience than previously. See www.mnsu.edu/studyabroad/links.html for more information for planning your education abroad experience.

How Will You Be Assessed in Women's and Gender Studies Coursework?

A student new to women's studies must often adjust to the emphasis on the integration of reading, research, and personal experience. There is an assumption in women's and gender studies analysis that the "I"—or the self—is a resource, witness, and aide to developing theory. Reading and reflecting on your own personal narratives (either through documentaries, personal essays, or fiction) and synthesizing that with data-driven research may feel like a stretch—it is! Women's and gender studies classrooms regularly probe material that creates emotion, tension, and conflict. Discussing difficult topics in a critical, sensitive, and confident way can be one of the biggest adjustments that a student can make. Some students may find this work uncomfortable or too revealing.

> WMST classrooms are very open and safe, which is liberating in terms of speaking up and encouraging debate. Sometimes this feeling increased when it was a class of all women but I don't think people held themselves back too much even if there were male students. For me, these classes were tangible proof of how feminism can change the way you feel by changing the

environment. This feeling is only an appetizer, however, because the goal is for the whole world and everyone in it to feel as accepted as I did in my WMST classes.

(Carla, 2008, UNC, Chapel Hill)

Katie highlights the different features of the women's studies classroom:

I learned to find MY voice. I learned to see the "big picture" by analyzing systems of oppressions and their interrelated connections to social institutions. I learned that the little things DO matter. I also learned that nothing changes if my voice is not engaged in being an advocate and part of the system changes that need to be made.

(Katie, 2008, Minnesota State, Mankato)

We asked our interviewees to reflect on what makes the women's and gender studies classroom unique for student learning. Matt, whom you met in Chapter One, echoes many other students' experiences:

[My women's studies class was a] Different type of experience within academe than I had ever been exposed to just in terms of how class was structured. Students facilitated every day in class with the graduate teaching assistant. We [students] would meet outside of class and we would talk about what we wanted to do and then we would do presentations and facilitate. It was just different . . . I didn't know education could be like that. It wasn't the model in every women's studies class that I had but, most of my classes in women's studies had an active and collaborative learning component to it even if it wasn't the dominant form.

Eva Marie, a women's studies major, builds on Matt's comment and names the guiding principles of feminist pedagogy (which are often in operation in many women's and gender studies classes) discussed in Chapter One:

What I found unique about a women's studies classroom was the feminist pedagogy. I did not know what the concept meant, at first. But as I gained access to the definition, it made sense to me. It [was] a way of teaching that exposed the instructor and the student to new information. The teacher along with the student continues to learn through class sessions. The new information that the professor acquired through the previous sessions may have an influence in changing the curriculum for the next semester. In my experience in women's and gender studies classes, they are not lecture classes. Professors learned from students as well. The environment that is created through feminist pedagogy helps students gain confidence in expressing their opinion.

The different experiences that are shared through concepts of the course can bring students together [and] may carry [over] into a common bond outside the classroom.

(Eva Marie, 2010, Minnesota State University, Mankato)

Conversely, it would be a mistake to think that all women's studies classes always stress personal experience or self-analysis as the only tools for students to use. Women's and gender studies is an academic enterprise that not only adheres to, but also accepts certain conventions regarding truth claims, whether ascertained through hypothesis testing and the conventions of the scientific method, critiquing truth claims through philosophical conventions, weighing evidence and arguments through legal processes, or engaging in textual analysis. Women's and gender studies faculty are trained in a variety of disciplinary perspectives, and we hold students to the same standards that are applied both internally and externally to women's studies scholars.

There is a variety of tools and skills that professors employ in the classroom, ranging from traditional methods of evaluation and assessment (such as exams and quizzes) to journals, group projects, and papers. Given the interdisciplinary nature of your learning, you may be asked to attend research colloquia held in women's and gender studies that invite guest speakers. Or you may be asked to attend seminars or special talks about research on gender and sexuality that your program co-sponsors with

WHAT'S COMPELLING ABOUT *YOUR* WOMEN'S AND GENDER STUDIES CLASSES?

As you move through your classes in women's and gender studies it may be helpful for you to reflect on the qualities about the class that you find compelling. Is it the way the instructor engages students? Is it the quality of the assignments that you're being asked to complete? Are you being asked to locate your own lived experiences as part of the learning process?

other departments. You may then be asked to summarize the main points from these talks and figure out how they translate into the work you are undertaking in the classroom.

Finding Womentors/Fementors

We in women's and gender studies aren't the only ones to recommend mentors. Finding and cultivating strong mentors is something consistently promoted in business, leadership, and professional development circles. As part of our continued quest for professional development, both of us have participated in a number of leadership development and mentoring programs. Cheryl had the privilege of experiencing two New Leadership programs (Tri-State in Morehead, Minnesota, and in Las Vegas), as well as participating in the Mankato YWCA's Women's Leadership Program.[27] Michele participated in an academic leadership program at UNC, Chapel Hill. Each of these programs highlighted the important role of mentors.

Sometimes, mentors are formally assigned to you as advisors and you develop a working relationship that extends beyond graduation. Other times, we are adopted and nurtured by faculty members, professional staff, community members, or past graduates of the program who may encourage us in one or more of the following ways: listening to our concerns, giving us tough love when necessary, forwarding educational and or professional opportunities, assisting in introducing us to others or social networking, helping us to think "outside the box," reigning us in, providing opportunities for research, activism, or publishing, and sharing in our joy in our accomplishments and/or providing support in the face of disappointments. Some mentors may be comfortable with "warm and fuzzy interactions," (where they disclose personal information about themselves and may invite you and other students out for lunch), whereas other mentors are comfortable with more formal, structured mentoring. Whether you actively seek a mentor or if the mentoring relationship emerges organically, these relationships, like friendships, may be short term and contextually bound or lifelong, mutually supportive systems. They are important to your development as a student and can serve you well as you leave your undergraduate experience, continue your education, or enter the job market.

The role of mentors was important for graduates in our study. Many people reported that the mentors who have been most influential have been the professors, staff, and advisors they met in their classes, through formal internships, and in community work. These relationships have been robust for our graduates years after they have formally graduated. At your campus there may be an official way to be mentored through a university program that focuses on college students' issues. Mentoring programs might be offered through the division of Student Affairs, Office of Residential Life, the Women's Center, etc. No matter how and where you find a mentor, their influence on your personal and professional life can be profound. Because we realize the importance of mentoring, we asked survey respondents about their experiences via the online survey.

Here are some of the responses we received to our mentoring question: "Who are your current mentors? Describe your relationship to them."

- "Most of my mentors are undergrad[uate] professors and educators who were and still are mentors and good friends. Also, many of my new mentors are my graduate departmental faculty and local community activists."
- "My former professor of gender and sociology at the university. She supported me in different ways: [gave me] contacts to other gender-scientists and institutions; I could participate at her university classes as a teaching assistant. And, she 'believed' in me."
- "Many of my former professors serve as my most influential mentors because I am a first-generation college student and they helped foster my education and showed me that I can live an intellectual life. Two of them are also my feminist mommas who showed me the light and have changed my life by giving a name to what I have already practiced."
- "My undergraduate advisors, one female and one male, with whom I still regularly email . . . I met with them at least weekly on an informal and formal basis, especially in my final two years when we spoke about my graduate school prospects. I also worked with the female mentor as a teaching assistant and a research assistant."
- "My mentor passed away in late 2008. Since that time I have relied on close friends to discuss intellectual, emotional and socio-political matters."

- "Former internship supervisor—provides professional guidance, wisdom, and best practice support within my chosen field of employment."
- "My current mentor is my undergraduate women's studies professor from University of Delaware. We remain in touch and she has truly been helpful and influential in my personal and professional development."
- "College professor—took classes on domestic violence and pornography with him and later TA'd [was a Teaching Assistant for] domestic violence course; former employer/college professor— worked at women's leadership center during college—took her women in politics course during college."
- "These people know me well and understand my strengths. Although different, they all have a good understanding of feminist issues and understand my passion for it."

Cheryl describes her unique and varied history as a mentee:

I had the fortune to be mentored by passionate and activist scholars at the University of Toledo while pursuing my MA degree. Because the department was fairly small in terms of faculty members and graduate students, it felt more like a family than a formal workplace. As a graduate student, I had access to the lounge, copying privileges, and felt comfortable visiting faculty members in their offices. When I first went back to school, I was unsure of my academic abilities after working for years in the nonprofit world. I was immediately befriended by Dr. Barbara Chesney, a sociologist whose work focused on health and medical issues. Not only did she offer me the opportunity to serve as her research and teaching assistant, but later she agreed to serve as my thesis chair. I feel I have emulated her style in my interactions with graduate students. Barbara and I would often go to coffee shops and other off-campus locations to grade papers and discuss thesis ideas. Aside from showing me the culture of academia, Barbara was there for me emotionally when my father passed away during the first week of my second year of graduate school. I knew Barbara would hold my confidences in my moments of grief, especially after I was surprised by her presence (along with two of my graduate colleagues and friends) at my father's funeral. Largely because of Barbara and later Barbara Brents—my mentor at UNLV—I feel that being a mentor is more than just imparting formal knowledge. A good feminist mentor listens to her students, is their ally and advocate, and continues the relationship after graduation. Another mentor at the University of Toledo was Dr. Patrick McGuire. Aside from intellectually engaging me in the topic of political sociology in the classroom, he was someone I could easily turn to when I had a question, concern, or just wanted to talk. I can remember stopping by Dr. McGuire's office to chat about ideas raised in class, to ask questions about graduate school and research, as well get affirmation about my choice to go back to school. Unfortunately, a few years ago Dr. McGuire lost his fight with cancer, but his influence on my life has been profound. Last, but not least, I had the honor of working with Dr. Cary Kart while at the University of Toledo. I was inspired by his medical sociology course and was able to work with him on revisions he was doing on his gerontology textbook. I can always count on Dr. Kart for his sense of humor as well as his fierce grasp of sociological concepts. I also felt that Dr. Kart would fight for his department and students—a trait that I also try to emulate.

It was through women's studies and the mentoring that I received under Ellen C. Rose (the former director of the UNLV Women's Studies Department) that I was able to co-teach my first (and only co-taught) course "Porn in the USA." Through fate or kismet, a newly hired assistant professor in Political Science and I met and found a connection over a multitude of ideas and issues. We bonded over a common interest in sexuality studies and were given the go-ahead to develop and teach a course on pornography. It was through this collaboration that Michele and I first worked together. Later, Michele continued to act as my mentor, collaborator, coach, confidant, conspirator, and friend. She not only served as one of my dissertation committee members, but Michele has always made herself available to me to discuss teaching issues in the classroom. She also helped me process the transition from graduate student to new professional while I worked as a visiting professor in women's studies at UNLV, during my time at Minnesota State, Mankato as an assistant professor of women's studies, and as a co-author on presentations. It was through these conversations, dialogues, gripe sessions, and my caffeine-fueled epiphanies that our concerns about women's studies and our students resulted in a book proposal for *Transforming Scholarship*.

We can highlight a few key points from Cheryl's story:

1. Professors are people, too—Cheryl talks about how accessible these mentors were, how you can have many of them, and how boundaries between school and life are blurred or even erased when mentoring relationships become friendships, too.
2. Personal is not a dirty word—Personal relationships/friendships abound between mentor/mentee—some students feel there's a taboo against getting too close to professors/mentors. Sort out what kind of relationship you both want—more or less distance?
3. Two heads are better than one—Cheryl talks about how she came to her own realizations about school, work, life, book proposals through conversation, dialogue, and the company of mentors.
4. You can write your own book, too, or whatever big dream inspires you!—Cheryl talks about living up to her potential with the guidance she received from these fabulous people.

Yet, as with any type of relationship, you need to be aware of your own conduct so that the relationship is one of reciprocity. Some mentees may not perceive interpersonal and professional boundaries of their mentors. They may unwittingly try to monopolize a mentor's time, expecting counseling or a therapeutic relationship. Much of the demanding work of being a professor happens outside the purview of what undergraduates see and experience. The demands on faculty time increase every year. Keep in mind that your faculty member has three jobs in their college or university: teaching, research, and service. Be respectful of the time that you work with a mentor. Think about how to be a good *mentee*.

It is as important to be aware of how you feel the mentoring relationship is going. You may feel grateful to receive support and help with your concerns and career planning, rather than feeling like it is an obligation that your mentor is fulfilling. But, unfortunately, mentors can sometimes possess unreasonable or unattainable expectations for mentees. If you feel bullied, pushed, or overly criticized, please trust your experience and find a way to extricate yourself from that mentoring relationship.

Co-Curricular Opportunities

Undergraduate student culture varies widely across campuses. We encourage you to investigate what other forums exist where you can talk about issues of interest to you as a women's and gender studies student. Rapport and friendship happen pretty naturally through courses as students bond through shared learning experiences. Your women's and gender studies program or department may offer informal and formal opportunities for students to meet each other and learn about research opportunities, fellowships, awards, and other important happenings (e.g. a major's night, an end-of-the-year celebration). Your program or department may also host an annual lecture or speaker series highlighting scholarship in women's studies or a topical speaker on women's issues. Inquire about a student listserve, bulletin board, Facebook page, or other ways that the program keeps students updated. Taking advantage of these opportunities will afford you the ability to expand your network. What you do on campus can also enhance what you are learning in the classroom. Applying what you know in a real-world context allows you to develop skills that can be transferred to future places of employment.

You may want to investigate other groups on campus that work on women's issues. You may be pleasantly surprised to find a number of active organizations that focus on women's issues and sponsor well-known events such as "Take Back the Night" (sexual and partner violence event) or "The Vagina Monologues." If you don't find something that interests you, create your own group! Fashion it to fit your own interests and goals, and share the passion you have with others. See the sidebar about students coming together to start an important campus group.

Additionally, find out if your campus has a women's center. There are many women's centers on college campuses across the country. Women's centers serve the needs of faculty, staff, and students through a variety of programs. For example, the Jean Niedetch Center at the University of Nevada, Las Vegas, offers a range of resources and services. They include discussion groups on health, sexuality, self-defense, and violence issues, and the center sponsors a film series, "Take Back the Night," and the Susan B. Komen "Race for the Cure."[28] The Women's Center at Minnesota State University, Mankato, is an important resource for faculty and students alike. Many of Cheryl's students worked as staff for the center and gained valuable experience planning events and organizing and leading groups.

We end this chapter with a focus on Moya Bailey, Spelman College alumna, national activist, blogger, and doctoral candidate (at time of

STARTING PROJECT DINAH

Project Dinah, a women's safety and empowerment initiative at UNC, Chapel Hill, has gained campus-wide press and attention in recent years. Its mission is to end all sexual violence on campus and in the community through education and advocacy. Women's Studies majors and minors at UNC often find Project Dinah an important organization to be actively involved in, because it puts into practice the academic knowledge about sexual violence that they learn in the classroom.

Project Dinah has grown to include many members and now offers a variety of programs, but it was founded in 2005 by a small group of passionate first-year students who were moved to activism after discovering the prevalence of sexual assault on college campuses—such as *one in four women* will be victims of assault or attempted assault as part of their college experience. Receiving seed money in 2004 helped this group of students to distribute safety whistles and resource cards on campus. Project Dinah later became an independent and officially recognized student organization.

Project Dinah took its name from Dinah, the daughter of Jacob and Leah, whose rape story is told in the Book of Genesis in only a few short verses and never mentioned again. Building from this story, the goal of Project Dinah is to end the culture of silence surrounding sexual assault and give a voice to those women who have been silenced. Today, Project Dinah still distributes safety whistles and resource cards, but the organization has grown dramatically and now sponsors a number of campus- and community-wide programs.

Since its inception, Project Dinah has organized the annual "Take Back the Night March and Rally." In 2009, Project Dinah incorporated a SpeakOut with "Take Back the Night," during which volunteers read anonymous testimonials of survivors. UNC students and community members were invited to post their stories online at www.speakoutunc.blogspot.com.

Another event, which is designed to promote healthy communication between sexual partners, is "I Love Female Orgasm"—Project Dinah's most well-known program. This event has attracted more than 500 students in each of the past two years. Other sponsored programs have included free self-defense classes and a benefit concert for the Orange County Rape Crisis Center, as well as a variety of initiatives co-sponsored with the Carolina Women's Center.

writing) in Women's Studies at Emory University. She highlights how she developed her interest in women's studies and how her activism on misogyny in the hip-hop world began as a discussion in her women's studies classroom. Her story is a compelling example of theory and practice coming together as a catalyst for change:

> I identified as a feminist in high school which was a bit differ-ent from my peers. And I had an Advanced Placement (AP) psychology professor who identified as a feminist [in high school] and we talked about lots of issues. I tried to organize pro-feminist actions. When I got to Spelman, I already had that leaning. And, it was difficult at first because I was in the sciences and also in psychology.

It was a difficult transition for Moya in the psychology department. She felt that the department was not interested in the kinds of questions and experiences she wanted to raise. In what she deemed as a negative and conservative environment in psychology, she felt like she was being "pushed out." During her first year on Spelman's campus, she quickly became active on campus:

> It was actually through activism and student networks that I got involved in women's studies. All my friends [in the] second semester of my first year were connected to activist organizations on campus and all the organizations were connected to the women's resource center and were tied to the women's studies department. And finally a professor asked me, "Why aren't you a women's studies major? You're doing all this organizing with the feminist groups on campus. You can be pre-med and a women's studies major." Oh, I said, I hadn't realized that.

Moya quickly changed her major from psychology and pre-med to pre-med and women's studies: "I was really happy and content in women's studies." It was a pivotal point in her academic career:

> When I got into my women's studies classes, I finally got the language that I needed to articulate what was happening in my world. So, growing up in an all white environment as the only black girl there were a lot of dynamics that were happening in many of my classes that I didn't have language for. So, getting into women studies classes I found out, "oh that's racism," "oh I have internalized some of these racist things and internalized sexism."

Having that language was really affirming to me because I could see, it's not me, it's the system. That was liberatory for me.

Moya came to national attention as a junior in college when she helped to organize against Nelly, a popular rapper, which sparked a national discussion on the role of misogyny in hip hop, rap lyrics, and videos. Below she discusses how this activism organically emerged from her women's studies class:

> Nelly was supposed to do a bone marrow registration drive and the Student Government (SGA) president told me that he was coming. His controversial video Tip Drill[29] was airing around that time, too. I said, "He's going to come to campus?" . . . The SGA president brought this issue up in a women's studies classroom and there was a discussion among the class and professor [Beverly Guy-Sheftall] about what should we do. Should something be done? At the time I was president of the feminist group on campus.

Given Nelly's popularity and support, at first Moya was not sure if anything would get the attention of students: "I was like, no one is going to come if we do anything . . . No one is going to come." Her class debated various actions they could take. "[At first] We thought we should write a letter. We finally settled on trying to invite him to have a conversation about sexism and misogynist images in his music when he came to campus." They thought a dialogue would be the most constructive approach rather than trying to organize a protest of his coming.

Around the same time that Moya and her classmates were strategizing about how to raise awareness about misogyny in Nelly's and other rap videos, some of Nelly's public relations people had come to campus to check out location and safety. They saw flyers that Moya's feminist student group had made. They had named Nelly the "Misogynist of the Month" because of the "Tip Drill" video. There were flyers of this "Misogynist of the Month" posted around campus. Although there wasn't a scheduled protest or demonstration, Nelly's people believed that there would be during Nelly's visit.

Moya and her group had decided against a protest, because at that point there were a small number of people who were interested in having a critical dialogue on the day that Nelly arrived. "Nelly's team decided to pull out and then went to press saying that they didn't want a protest at Spelman and it erupted into this huge thing." Nelly's team also put pressure on the SGA president to guarantee that there wasn't going to be a protest if Nelly did come. "And the SGA president said we can't guarantee the students won't do anything," and so the SGA stood up for this small group of students.

> And then it didn't end up happening. So, all of this erupted from an event that didn't even actually take place. We decided to show the video on the day [that Nelly was supposed to arrive] so people could see what we were upset about and [we] had signs up. Because [the] press had gotten wind of the story, [and] they still came to this non-event. It was huge, all the press came up . . .
>
> It was really something that happened in a classroom with a few students—it was not the majority of campus and so in the public frame it was "Spelman Says No to Nelly," but a lot of students were upset with us because they wanted to meet him and they wanted him to come. What was so powerful to me [was] that just a few vocal students were able to scare Nelly into not coming and being accountable for the music he makes.

This critique of how hip hop and rap videos position women, especially African-American women and women of color, created a ripple effect that Moya could not have anticipated—it opened up a national dialogue and launched her and others into critical and public conversations. Some outcomes included that *Essence* magazine started a year-long "Take Back the Community" campaign, and the television channel BET developed specials on "Hip Hop in America" and had ongoing discussions about artistic responsibility.

Moya believes in the power of a few committed people to take action against inequality: "I'm just amazed at the ripple effect of something so small." Moya's experience is an important reminder of "the power of a vocal few—it doesn't take a lot of people to make something happen." She was able to challenge status-quo thinking about the portrayal of women (especially African-American women) in contemporary videos.

And there is another important takeaway to her story—that the women's and gender studies classroom provides an intellectually engaging form for emerging debates and issues central in students' lives. Not every class will lead you to mobilize others on behalf of a cause, but it will sharpen your ability to think and debate about contemporary critical issues that affect women and men's lives.

YOUR TURN: EXERCISES

1. UNDERSTANDING THE COMPONENTS OF YOUR EDUCATION

Now it is time for you to critically assess all of the components of your education. Find a time when you will not be disturbed and gather the materials for your program that you acquired through your initial visit or from the department's website based on the exercise in the last chapter. Maybe you haven't decided yet whether to major, minor, or concentrate in women's and gender studies. Take some time and think about what kinds of questions and ideas excite you. Reflect on the following questions:

- Are there issues that you find yourself drawn to in women's and gender studies?
- Is there a type of research that you have been exposed to that excites you?
- What kinds of courses will you need to take to build on your interests?
- What types of internship opportunities are available to you through the program or department?
- What courses are being offered during the next two semesters?

2. FUN QUIZ

It's time now to have some fun with this brief quiz based on the chapters you have read thus far and your classes in women's and gender studies!

1. **What is Women's Studies?**
    a. Feminist propaganda and the research wing of the women's rights movement.
    b. The interdisciplinary study of power and gender relationships, which is emphasized through an interactive learning process.
    c. Women's studies? Where's Man's Studies?!
    d. Where you check out women—ha-ha-ha!

2. **What is sex?**
    a. A biological classification used to categorize humans based on chromosomes, anatomy, and gonads.
    b. We're talking about sex now?! Thank god! This quiz was getting boooring!
    c. A biological classification used to separate humans into distinct categories, such as male and female.
    d. (a) and (c).

3. **When asked what you want to do with women's and gender studies after you graduate, you can reply:**

    a.   "Um, there's life after college?"

    b.   "Well, I could become a lawyer, doctor, politician, professor, teacher, or choose any number of other successful professions!"

    c.   "I'm never graduating college!"

    d.   "I plan on traveling around the country in my van for the rest of my life. I'll sell homemade hemp jewelry when I need money and become one with nature."

4. **What are the "waves" of feminism?**

    a.   A way of charting different periods of feminism characterized by different goals and activities going on during those time periods.

    b.   An ocean of feminism!

    c.   A cool new surfing style, dude.

    d.   Was that in the movie *Jaws*? That mechanical shark was SO COOL!

5. **The French author and philosopher Simone de Beauvoir wrote a book called:**

    a.   "Je suis Francaise, huh huh huh!"

    b.   *The Idiot's Guide to Feminist Existentialism*

    c.   *The Second Sex*

    d.   *NEWSFLASH: Sex and Gender are not the Same Thing*

6. **In Anne Fausto-Sterling's piece, "The Five Sexes: Why Male and Female Are Not Enough" she names the five sexes she describes. Those names are:**

    a.   Einie, meanie, miny, mo . . . moo?

    b.   Grover, Kermit, Bert, Miss Piggy, and Animal.

    c.   Five sexes!? No such thing!

    d.   Males, merms, herms, females, ferms.

7. **A women's and gender studies curriculum is made up of core courses and cross-listed courses across different departments and programs because:**

    a.   Professors can't make up their minds what to teach.

    b.   It's more interesting to take courses from everywhere.

    c.   Interdisciplinary courses intellectually support women's and gender studies training, because no one discipline has the answer.

    d.   It's just the way they do things in women's and gender studies.

8. **Moya Bailey is an example of the connection between theory and action demonstrated in women's and gender studies classes because:**

    a. She stood up for all bone marrow donors' rights.

    b. She and her peers used what was happening in their lives as a discussion point in class and then as a launchpad to begin an activist project.

    c. She and other women's studies professors don't like hip hop artists.

    d. She got angry, but it did not accomplish anything.

9. **If you were a women's and gender studies major and you wanted to travel abroad:**

    a. You would be out of luck.

    b. You would be able to research a number of programs that offer women, gender, and sexuality themed courses.

    c. You would have to finance the whole trip yourself.

    d. Why would you want to leave your campus?

10. **"Women and Creativity" is:**

    a. The title to the kind of upper-division class that you'd find in a women's and gender studies program.

    b. A show on Lifetime.

    c. Never-ending.

    d. The same thing as saying "Men and Creativity."

SECTION TWO

YOU'VE COMMITTED TO LEARNING IN WOMEN'S AND GENDER STUDIES: GREAT! NOW WHAT?

3
HOW *YOU* CAN TALK ABOUT WOMEN'S AND GENDER STUDIES ANYTIME, ANYWHERE, AND TO ANYONE

Picture this: you have just arrived home for winter break after your fifth semester at school. As you sit down to your first home-cooked meal in weeks, you proudly announce to your family, "I've decided to switch my major from pre-med to women's and gender studies." Across the mac-and-cheese, your parents drop their forks and knives, eyes popping out of their heads and remark, "What the heck are you going to do with a women's studies major? And what IS it anyway!" Their pre-med doctor-to-be has just transformed before their very eyes into a "bra-burning, man-hating feminist" and they want answers—now.[30] Good news—we're here to help!

At this point in the book, we're assuming that you have made an academic commitment to women's and gender studies in your college career. Maybe you have taken courses in high school, your first year of college, or even come to women's and gender studies later in your undergraduate education as a junior or senior. We believe that one aspect of this incredible journey is to become your own best advocate. This means communicating effectively with others about women's and gender studies and your decision to pursue a career in the field.

Although the dinner-table scenario may not fit your own personal experience, you may have struggled with how to explain your choice of academic major to family, friends, and the "nice old lady" sitting next to you on the airplane. And you may ask yourself why you should care about the person on the plane. Every opportunity to talk intelligently about women's and gender studies is a useful thing to undertake, because that person you talk to about women's and gender studies may be a potential employer, chairperson of an awards committee, or philanthropist. By talking with them about women's and gender studies in an easy, positive, and understandable way, you do your part to make this field of study visible, demystified, and legitimized. That random person you speak to may be, at some later date, in a position to make a decision that could affect someone with a women's and gender studies background. We think that communicating well about women's studies creates a ripple effect that has unknown positive ramifications.

You are not the first person to face these challenges. Many other students before you have had to talk to others about women's and gender studies. In this chapter, we will hear from former students about their experiences meeting these same challenges. As we stated in Chapter One, we think it's important to communicate with others about the role and value of women's studies in your academic training, because it offers you an opportunity to provide a compelling and positive frame for women's studies and issues of gender equality. Although an overwhelming majority of graduates found that many people supported their interest in women's studies, there were also students who reported otherwise. This chapter prepares you for communicating these aspects of your chosen field of study to others who are interested and supportive, and some who may be unaware of the existence of women's and gender studies as an academic major or who may hold misconceptions about women's and gender studies.

We hope that you are eager to talk about women's and gender studies, and that you will strongly value communicating both the concepts and skills that you are learning and the overall importance of your education. Language shapes who we are, how we see ourselves, how others perceive us, and our very actions and behavior. We want you to harness the power of language consciously to serve you.

We devote an entire chapter to this topic because we believe that communicating with others about one's field of study is a skill that is undervalued not only in women's and gender studies, but in most undergraduate fields. In other words, students are not typically encouraged or coached on how to discuss their chosen academic majors. One of the core goals of this book is for you to learn how to be your own best advocate as you pursue your career, including the time you spend as a student in women's and gender studies as well as in postgraduate life. Being your own best advocate and ally involves becoming comfortable with communicating. You will feel more confident about your choice and others will see that.

In this chapter, we first discuss the kind of "constituencies" that you'll be regularly speaking with about your women's and gender studies education: family, parents and relatives, partners (e.g. husbands, wives, domestic partners, and significant others), friends, and the general public (e.g. potential employers, co-workers, professors, and, yes, the "nice old lady" on the plane). Some of these folks may know a lot, while others may know nothing about women's and gender studies in higher education. We highlight and help you anticipate some of the questions you may be asked and the responses that you might receive from each group.

Learning how to communicate about women's and gender studies takes practice, time, and, like most things, it's a process. Think of developing your communication skills as a type of workout. Just as it takes focus, practice, and determination to run a marathon or keep up in yoga class, these same characteristics apply when trying to become comfortable with various types of public speaking. If you can think of communicating about women's and gender studies as a muscle to develop and flex, you're more likely to get inspired, to practice, and to get creative about your responses. It takes time to think through and answer questions from family and friends and the neighbor next door. The exercises at the end of this chapter are designed to help you practice communicating with others.

The Five Questions

Drawing from our own experiences as educators in women's and gender studies, we have identified five basic questions that are consistently posed to women's and gender studies students. We explore them throughout the chapter:

1. If women's studies centers on women's lives, is it anti-male?
2. Given the enormous progress women have made over the past three decades, why would you need a degree in women's and gender studies?

3. What kind of employment can you find with a degree in women's and gender studies?
4. Is women's studies biased because it has a political agenda?
5. Does women's studies create victims by arguing that women are victimized in different ways?

Do any of these questions sound familiar to you? For clarity and ease of classification, we provide examples of how various groups of people might raise these questions. However, in your everyday experience you are just as likely to be asked any one of them from any person. Let's see how these questions might emerge for you.

Talking to Family

We begin our discussion with the important core group with whom you will most likely have to discuss your choices about an educational degree: your family. Just as there is no typical undergraduate student, there is no easy category for what constitutes "family" for all students. The student experience in higher education has shifted dramatically over the past two decades. Only about a quarter of all students are "traditional": that is, they enroll in college right after high school, rely on parents for financial support, and don't work or work only part time. Many students do not fit these criteria. They are financially independent, attend school part-time and work full-time, and may have dependents to support (e.g. children, partners, parents). Our definition of family includes parents, partners, and extended kin networks (aunts, uncles, godmothers, family friends, etc.).

Family tends to have a vested interest in our college experience. They often provide emotional, financial, and social support for us while we attend college. So, when you think of family, what people come to mind? Are you thinking of your:

- parents
- husband, wife, significant other, or partner
- teenage son
- great aunt
- godfather?

Get a clear image of that person or group of people. We would like you to keep their image in mind throughout this section. They are the people you will most likely talk with about women's and gender studies at some point during your college career.

One of the most stressful experiences that some students have during college is sharing their decision of an academic major with family members. Why? Because for some students, especially traditional students, it can mean choosing a very different path than the one their parents thought they were taking. It can bring up a difficult conversation about family expectations that were perhaps, up until this point, implied but not explicitly stated. For example, if you were always strong in the sciences throughout high school and had taken lots of science classes in the early part of college, there might have been an expectation that you would pursue a career in medicine or the health professions. Much as with the scenario in the opening of the chapter, if you come home and announce that you are now a double major in women's studies and anthropology, your family may be completely surprised and confused. Choosing a major with intention and purpose can feel both disorienting and exhilarating, because it marks perhaps the first time that you embark on a learning process that you have defined for yourself. It can be disorienting, for example, if you always thought of yourself as a zoology student but have, over the past two years, become obsessed about the role of masculinity in nineteenth-century British novels. That kind of change can feel like a dramatic shift for everyone involved.

The challenging path for a student is to illuminate their decision-making process to someone who does not share the same day-to-day academic experience. Some students inform their families of their decisions about classes, majors, and minors throughout their college career. Others have longer conversations about academic matters over holidays, summer, fall, and winter breaks. First-generation college students may have the additional challenge of talking about the college experience to family members who do not understand or identify with that experience. This may be especially acute in working-class families, for students from countries where education is seen as a privilege and not a right, or in families where a college education is seen as tied solely to creating economic opportunity rather than personal self-development or fulfillment. If a family member is helping to pay for college, there may be significant expectations that they get to shape what you decide to major in and the opportunities that you pursue during college.

For other, non-traditional students, the concern over what a particular family member thinks may be less of an issue because the student may not live at home or rely on any monetary support from parents or extended kin. These students may find themselves having conversations with their intimate partners, which can produce some similar dynamics.

Many students find that when they talk to their family members about their interest in women's and gender studies, they receive positive and supportive responses. This can be your experience, too. We will give you tools to increase the likelihood of a positive outcome.

Affirmative responses about women's studies from family members can feel deeply supportive. Carol shares her experiences of talking with her family:

> As the first person in my family to earn a four-year degree, it has been rewarding to tell family members what I do as a women's studies student. Granted my great-grandmother and great aunts have no need for the jargon of academe (hegemony, discourse, constellation of identity, etc.). However, these women very well understand what it means to be discounted because of race, class, and gender. And when I tell them that part of my work is "acting like women count" through research and writing, for example— they care and understand and are, I am gratified to say—deeply proud of me.
>
> (Carol, 2007, UNC, Chapel Hill)

Marci,[31] a former student of Michele's, had a startling experience when she talked with her mother about becoming a women's studies major. Marci talked about her commitment to issues of sexual violence. It was then that her mother revealed a life-changing story to Marci. Marci's mother had been raped in a bar when she was in her early twenties and before Marci was born. Her mother lived in a small town and detailed the negative experiences that she faced in seeking support and justice. She felt that even the local support services aimed at sexual assault survivors were judgmental. Her mother explained that she felt judged because of her prior sexual behavior and also felt others looked down upon her because of her class status. She had a very difficult time bringing a case against her attackers. Marci had never heard this story before. Her mother was thrilled that Marci had found women's studies and noted that she had taken some women's studies courses at a community college. Her father was also supportive of her decision and encouraged her to conduct an internship at a rape crisis center near campus.

We have found that many students who have decided on women's and gender studies have seen themselves as walking in family traditions of study. Carla, a women's studies minor said:

> My mother was a women's studies minor at SUNY-Geneseo in the late 70s/early 80s, so in a way I was continuing the tradition. Being a third-wave feminist was like being a chip off the old block. I am proud to come from such a forward-thinking family, men and women included.
>
> (Carla, 2008, UNC, Chapel Hill)

Graduates have also reported that parents make very supportive statements about their choice to pursue women's studies such as, "I wish they'd had women's studies when I was in school. I would have taken it!"

It is completely normal for parents and family members to be interested in their loved one's education. If family members don't embrace your choice of women's and gender studies, several factors may be involved. For example, family members do not always know or understand the changes that have happened in the academic world. We have found that some parents in particular reflect back to their own experiences in college and project them onto understanding the choices their children make. People's expectations of what constitutes academic work are usually heavily influenced by their own personal experiences. This perspective can sometimes position perceived "new" majors unfavorably. Some parents may assume that if it did not exist "when I was in school," then the major or area of academic study is somehow less legitimate.

For instance, if a student's parents went to school during the 1970s, depending on what college or university they attended, they probably did not have campus departments and programs dedicated to the study of the environment, peace, or ethnic studies. However, these academic fields have emerged over the past forty years and have thriving majors that are well established on many college campuses and universities. Another example: perhaps your mother attended a state university around 1990. It is likely that there was not a women's studies program established there at that time (or if there was, she did not know about it), and it is quite possible that she never even had a female professor during her college career. If so, her experience might make her skeptical or less receptive to understanding why you have chosen women's and gender studies. If this is the case, you may find yourself having to talk about how women's and gender studies developed in higher education, drawing on material from Chapter One.

Parents also feel an enormous responsibility to make sure that you are successful in the world. Sometimes parents ask: "How is this major going to help you find employment?" They obviously want you to graduate with a degree and set of skills that can translate into a global market. Therefore, it may be useful for you to have a sense of what kinds of positions you can apply for with your degree. Finding this information in our book or on your school's website would be a start. It might also be useful for you to spend some time finding out who are the most successful graduates of your school's program—you'll get lots of useful information from Chapters Five and Six, which focus on employment and career pathways. Women's and gender studies graduates work in a variety of fields and succeed in the public and private sectors. Some parents and relatives may welcome such concrete information and be more supportive of your decision when this is included.

It may also be helpful to remind family members that you will enter into a very different labor market than the previous generation. Employment in one sector over the course of one's life is rapidly becoming a thing of the past. For example, your career path is most likely going to be a fluid experience as opposed to a stable one. It would be helpful to share with family members who may not know that nearly half of all graduates change their career plans after they finish college and the average person changes careers nearly five times in his or her lifetime. This trend will probably remain stable for the next several decades. You might also stress to your family that women's studies (as with other liberal arts majors) is preparing you to be adaptive and responsive to larger trends in the marketplace. It does not prepare students for one specific job, but is a way of preparing to harness one's individual talents and abilities in a broad variety of careers.

Talking openly about what women's studies means to you, why you value it, and what you think it might mean for your career can create a level of closeness between you and your family. It also means thinking ahead about how to tell the story of your experience of women's and gender studies. We agree with best-selling author Mary Pipher about the

CHARTING CAREER CHANGES: RESEARCH AND MYTHS

When discussing future careers and the labor market, you may come across information that says that the average person changes their career three to eight times over their life. Actually, there is no accurate statistic that charts workers' changes over time with that predictability. The problem with this estimate is two-fold. There are not only issues with "operationization" or how one defines and measure the terms one is using (e.g. an occupation versus a career; a shift within the same field to another job type or a promotion) but with collecting the data as well. According to the US Bureau of Labor, there is a paucity of longitudinal data measuring the average number of jobs/careers held by the average citizen. A Bureau of Labor Statistics (BLS) news release published in June 2008 examined the number of jobs that people born in the years 1957 to 1964 held from age eighteen to age forty-two. The title of the report is "Number of Jobs Held, Labor Market Activity, and Earnings Growth among the Youngest Baby Boomers: Results from a Longitudinal Survey." The report is available on the BLS website at: www.bls.gov/news.release/pdf/nlsoy.pdf. These younger baby boomers held an average of 10.8 jobs from ages eighteen to forty-two (in this report, a job is defined as an uninterrupted period of work with a particular employer). On average, men held 10.7 jobs and women held 10.3 jobs. Both men and women held more jobs on average in their late teens and early twenties than they held in their mid-thirties. From ages eighteen to forty-two, some of these younger baby boomers held more jobs than average and others held fewer jobs. Twenty-three percent held fifteen jobs or more, while 14 percent held zero to four jobs.

However, it is important to convey to worried family members that the trend in employment is that workers need to be prepared to change jobs often. And many studies suggest that there is not a direct correlation between choice of major and a specific employment position post graduation. We strongly believe that training in women's and gender studies prepares students to think creatively and dynamically about matching their skills and interests to the working world. We explore these ideas further in Chapter Six.

For additional statistics on the number of jobs held, see the tables at www.bls.gov/nls/y79r22jobsbyedu.pdf, and look at www.bls.gov/nls/nlsfaqs.htm#anch41 for further information as well.

importance of stories as ". . . the most basic tool for connecting us to one another" (Pipher 2006: 11). Stories evoke strong emotions in our listeners and can trigger powerful stories from our audiences in return. We encourage you to become intentional in how you tell the story of your interest in women's and gender studies. People often respond favorably when you tell them why this academic field of study has meaning to you. It also gives you time to reflect on its meaning, as it did Courtney, a double major in journalism and women's studies, who discusses her experience talking with family:

> When I told my parents I was a feminist they had a lot of questions. Dad wanted to know if I was dropping my journalism major, if I was planning to miss class to attend bra burning rallies and if I considered what a male boss might think in the future. Mom wanted to know if I was still going to shave my legs, if I had been to church lately and if she was still going to have grandchildren—"not adopted ones"—"real ones." They both wanted to know if I had actually thought about this decision.
>
> That was three years ago and, thankfully, my parents have a better understanding of what being a feminist means—and what it means to me. Though most of their original questions were thoughtless and unfounded, asking if I had thought about my decision was extremely relevant.
>
> It wasn't until I enrolled in Introduction to Women's Studies my sophomore year that I begin to think about anything. I consider myself to be an intelligent person, but until that point I was not an intellectual person. I had never considered motives or experiences before accepting information as "the truth." I had never thought about the ways in which I was privileged or oppressed. I had never thought about activism or agency. I had never even thought about my own racial identity as a person who is half-White and half-American Indian.
>
> (Courtney, 2010, UNC, Chapel Hill)

Although, initially, Courtney's parents were not supportive of her decision, Courtney was able to talk with them further about her academic interests, and in time the stereotypes that her parents held dissolved. Over time they also could see the positive changes that occurred in Courtney's life as Courtney truly claimed her education.

Frank conversations about the role of feminism and women's studies will probably come up at some point with your parents. You can view discussing your interests with your parents as a process, one that can have an impact on yourself and your family in interesting and sometimes unpredictable ways. Diana Rhodes is a graduate in women's studies and sociology from UNLV and is profiled in Chapter Five. Diana's experience provides a useful illustration of how conversations about women's and gender studies can contribute to new ways that family members experience their own reality:

> My mom always raised me as a strong independent person. My mom was raised in Texas and she came to the US in the early 1970s, from Vietnam, when she was eight or ten. She came right at the end of the war and she was the youngest of twelve siblings. My mom is a bad ass!
>
> At first they did not quite get it [her feminism and interest in women's studies] but they are now cool with it. I realized that my parents have always given me choices, they always let me choose what I've wanted do. It was funny because my mom didn't identify as a feminist. I would buy my mom bell hooks books and stuff for birthdays and she would never read them. She was like, "it's not really my thing," which is interesting, because when I first started getting into my activism, my feminism and my women's studies world is when she more rapidly began moving up in her career. She works in gaming [in Las Vegas]. She started in the cage [as a cashier] . . . and now she's a senior shift supervisor. The more she got promoted and started moving up, the more she started seeing these very gendered things and how male-dominated her world is. She saw the choices and the compromises she would have to make. She stopped wearing skirts and started wearing suits. She would buy her pants a size too big so it would hide her curves. She shared with me these little things. We'd talk about it and now she tentatively identifies as a feminist. The more she got into higher positions she started to see the things I'd talked about, which was really not good and she had to face those things. But she started dealing with those things and asking why things were happening, [asking about] "this very power structure, patriarchy," the kind of words I was talking about, and now she's very, very proud of me.
>
> (Diana, 2006, UNLV)

You never know where a conversation about women's and gender studies will take you!

SPOTLIGHT: MOYA BAILEY

You met Moya Bailey in Chapter Two. Here, she reflects on her parents' understanding of her pursuit of women's studies and her passion and commitment to feminism—interests that don't easily map onto a traditional career path:

> It's difficult because they [her parents] see feminism as a constant critique (which it is), but they see that as negative thing. They say, don't you get tired of pointing out negative things on TV and in the newspaper? And I'm like, don't you get tired of taking this in and it not being healthy? But then we've joked about that and even my dad will sometimes say, "You think I'm this patriarchal man," and he'll say it in a joking way—it's a joke but with an edge. But I think my relationship with women's studies does challenge the way women are supposed to be and he knows that. What's interesting is that as an only child, I think the way my mom and dad raised me was to be independent and take care of yourself (not to depend on men), which is a feminist principle. It's interesting to me that they cultivated [that in me] but then they are surprised how that gets carried over—they didn't connect what they were doing to feminism explicitly.

Moya said in her interview that her parents believed that being a doctor was a very clear career choice for their daughter, so they were surprised when she changed her major (from pre-med and psychology to pre-med and women's studies) and focus.

> I loved science, it came easily to me, I did lots of summer science programs, went to hospitals and did lots of programs related to medicine, so it seemed like a big switch to them. But I couldn't really see the systemic change that would happen for me, becoming a doctor. I could be a practicing physician who did things differently as an individual practitioner, but in terms of the system itself, it didn't seem like [being a doctor] had enough impact, and that was one of the things that made me shift. So, they are concerned about my individual livelihood, but feminism made me think beyond myself in many ways. And that is one of the tensions that they have with feminism is that it is global and focuses on the big picture and community. And, I think in a lot of ways they don't trust a lot of people and rightfully so—they grew up in Birmingham [Alabama] during all of the social unrest [of the civil rights movement]. Those experiences have made them very interdependent upon each other and my family. I don't necessarily have that same sense, so my sense of "Let's change the world on a global scale" is not where they are.

Moya charts the evolution of discussions about women's and gender studies and feminism with her parents, with these discussions encompassing humor, their concern, and her sense of what's right for her life. Moya makes an important connection between how her women's studies training and feminist practice encouraged her to think differently about career choices. We'll come back to this point in Chapter Six. Your training in women's and gender studies is going to encourage you use a different lens to think about what's next after graduation. Moya found that this type of critical thinking led her down a new and interesting path.

Conversations about women's and gender studies can become inflamed quickly when issues of sexuality or politics unexpectedly arise. Some family members may question your political beliefs and even your sexual orientation if you show an interest in women's and gender studies. Respondents in our survey and interviews revealed stories of initially feeling harassed when talking to some family members about their choice to major in women's and gender studies. Some graduates have felt that women's studies can be used as a scapegoat for parents and relatives to suggest disapproval for other beliefs and behaviors that some might feel are unacceptable.[32]

More specifically, some female students are concerned that a family member may accuse them of being a lesbian if they discuss an interest in women's and gender studies. "Lesbian baiting" has had a long history in feminism and women's studies and we live in a society where LGBT issues are still suspect. Graduates mentioned that being accused of being a lesbian was a response from some family members (and peers). It is our belief that this is a homophobic response and can provide for a tense conversation. It can also be additionally challenging for students who feel that they *have questioned* aspects of their sexual and/or gender identity through the synthesis of material and critical reflections in their classes.

Although we emphasize in this chapter the importance of face-to-face verbal communication, we also believe that other types of correspondence play important roles in communicating your ideas. If you find yourself accused and attacked about sexuality and/or political views after talking about your interest in women's and gender studies, and you have tried to respond respectfully and cogently (using some of the techniques that we offer at the end of the chapter), it may be important to allow for a cooling off time between you and that family member. During that cooling off period, we suggest that you try writing them by email, card, or letter some of your thoughts about how that person responded. Written

STRATEGIES FOR DEALING WITH LESBIAN BAITING

The term "lesbian baiting" in this context refers to the interpersonal experience some students who express interest in women's and gender studies face from family, peers, and others who assume (or accuse) that the student identifies as a lesbian or bisexual person. The person might respond, "NO! I'm not a lesbian!" and by doing so she's validating that such a thing would be terrible. Indeed, it validates the homophobia that propels the comment. This is a very common strategy to shut down women's and gender studies students.

Lesbian baiting is tough. A guy at my work assumed I was "man hating" because he knew I was a women's studies major. I think the best way to deal with it is to train yourself to be calm and not get defensive over such things. Depending on the person, maybe you can ask them to explain how women's studies makes you a lesbian. Sometimes when people are forced to explain their ABC thought processes, they realize how dumb it sounds.

(Tucker, 2008, UNC, Chapel Hill)

communication allows for some time to elapse between strong feelings that might have been shared by you and a family member. Writing also helps to clarify one's thoughts and allows for reflection, unlike direct communication. If you decide to write a letter, you might want to express disappointment at the tone of conversation, about what allegations or assumptions were made, and about how that made you feel. This allows for the person to look at their assumptions and to distinguish between what you would like to accomplish as a student and being labeled in a category that may or may not reflect your immediate experience. There is, of course, no guarantee that your letter will be heard and received with the intentions you meant, but it provides another way to communicate your ideas and feelings with someone who is very important to you.

The best preparation for family discussions is to take some time anticipating their responses. As you reflect on the person (and people) who constitute your family, can you begin to imagine what kind of response they might have when you tell them about your interest in women's and gender studies? Will they be supportive or uninterested or ask for more information? Have they expressed strong feelings about your career path throughout high school and college? By anticipating the types of responses you may encounter, you can begin mentally to script your answers to your family member's questions. Also, as you begin to create a ready answer for someone you know and love, you will be able to recycle and reframe your answer for other groups (such as friends or the general public). The exercises at the end of this chapter will help you to do just that kind of work.

Talking to Friends

Learning from and being with other students who become your friends is one of the special gifts of a college education. In college, friends are often a mirror of our interests, academic and personal passions, likes and dislikes. Friends play a key role as sounding boards and advisors as we navigate both the academic and social life that is part of a college experience. We've heard a range of responses from our respondents about the role of peers in their college influences. For some students, many of their friends have taken women's and gender studies classes and are encouraging them to explore the field. Others had friends who had never heard of women's and gender studies and made pointed remarks about choosing it as a course of study. Students can feel confused and isolated when peers are not accepting of their personal and academic choices. If you are not prepared for it, navigating the range of possible comments from friends about women's studies can feel overwhelming.

April, a double major in psychology and women's studies, discusses her experience:

> While I was in school and had only taken a few women's studies classes I didn't know what to say! Then I started to tell people to imagine taking a history class where the perspective was only from women—which I think was helpful, but it still confused some people. Now, I've added that it's more than just reexamining our past to include women's p.o.v. [point of view] but also examining how gender and sexuality shape all aspects of our lives.
> Also, I've found that male students tend to ask more [questions] than female students, and they assume that all we talk about [in women's studies classes] is feminism or man-hating ideas. Crazy!
> (April, 2009, UNC, Chapel Hill)

From peers, you might experience comments and questions that sound something like this:

- "Being a women's studies major—isn't that like being a double feminist?[33] That's going too far."

- "Isn't women's studies just for women? Isn't that against men?"
- "Doesn't women's studies just blame men?"

The idea that "man-hating" ideas comprise all of the discussion in women's studies courses is a familiar one.

Many people may also conflate feminist political activism with the role of women's and gender studies as an intellectual pursuit. And while it is clear that an aspect of inquiry in women's studies is concerned with change that benefits all, it is also an interdisciplinary field of study that is accountable to the standards of good scholarship and insights that govern work in colleges and universities. To this point, we think that reminding your peers of the academic outcomes and learning goals that women's and gender studies seeks to teach would be helpful as a response to questions about its relationship to politics and activism. We like how scholars (and activists) Gwen Kirk and Margo Okazawa-Rey grapple with this first question, "Good scholarship is about looking at analytical patterns and asking difficult questions" (2010: 5). During some point in your academic career, you may very well be interested in activism, but it is far from a given that all women's and gender studies students define themselves as activists.

Unfortunately, feminists and women concerned with gender equity are often largely portrayed as being unfeminine, bra-burning man-haters. This distorted notion can affect how some friends may view women's and gender studies and your interest in it. In Chapter One, we documented the role of women's studies in demanding the inclusion of women into traditionally male-centered curricula—classes often centered on subjects that were ignored in other courses. Rather than addressing the lack of parity, some educators and the general public think that feminists and the women's studies community wanted to make men as invisible as women had been in the academy. Comments by friends questioning how women's studies addresses men's lives might mirror this same concern.

Yet, as women's studies has flourished in the academy, it has also opened up new spaces for examining the complexity of both women's and men's lives. Looking at men's lives and asking critical questions about gender has enabled scholars to examine the concept of masculinity and to develop men's studies. As Michael Kimmel states in his provocative essay "Men and Women's Studies: Premises, Perils, and Promise" (1996):

THE MYTH OF BRA-BURNING FEMINISTS

If you have talked to someone about feminism and/or women's and gender studies, there's a good chance that you will have heard the ever-famous phrase "bra burning" at some point. This phrase might arrive in front of you as the question: "Do you want to be like those 'radical bra-burning feminists'?" Or as a phrase: "Those 'bra-burning feminists' were really angry way back when." In many people's minds, feminist activism of the 1960s is often reduced to women burning their bras. You will find in your studies that this idea is narrow, simplistic, and UNTRUE. During the 1960s and 1970s, women and men were actively challenging gender roles and ideas about men and women in society in a variety of ways and places. Yet, the media framing of that decade of feminism was all about bras. So, what did really happen?

Although some people may equate bra-burning as a necessary adjective before the term feminist, there's been a lot myth-making between the two. Many second-wave feminists took aim at the normative standards of beauty, including critiquing the role of beauty pageants as ritual of reinforcing norms about ideal womanhood. A few days before the 1968 Miss America pageant, a number of women protested (including members of New York Radical Women) and threatened to burn all "instruments of torture" (i.e. girdles, curlers, bras, and issues of *Cosmopolitan* and *Playboy*). This was one of the first public, organized protests by women to critique a big and popular event. They did not, however, burn any bras (deciding in favor of fire safety). A reporter quoted Robin Morgan, an activist there, and she indicated that it had been a "symbolic bra-burning." Although no bras were actually burned at this event, the reports in the paper just a few days after the event connected feminists with "bra-burners." Most historians of this time period suggest that very few actual bras were ever destroyed during the women's liberation movement. However, once that symbolic frame was presented as a way to understand "women's libbers" and feminists, it stuck as a dominant one that did bring national attention to the women's liberation moment, thus creating allies. Indeed, women around the world began to protest beauty pageants. But the "bra-burning feminist" label created a frame for parts of the public to delegitimize and dismiss important concerns that many women were raising through the beginnings of a mass movement.

For more information on this topic, see Ruth Rosen (2000) *The World Split Open: How the Modern Women's Movement Changed America*, and Estelle Freedman (2002) *No Turning Back: The History of Feminism and the Future of Women*.

". . . without women's studies there would be no men's studies." Women's studies made gender a lens with which to understand the world. Through critically evaluating the roles of men in society, scholars could look more closely at how men also occupied multiple social statuses (including age, race/ethnicity, nationality, sexuality, ability) that affect their experiences with power and privilege in contemporary societies. Concepts like "hegemonic masculinity," as explored by scholars such as R. W. Connell and James W. Messerschmidt (2005), Michael Kimmel (1994), and Michael Messner and Donald Sabo (1994) have challenged masculinity as a universal experience and instead presented it as an ideal type, which many men aim toward (due to multiple rewards and pressures) but few men can attain. As discussed in Chapter One, besides men's studies, gender as the key organizing focus of inquiry helped in the creation of gender studies, transgender studies, and queer studies. Thus, rather than being exclusive or narrow, women's studies has advocated for and supported a more inclusive and complex analysis for all human beings.

So, if you are confronted with questions specifically about the role of men in women's studies, you might respond with a statement like the one offered by Gwen Kirk and Margo Okazawa-Rey, who smartly addressed this topic (paraphrased and imagined here): "Sounds like you've got a misperception that by focusing on women, men are left out of the picture. First, women's studies is about looking at gender, which includes women and men's roles in societies. Women's studies doesn't blame everything on men of any particular background. That's anti-intellectual. I find women's studies personally empowering and useful in how to critically evaluate the ways that longstanding patterns of inequality affect us all. I see women's studies as committed to seeing how experiences of inequality and privilege shape people's everyday lives" (see Kirk and Okazawa-Rey 2010: 5).

A slightly different way to respond might be:

> Women's studies is not as narrow as you might think. Although it places women in a center of analysis, it does not ignore or diminish men. This analysis benefits everyone, regardless of their gender, and it looks at a range of issues. Women's studies has taught me the ways that men have played key roles in promoting

THE WHITE RIBBON CAMPAIGN

In the early 1990s, a handful of men in Canada decided they had a responsibility to urge men to speak out about violence against women. Wearing a white ribbon would be a symbol of men's opposition to violence against women. In less than two months, 100,000 men across Canada wore a white ribbon, and many men found themselves talking about the root causes of sexual assault. This effort was incredibly effective and through it the organization was born.

> The White Ribbon Campaign (WRC) is the largest effort in the world of men working to end violence against women (VAW). In Canada the white ribbon campaigns take place throughout the year. In over fifty-five countries, campaigns are led by both men and women, even though the focus is on educating men and boys. In some countries it is a general public education effort focused on ending violence against women.
>
> (www.whiteribbon.com/about_us/)

The WRC is a small organization that encourages chapters to be started and run around the world.

the advancement of women generally. For example, it was in my women's studies class that I learned about the White Ribbon campaign, which is about men fighting sexual violence. I've also discovered the ways that men have been actively fighting for fair pay for women and women's health issues.

Men Talking about Women's and Gender Studies

Both heterosexual and queer men who take women's and gender studies classes and choose to major or minor in it can face unique and particular challenges when talking with peers about their academic commitment to women's and gender studies. For example, heterosexual men may face homophobic remarks from some male peers who question their sexual identity. Heterosexual men may also encounter skepticism from their female colleagues who question their motives about majoring in women's studies. Some comments that our respondents have heard concerning men in women's and gender studies include: "they're just acting like sensitive men in order to get into women's pants" or "because they're

privileged as men they can never truly understand a feminist perspective."
We have also encountered heterosexual men who are trying to define
themselves as men in a culture that often asks them to demean the very
women who have raised them, women with whom they have raised
families, women as partners who have survived sexual assault, and women
who are their children.

Homosexual men also must deal with issues of sexism both within the
larger social environment and within gay male culture. Homosexual or
queer men might also be mistaken for or presumed to be transgendered
individuals wishing to become transsexuals—since they are interested in
"women's issues."[34]

We turn now to Matt (whom you met in Chapter One), who reflects
on the comments he received from peers after he declared his women's
studies major:

> A lot of the men in my life at the time I was getting into it
> [women's studies] had no idea of what to make of it: They would
> either say: "What are you going to do with that? What the hell
> are you thinking?" Or, "it's a great way to meet chicks." It was
> always one of those three responses. Or, maybe not stated as
> directly to me as often but raising . . . questions about my sexual
> identity. Of course men learning about women's experiences
> means we want to sleep with men. That's not even logical! But
> lesbian and gay baiting is a common response to women or men
> who get involved in feminist projects.
>
>   (Matt, 1999, UNC, Chapel Hill)

As we've noted, men who are interested in women's and gender studies
issues might encounter open skepticism and hostility from other men (and
some women). Matt has spent the past decade working on issues of sexual
violence and motivating men to become allies in the struggle against
violence. He thinks it is imperative for men to become active in feminist
struggles. He provides these tips to encourage male students to deal with
peer pressure:

- Find other men who are doing anti-racist, anti-sexist, and anti-
  homophobic work. It helps to build a community of supportive
  male allies. It is critical for men to do work within the communities
  of privilege they occupy so that they can be better allies.

- Become engaged in activist projects. Men in women's and gender studies who might identify with feminism can deepen their commitments to feminist work by committing over a period of time to projects in which they are interested. This can support their interests and help build friendship and ally networks with both women and men. We think this is sound advice. The other advantage of getting involved in projects on or off campus is that it will also build your confidence in talking to other people!

Unfortunately, there are no easy remedies for challenges raised by peers. We hope that after discussing the importance of women's and gender studies in your life with your friends that they are better able to understand your motivations and perhaps look at their own misperceptions in a new light.

Talking to the General Public: Employers, Co-Workers, and Casual Acquaintances

When I applied for the Marshall scholarship, I had to attend a panel interview on campus. I was interested in pursuing a Master's degree in Gender Studies at Leeds University, home to the Centre for Interdisciplinary Gender Studies. I imagined there wouldn't be much competition for this particular degree in a college that was outside of London.

One woman on the panel asked me why I wanted to study gender [and] what the validity of the subject was. She asked in a respectful way, saying that as a person who had studied math, she really didn't know what to expect in such a course of study. I wasn't prepared for the question at all. [I thought] If Leeds and many other universities devote faculty and centers to the subject, then it must obviously have some validity beyond my mere opinion on the subject, not to mention the effects of grassroots feminist movements across the planet.

I recovered quickly and gave a decent answer, but I was in no way prepared to defend the entire academic pursuit of gender studies. [I wondered afterwards] Are other masters programs questioned this way?

(Carla, 2008, UNC, Chapel Hill)

You encounter many people in your life in a variety of situations. In this section, we want to spend some time encouraging you to think about how you will communicate with people who are not your family or friends. We mean casual acquaintances—potential employers, co-workers, people you meet on a plane, professors (not in women's and gender studies), and passersby. In our experience, it is very common that students meet and casually talk about their academic interests with people outside their immediate family and peers. You may even meet people inside your university, other faculty members and staff, who do not know about the women's studies department or program at your college or university—as Carla's example above demonstrates.

We think it's important for you to gain some measure of confidence in talking about what women's studies means to you in brief exchanges with people you meet casually. Again, you may encounter people aside from your peers or parents who do not know much about women's and gender studies. Many students have these encounters early on in their academic careers.

Tucker, a graduate whom you met earlier in the chapter, reflects on her experience:

> So when people have absolutely never heard of women's studies, I try to explain it as the study of all different types of people that have been historically left out of academics; that the [women's studies] degree is about raising awareness of the oppression of different races, religions, genders, ethnic groups, socioeconomic backgrounds, etc. So, if I think people aren't going to be very receptive to hearing about women's studies, I try and explain it in a more all-encompassing way.
> (Tucker, 2008, UNC, Chapel Hill)

Thinking about how to talk to others about women's and gender studies was very important to Tucker as she began interviewing for positions after graduation:

> When I applied to my current job at a technical college they had explained to me that many of their students were from different socioeconomic and racial and ethnic backgrounds. Later on one of the people interviewing me asked me what exactly women's studies was. He made some joke about living with his wife for 25 years and if that counted, ha-ha. I explained to him that it was about being aware of the different types of people in this world and used it to support why I would be a good candidate for this position—because of my sensitivity and awareness of other people's differences.

Meeting people who don't know what women's and gender studies is can also happen if you travel out of your home country, as Katelyn, a women's studies major, relates below. She traveled to Guatemala both while she was a student and after she graduated:

> Whenever I told peers I encountered while traveling that I was a women's studies major, the most common reaction I would receive was a blank face. They would look at me as though I had somehow misspoken and wait for the real answer. When I began to explain what a women's study major was they would continue to stare blankly until I finished, and then would say, okay, but what is your career going to be? This would then launch into a discussion of the numerous paths that you can take as a women's studies major and after I told them the path that I was planning on taking with my degree they would tell me an anti-woman joke. It's amazing how after telling someone that you're a women's studies major they think that the most appropriate response is to tell you a joke about how women belong in the kitchen. Yet after many different times of hearing almost the exact same response, I've developed a pretty good answer for the blank stares [when people don't know what women's and gender studies is], and have heard almost every anti-woman joke that there is. The answer that I almost always give people when they ask what women's and gender studies is, is that it's the study of the past and current struggle of equality for women and men. It looks at our history from a gendered perspective and aims to gain a better understanding of what happened to all members of our population and not just those writing the history books. It also integrates a social, racial, and economical lens when examining society. Women's and gender studies is not just about trying to re-write history from a female perspective as people often claim, but really a chance to look at our history and try to understand why certain inequities still exist today and how we can work to change these.
>
> (Katelyn, 2008, UNC, Chapel Hill)

Although we hope that your international experience will go more pleasantly, Katelyn's experience is a good reminder that it is important to be prepared to talk calmly and intelligently about women's and gender studies.

Bias

You may encounter people who believe women's and gender studies does not constitute a real discipline, produce useful knowledge, or that it is inherently too political to be an "unbiased" discipline. Some people might hold the assumption that "women's studies is not 'real' scholarship but, instead, is feminist propaganda" (Kirk and Okazawa-Rey 2010: 5).

The word "bias" is one that you might hear occasionally when you talk about women's studies in particular. People may imply that it is biased to begin inquiry with questions that center on women, their experiences, and implications of living with inequality in a variety of forms. For example, women's studies classes often ask the question, "Why do we see different and negative global outcomes for women in the areas of health, economics, and political spheres?" Someone you meet might not like the starting point of talking about unequal outcomes. They might come from a research tradition that assumes an "objectively" knowable world where all questions are equally legitimate and are unconcerned with the "real world." So, bias can emerge as a type of critique that is used by some when all research is presumed to be conducted "objectively," or without reference to or interest in lived experience.

Women's studies research in the academy emerged in part to counter truth claims by researchers who, on the face, seemed "unbiased," but systematically ignored or distorted women's experiences. Often, the neutral and unbiased observer was revealed to have power to direct and communicate research findings in specific ways suitable to them and to not be neutral at all in portraying ideas about human history. Research that appeared on the surface to be neutral often reproduced sexist ideas about men and women. Women's and gender studies scholars instead enter research from the perspective that all knowledge has a type of built-in lens with which everyone enters the research process. Indeed, many women's studies scholars would argue that all research has a perspective that should be acknowledged and made transparent, and that all results must be questioned. The research process is thereby seen as a type of self-reflexive exercise as well as inquiry—offering insight into your own self and your position as researcher. Women's and gender studies scholars acknowledge that their work comes out of a perspective that challenges power and assumptions that knowledge is neutrally pursued in research. Women's and gender studies makes an explicit claim that knowledge can never be neutral.

There is also a political dimension to how particular ideas about the role of women's studies in higher education have been formed in the public. In "Sticks and Stones" Martha McCaughey describes the attacks in the

US against women's studies—conservative arguments waged by scholars who suggest that women's studies is not intellectually rigorous. These attacks try to delegitimize research that exposes inequities along race, class, and gender fault lines. Other challenges to women's studies have emerged in political hearings from legislators who question the legitimacy and, ultimately, government-sponsored funding for what they would call feminism and sexuality research (McCaughey 2009: 70). While this is not a new phenomenon, economic downturns as well as changes in legal and political environments present ongoing challenges to women's studies faculty and students alike. Political and social attacks on feminism and women's studies in higher education are cyclical and often reflect broader attacks on women's growing political and social power.[35]

Norway's recent national debate and furor about the value of studying gender is an important illustration of how questions about the role of women's and gender studies in higher education manifest in contexts outside the United States. In the early part of 2010, *Brainwash*, a television show, aired that proposed to take up topics about biological- and social-explanation models of human behavior, especially within the realm of gender and sexuality. The show proposed exploring questions that included: Are men biologically destined to be rapists? Is one born gay or does one choose to become gay? Why are so few women choosing careers in male-dominated fields? The show was heavily favored to present biological explanations over socially situated ones. And, although gender experts were consulted, they and other interviewees were seemingly kept in the dark about the overall motives of the show. Gender scholars offered answers that relied heavily on looking at gender as a type of social construction, and they minimized the role of biology as the sole factor in understanding human behavior. When the show was broadcast it erupted into a national debate in Norway about gender and the role of gender studies programs in producing research. Many in the academic community believed that the scholars were unfairly presented (and then attacked in the media) as having no interest in science or biology, which was not accurate. Some citizens and political pundits called for the closing of research centers on gender and sexuality; others believed that the gender research was less legitimate because it did not explicitly rely on the biological sciences. Many in the scholarly community perceived this to be an unfair criticism as gender research (in Norway and globally) is connected to the sciences, but the starting point for the types of questions being asked often differ. Gender scholars do not take science at face value when understanding human sexuality and gender arrangements. Jorunn Økland, director of the Center for Gender Research, was in the maelstrom of these debates and has written several blog entries about the outcome of these debates:

> The debates have focused on the importance of natural sciences in explanations of sex; other main theories about gender and sexuality; main topics in gender research—what falls outside its remit?; the role of gender scholars in a state feminist country— are they supposed to be in opposition to the government or help them introduce research-based policies? The debates have also raised issues of media ethics, and how to produce catchy popular science programmes. The debates have on the one hand shown all the characteristics of a scapegoat chase (after all, only 4–5 gender researchers were interviewed, altogether there are less than 50 academics, Ph.D. students included, working at gender research units in Norway). On the other hand it has provided gender researchers with a unique opportunity to spread awareness about their existence and to convey some of their research to the general public.
>
> (Økland 2010)

In responding to a question or remark about bias, you could emphasize that women's and gender studies is taught globally in over 700 different kinds of institutions. You might say something such as:

> Given the diversity and longevity of the many institutions that currently encourage and support work on gender and women's studies scholarship, it's not likely that they could survive in the academy this long without presenting useful information to scholars outside of women's studies and the public. Academic research on women and gender is published widely in the academy and is often used by policymakers. These factors suggest that the academic community works hard to secure the highest quality work from scholars in their fields.

Talking and debating about gender and sexuality often makes people uncomfortable. Women's and gender studies scholars have argued for the past thirty years that gender arrangements are neither neutral nor without consequence. A critique of societal power has also been a component of women's and gender studies research. Therefore, as students pursuing work in this area, you should not be surprised that women's and gender studies has fended off its share of attacks and criticisms. We do not feel discouraged by such cyclical issues, as they are part of being involved with fields of study that seek to challenge the status quo, and we hope that you are not disheartened either. Instead, we encourage you to be a well-informed student who can respond to sometimes pointed questions in a calm and thoughtful way.

Creating Victims or Identifying Inequality?

Another question that you might encounter from someone in the general public is: "Doesn't women's studies create victims by arguing that women are victimized in different ways?"

Many of our respondents faced this question at some point in their women's and gender studies training and have provided interesting responses. Eva Marie, a women's studies major who you met in an earlier chapter responds:

> From the introduction of terms and definitions, some studies use the issue of victimization as a self-awareness tool to inform students how to recognize the meaning [sic]. It is my belief that women's studies does not breed victims, but gives its students a way to explain why victimization occurs and how to prevent it.
> (Eva Marie, 2010, Minnesota State University, Mankato)

Beth, a former student of Cheryl's, builds on this point:

> The importance of women's studies is to recognize our place in the world, how we contributed to the current state of society, and to promote the option (through knowledge), to act. Furthermore, although women's studies may bring the acknowledgement to individuals that they have been victimized, it also gives the knowledge and strength to turn victims into survivors and to make oppressors (in many forms) aware of their contribution to victimization (of themselves and others).
> (Beth, 2008, Minnesota State University, Mankato)

Carol, whom we met earlier in this chapter, comments:

> Women's studies equips women to critically engage the world by asking sometimes very simple questions like, "Why do people warn

their daughters about being out at night alone, but not their sons?"
Such questions do not make women victims as much as equip
them to interrogate the various discourses that (in this example)
make parents' fears "real."

(Carol, 2007, UNC, Chapel Hill)

We know that women's and gender studies graduates are up to the
task of finding skillful ways of responding to questions, concerns, and
even skepticism about their academic interests. In Luebke and Reilly's
(1995) study of the first generation of women's studies graduates, they
found that the majority of students were undaunted when faced with
indifferent or even hostile feedback about their choice of major.

As with anything, a new skill requires practice, practice, and more
practice. You may go through cycles of working on your communication
about your academic interests. It might be helpful to think of this as a
process that will continue even after graduation.

Communicating about women's and gender studies is not just your
responsibility. We, as professors, find ourselves in similar positions because
we encounter people who know little about women's and gender studies
or have uninformed perceptions of what we do as professors. In other words,
your women's and gender studies professors may confront the same kinds
of challenges that you may face. We feel that communicating about
women's and gender studies in an accessible way is part of our role as
educators. Just like you, we've had to practice and find ways to make
communication fun for us. Michele has been inspired by Jane Burns, one
of her senior colleagues, who makes a point to travel with a copy of the
department's complete course listings. When Jane sits down next to her
seatmate on the plane and is asked by her: "What's women's studies?"
she pulls out the course listing and says, "Here are all the courses that we
teach." She also rattles off information about how women's studies has
courses cross-listed with every major school on campus at the university
(e.g. School of Social Work, School of Medicine, etc.), how the department
teaches over 250 students each semester in the "Introduction to Women's
Studies" course, and the ways that women's studies contributes to the
mission of the university. For her, having a visual reference is quite helpful
and allows her to feel relaxed while talking about what she does as a women's
studies professor. We've suggested some exercises below to get you started
as you think about your communication of women's and gender studies.

YOUR TURN: EXERCISES

Elevator Speeches

One way to become more comfortable and proficient in talking about your academic passions is to practice a technique of communicating that is called the "elevator speech." The elevator speech began in the world of business. It is used to help prepare people to sell their product in a short amount of time—usually the time it takes an elevator to ascend a few floors. An elevator speech presents a sizable amount of information in a compressed way. Having a short speech memorized can be very helpful when you meet different people and want to convey important information in a quick and concise way. Cheryl and I have adopted the elevator speech as a teaching tool in our classes. For example, we will suggest a role-playing scenario where the student imagines he or she is in an elevator with someone (perhaps the dean of the college), and they have just a few minutes to verbally explain a concept we are discussing in class using jargon-free language. In this scenario, one student plays him or herself and the other student acts as the dean of the college. Students have told us that this exercise helps them to think on their feet and learn how to talk about complex terms in everyday language.

The elevator speech is highly adaptable. You can use this tool as a way to introduce yourself, to build professional and personal relationships, and to have a confident answer to the potential questions that you may face. The elevator speech has a few key components:

- The speech is not longer than 30 seconds.

- The speech is usually under 100 words.

- The speech is no longer than 10 sentences.

The best way to begin is to develop an elevator speech that centers on your interest in women's and gender studies by way of self-introduction. One way to begin constructing your elevator speech is to think about what your academic study means to you. In order to do this, you may want to look over your notes from Chapters One and Two. You also might want to set aside about 30 minutes to play with the following questions, which are designed to help you reflect on some of your experiences in women's and gender studies thus far.

In adapting this tool for your everyday interactions with others, reflect on the following questions:

- What benefits does a degree in women's and gender studies provide you with as a student?

- How have you made connections between what you study and everyday life?

- Is there a vignette/story you can tell that would communicate your personal experience as a women's and gender studies major (or minor, etc.)?

Once you have reached a place where you have some answers to the above questions and better know the information and feeling you want to convey in your elevator speech, we would like you to take each of the questions that we posed at the beginning of the chapter and create versions of your elevator speech for the different audiences that we have discussed in this chapter: family, friends, and the general public.

a. If women's studies centers on women's lives, is it anti-male?

b. Given the enormous progress women have made over the past three decades, why would you need a degree in women's and/or gender studies?

c. What kind of employment can you find with a degree in women's and gender studies?

d. Is women's and gender studies biased because it has a political agenda?

e. Does women's studies create victims by arguing that women are victimized in different ways?

Much of your communication style involves not just the words you use but also your body language. To deliver an elevator speech effectively, you will need to be calm in your delivery. Be conscious of fidgeting and work on eye contact. Write your elevator speech out and, if possible, record it or film yourself. Practice on friends who don't know much about women's and gender studies. Remember that in casual conversation there will be some give and take, and you can always add to your response if someone asks you a question.

Remember Kendra from our introduction? She was having a hard time communicating with her mother about her interest in women's studies and what women's studies is. We've started some prompts for you to complete:

> *Kendra*   Women's studies puts women's concerns and experiences at the center of academic study. And, Mom, that's the great thing about this major, I can take all sorts of courses that are cross-listed between the women's studies department and the political science department. I can study women's political participation in Latin America or in the US, for example. Or, I could take a political theory class that focuses on what women have considered important about democracy and citizenship.
>
> *Kendra's mom*   And you can major in that?"
>
> *Kendra*   Yes, definitely. Women's studies is an academic major just like theater.

• "The value of women's studies as a major is . . ."

• "Graduates in women's studies from my program go on to careers in . . ."

Examples of Elevator Speeches

Cheryl's Elevator Speech

> *Q* So, you're a women's studies professor. What exactly is Women's studies?
>
> *A* Women's studies begins with the assumption that we are gendered, or that we are socialized to see and classify ourselves and others in often "masculine" or "feminine" terms. Gender is not only

something we are assigned at birth, but something we constantly achieve and perform throughout our lives. It is also reinforced through laws, ideology, and language. But, even as gender plays a major role in our day-to-day lives, we don't often question it or its impact on our interactions. Women's and gender studies asks us to consider the impact of other statuses on our identities, such as race, ethnicity, sexuality, age, ability, nationality.

Michele's Elevator Speech

Q So, you're a women's studies professor. What exactly is women's studies and what do you teach?

A Women's studies is an academic interdisciplinary field interested in producing new ideas that challenge existing ones about women's and men's lives. For me, that means that much of my teaching and research is about rethinking assumptions about women as political actors and examining issues of power and dominance. It is a solutions-based investigation tackling some of the most pressing global problems of inequality in our time.

You want to take your time in crafting different versions of the elevator speech. It will be important to practice the speech(es) until you feel comfortable with your delivery. There are a number of resources on the web where you can find more information about elevator speeches.[36] Another benefit of crafting elevator speeches is that they are also great practice for job interviews!

Word Play

So, when discussing women's and gender studies with your various audiences, ideally you want to use language that is easily understood and connects with people's everyday experience. Talking about power, oppression, and intersecting identities in a simple and straightforward way is not easy! Think of this task in relation to something that's really fun, such as playing with magnetic poetry/word sets. You have probably seen these magnetic poetry refrigerator kits either in your or a friend's home. The kits are subject-specific (e.g. London, gardens, beat poetry, dogs, etc.) and contain a number of words that relate to the subject. These kits can be fun and allow for creative expression as you try out new sentences, word forms, or haiku. Unfortunately, no such magnetic word kit exists for women's and gender studies.[37]

You can use this tool to kick-start your own innovative thinking. In order to do this, first think of approximately 200 concepts that you'd commonly encounter in women's and gender studies classes. This sounds like a lot, but you can quickly search through your class notes or the indexes in some of your favorite books. A good place to begin might be the texts that you used in your introductory classes. You'll also need to add a few prepositions and other connecting words to your list (e.g., of, the, and, have, etc.). It may be easier to type these in a file and then, when you're ready, place the words in bold or use a large font size. Next, print your sheet and cut out the words. Spread the words around. Use your imagination. Move them around to make patterns and stimulate thinking. Look at the words: how would you use them in general conversation? What words are you drawn to? What concepts still feel too hard to explain in general conversation? This might be a fun and rewarding exercise to do with your women's and gender studies classmates and friends.

4

DISCOVERING AND CLAIMING YOUR INTERNAL STRENGTHS AND EXTERNAL SKILLS

In Chapter Two, we devoted some time to helping you understand how undergraduate programs and curricula in women's and gender studies are typically organized—as interdisciplinary fields of study. You learned about the aims and goals of women's and gender studies, both inside and outside the classroom. In Chapter Three, we discussed the many ways in which you can communicate with others about your experiences in women's and gender studies, and provided you with techniques to enhance your own understandings of concepts you have learned in your undergraduate program. Now we want to explore how you translate all of the great training you have had into skills and strengths for the postgraduate and working worlds.

As we argue in Chapter One, you are part of an intellectual tradition and legacy, one that produces a student with a particular set of skills, ways of problem solving, and worldview. That intellectual tradition, like others, has produced a distinct set of ideas and concepts that students learn through coursework and other learning experiences. In this chapter, we begin with a discussion of the top concepts that graduates identified in our survey as important to their professional work. They will look familiar to you, as they emerge from the feminist classroom. We also show you how these concepts are used in respondents' professional lives.

We suggest how you might begin to organize what you are learning (e.g. concepts, theories, frameworks, etc.) through the framework of "internal strengths" and "external skills." Skills and strengths grow out of the work that is done both inside and outside the classroom.

Here's what we mean. An "internal strength" is a quality, feature, or characteristic that is not always readily apparent, but perhaps feels like an inclination or talent. The term "external skill" or simply "skill" is probably familiar to you as the ability to do something well and/or something that requires training to do well (*Oxford Color Dictionary* 2001).

You might ask yourself: What core skills and strengths have I developed during the course of my education? How do I begin to assess the skills I'm developing from my interest in women's and gender studies? What kinds of topics and projects do I find most intriguing? What excites me? Conversely, what are the topics and assignments that make me want to down a triple espresso because they feel like chores? What are my core interests (e.g. Do you love studying the 1970s feminist arts movement or prefer nineteenth-century colonial legal history in West Africa)? What kinds of information do I gravitate toward when given the chance (e.g. Do you read every blog you can find about human rights issues in Latin America or do you follow the latest breakthroughs by female scientists)?

SKILLS OR COMPETENCIES?

Competency is a term that you might see in employment descriptions. A competency is an ability to do something, and is often measured against a standard. "Core competencies" typically refers to expertise that is fundamental to job performance and how an employee uses that in an organizational context. Some people use the terms skill and competency interchangeably. We prefer the term "skills." In this sense, skill refers to both the identifiable and measurable actions and behaviors that you are developing as a student, which you will take into the working world, and your own commitment to lifelong learning, which will lead you to your most promising and fulfilling future. Your future is defined by you and can include thinking about a temporary position, a career, continued education, leadership, and activism or a combination of all of these activities and experiences.

What women's and gender studies related activities do I find myself pursuing in my free time? Do some of my passions outside the classroom overlap with concepts from—or were possibly even inspired by—my women's and gender studies classes?

These are questions that are important for you to consider as you move through your educational and professional career. They are the basis for thinking about future employment, post-baccalaureate education, lifelong advocacy, and long-term happiness.

Exploring and developing what could be core strengths and skills provides an important learning opportunity for you both now and in the future. Throughout this chapter we ask you to reflect on your talents, interests, and abilities in order to clarify what your internal strengths and external skills are and how they might translate into other professional contexts.

Top Concepts Listed by Women's and Gender Studies Graduates

For many graduates, it is difficult to narrow down the one most important concept learned during an undergraduate women and gender's studies education. Often the concepts and ideas we learn are intertwined with other concepts and make it difficult for us to say which had the most impact on how we perceive ourselves, our daily interactions, and our world. In addition, the women's and gender studies "canon" has been changing, since the inception of the academic field and existing key concepts have been affected by new theoretical perspectives and research that becomes incorporated into texts, classroom discussions, and lectures, as well as in our classroom pedagogy and praxis.

Reflect for a moment on the concepts that you have been learning in your women's and gender studies classes. What are some concepts that emerge as important and that perhaps you have found repeated in various classes?

Despite the challenges of a changing canon and of figuring out what exactly constitutes a "concept" (see *Sidebar*: Critical Thinking about Critical Thinking: Concept or a Skill), we were interested in what aspects of women's and gender studies training stays with graduates and is used in their professional and personal lives. In our survey, we specifically asked our respondents "What is the most important concept that you learned in your undergraduate gender and/or women's studies coursework?"

When we think of concepts, we think about ideas and analytical frame-works or lenses that you might find in your coursework. Below we discuss the top five concepts that women's and gender studies undergraduate participants in our survey indicated had the greatest impact on them.

Gender as an important category of analysis is one of the top concepts to emerge from our data. In all women's and gender studies classes there is discussion of why it is important to pay attention to the way social and institutional norms about gender and gender roles affect everyone's everyday experience. Gender as a category of analysis is a fundamental concept that has emerged over the past twenty years.

A subcategory of this concept involved responses that listed "the social construction of gender." The social construction of gender has been a dominant theme in the field of women's and gender studies, especially within the past twenty years: Judith Lorber (1994), in fact, explicitly makes the case for the concept in her influential piece "Night to His Day: The Social Construction of Gender." Drawing upon the earlier scholarship of Candace West and Don Zimmerman (1987), Lorber believes that the process of engendering people is so commonplace that we only become aware of its impact when something is outside of the norm.

Similar comments received from students on our survey included:

- For me, the most important concept is the social construction of gender, especially in science.
- My concentration was on the history of sexuality and gender roles. The most important thing I learned is that these concepts are fluid and change over time and across cultures.
- Gender is a creation, not a truth.

Intersectionality is another key concept that was mentioned by our survey's respondents. According to Berger and Guidroz (2009) race, class, and gender, as well as sexuality, age, ability, nationality, and ethnicity are integral to one's position and status in society. Intersectionality approaches argue that individuals can locate their lived realities in relation to how structural forces and systems of oppression create and maintain differ-ences based on these socially constructed identities (Berger and Guidroz 2009: 1). Intersectionality is an umbrella term to a host of theoretical and methodological approaches. This term emerged from the theorizing of women-of-color activists and theorists, who argued that gender could not be understood in isolation from other complex systems of oppression (e.g. race, sexuality). Analysis and activism are strengthened by an attention to approaching problems through an intersectional lens. Besides intersectionality, other terms have become synonymous with this concept, including: race-class-gender matrix, multiple axes of inequality, the intersection, and the intersectionality approach. Our survey respondents echoed this multiplicity of terms associated with the concept of intersectionality, so we organized those terms under this concept.

Below are typical responses from our survey:

- Intersectionality—how multiple oppressions can affect people and have to be considered by social justice advocates who want to achieve full equality.
- That various axes of oppression intersect one another on multiple levels depending on the body, subjectivity, and position in society where they intersect.

The third concept is that of *inequality*. For many women's and gender studies students, their readings and assignments make them more aware of the concept of inequality—how economic and social rewards are distributed across a society often unequally:

- I learned that some issues I saw as personal shortcomings were actually the result of structural inequality directed at women. It also helped me to interpret the situations of other women in my family in this light. This was liberating, to say the least.

Undergraduate students stated that they learned as part of their women's and gender studies education ideas about compassion, fairness, justice, and equality. We grouped these together under one umbrella that we are calling *equity*, our fourth concept. One respondent wrote "the concept of fairness, justice, and treating people with equality and with respect including the ability to understand other paradigms than the one you were raised with." In many women's and gender studies classrooms there is much attention given to discussing how to understand and remedy contemporary situations that have their roots in historic structural arrangements that favored one community over another. As women's and gender studies curricula has maintained its connection with social movements and stresses applied learning through praxis, it is little

CRITICAL THINKING ABOUT CRITICAL THINKING: CONCEPT OR A SKILL

In many of your classes you might have come across the term "critical thinking." Professors or teaching instructors might stress how important critical thinking is for the class. Critical thinking as a goal for the class may even be mentioned on a syllabus. When we think of critical thinking, we tend to categorize it as an activity—as something that students do in the way they approach and synthesize materials. We did not view it initially as a stand-alone concept because of its very broad definition. Many people in the survey, however, listed critical thinking as one of the most important concepts gained from their training—this got us thinking about the term. One reason why participants might list critical thinking as a concept is because women's and gender studies introduced them to the role of critical thinking and its emphasis in women's and gender studies classes. When conducting research, it is important to honor and make sense of information that participants provide. Related phrasings that we coded under critical thinking include: critical analysis, critical writing, etc.

Here are how some graduates talked about critical thinking:

- The ability to challenge a dominant/mainstream narrative—critical thinking.
- How to think critically and question authority.

wonder that many of its students have internalized notions of equality and justice.

The fifth important concept listed by survey respondents was that of *empowerment*. Standard definitions of empowerment are (1) give authority or power to, and (2) give strength and confidence to (see *Oxford Color Dictionary* 2001). Other terms associated with this concept include "agency," "self-determination," and "choice." Often, when a graduate listed empowerment, it was coupled with a reference to their gender identity (e.g. being a woman). As we stated in Chapter Two, many women students explicitly find women's and gender studies useful in coping with some of the challenges and stressors of being a woman in sexist and male-dominated societies. Thus, we should not be surprised that we see this reflected in what concepts some students found useful. Moreover, with the emphasis that women's and gender studies scholarship places on the importance of understanding and advocating for oneself and others through feminist and collective struggle, empowerment is a salient concept.

Other important concepts for women's and gender studies graduates, as raised by our respondents, include: patriarchy (and capitalism), "internalized oppression," the "Birdcage" metaphor, collective action, choice, voice and active listening, respect for women, media bias, power (external as well as perpetuated by women toward women), gendered violence, privilege and the politics of location, "the personal is political", omissions and silences, mind/body split, dichotomous thinking, and feminist research and knowledge production.

These concepts that the graduates identify are probably familiar to you. There is not a clean, direct one-to-one correlation between women's and gender studies concepts and strengths and skills. However, examining concepts that are salient for graduates helps us to understand how these concepts might translate and be put into practice outside the classroom. By asking graduates about the concepts that have had the most influence on their thinking, women's and gender studies faculty can better understand these ideas as shaping problem-solving skills in students. It also gives students and professionals an indicator of what ideas have longstanding power, what concepts are being challenged, and what ideas are emerging in the field.

Internal Strengths and External Skills

Our research builds upon prior work that demonstrates that people who major in women's and gender studies see themselves graduating with distinctive "skills" (Luebke and Reilly 1995, Dever 2004). However, we believe the term "skills" does not capture the complexity of what you have learned, because the term "skill" focuses on the more tangible and quantifiable aspects of your training, and therefore we make a distinction between internal strengths and external skills. An education in women's and gender studies helps build both internal strengths and external skills in different ways. This discussion is grounded in how graduates talked about the strengths and skills they learned through their women's and gender studies education.

If you polled everyone in your women's and gender studies classes, they would reveal very diverse dreams and life goals. However, they would also report learning several skills in these classes that give them many different "tools for success" and that can be applied to a variety of situations. As mentioned earlier, internal strengths are those core talents you may possess but are not always aware of. An internal strength, however, is not always a preference or a talent. It may develop through the course of your training. Internal strengths can create a feeling of positive behavioral change inside a person that might not easily be measured. The internal strengths that are difficult to quantify accurately are reflected in graduates' understandings of how they interact with the external world because of the training they received.

Identifying internal strengths may take a process of reflection through self-administered tests or the verbalization by family members, peers, professors, employers, or others to make you aware of an internal strength. Strengths can be overlooked or neglected because they are taken for granted. Often in educational and occupational environments, we are critiqued on our deficits. Our "faults" are readily pointed to as areas for improvement. Yet rarely are we praised for our internal strengths and/or preferences. Here are some questions to start you thinking about your strengths:

- What kinds of feedback have you received on your research papers, activism projects, and/or internship memos?
- What areas have you been encouraged to pursue and by whom?
- In what areas do you consistently receive the highest ratings when evaluated by your supervisor at work?
- In what kinds of situations do you tend to thrive?

Unfortunately, we are seldom reminded of how important and valuable our inner strengths are in relation to the types of occupations in which we are interested. For you, your inner strengths might be amplified by your experiences in the women's and gender studies classroom. With conscious recognition, you may be able to translate your internal strengths into a launching pad for the development of your external skills.

Everyone has inner strengths; they simply differ from person to person. Ideally, instead of focusing on our shortcomings, we should be promoting our inner strengths as areas to draw upon within an organization or cause. For example, you may have always been comfortable meeting new people and like to connect individuals with others. According to Buckingham and Clifton (2001) you may have the gift of "WOO" or Winning Others Over. You may have been that young student who was never too shy to give a speech in the school auditorium or would gladly run for class president in high school. You may have a knack for motivating others in any activist work that you are currently doing. You may find it easy to speak often and persuasively in your classroom settings. On the other hand, you may not be as comfortable meeting new people, but prefer instead to work with smaller groups with whom you are familiar, or maybe you prefer one-on-one encounters or even working alone. This internal strength, of being "deliberative," allows you to approach situations strategically and weigh the various elements carefully. So, you might also think of an inner strength as a tendency, preference, or a leaning toward a particular behavior. In order to explore your own inner strengths, you may want to reflect on the following questions on everyday aspects of your life:

- Do you like to study alone or with a group of others?
- Do people tend to describe you as independent and self-reliant?
- Do you tend to seek help when confused with class work, or do you prefer to try to figure it out before asking for help?
- Have you sought out mentors or have people actively engaged you as a mentee?

Knowing one's internal strengths is important. Not only will this knowledge guide you in looking for employment opportunities that (ideally) match your internal strengths and talents, but finding a good fit can also complement those external skills of your colleagues, collaborators, and employers. Utilization of your inner strengths will not only help you professionally, but as you learn to maximize your inner strengths you will be able to bring out the best qualities in those around you. This seemingly simple understanding can bring you much success and happiness.

Now let's move from reflecting on your own personal inner strengths to looking at the internal strengths and external skills that many women's and gender studies students generally possess. First we'll address internal strengths, including: critical self-reflection; self-confidence and empowerment; leadership; ability to create community.

Internal Strengths

Critical Self-Reflection

An important internal strength is the ability to engage in *critical self-reflection*. Knowing how to engage in critical self-reflection helps you to assess your interests and talents accurately, as well as identify interpersonal areas that still need development. Your training in women's and gender studies encourages a deep self-awareness about how one makes decisions in the everyday world and how they are connected to ideas of equality, fairness, tolerance, and social justice. Moreover, it illuminates the different institutions that shape how we experience the world.

For example, due to your education in women's and gender studies you are probably well versed in the notion of interlocking oppressions. This ability to view the ways in which institutions and systems are interconnected and how they impact one's experiences based on social status is a powerful tool with which to view the world. Yet, as Patricia Hill Collins states, "we all live in social institutions that reproduce race, class, and gender oppression" (Collins 1993: 727). This basically means that we are born into an ableist, racist, classist, sexist, homophobic world, and we need to be able to evaluate internally our prejudices, stereotypes, and part in maintaining systems of oppression. As Cheryl's friend Diana Rhodes, a women's studies activist (profiled in Chapter Five), states, "you need to check yourself." Much as with your computer's anti-virus program, you need to do a self-scan periodically to see what you are "infected" with and what areas need direct action and what areas can be quarantined and addressed later.

You might want to pause for a moment and think about the role of critical self-reflection in your life. Have you come across this term in your women's studies classes? If so, in what ways have you found it useful for navigating the social world?

When we asked graduates about how they have used their degree since graduating, many respondents noted how important critical self-reflection was in their personal and professional lives:

- Oh, I use it [my women's studies training] all the time in the way I interpret situations and act in them. Professionally, I created a staff training for an environmental education program utilizing feminist and queer theory and activism.
- [I found self-reflection useful for] the ability to examine my own privilege, my own assumptions, and the part I play in broader systems of oppression.
- [I use self-reflection] to analyze my relationship, guide the way I raise my children, and form the basis of my analysis of family law, and inform my interpretation of media.

As our respondents indicate, critical self-reflection is not only vital in their personal lives, but in their professional environments as well. As many women's and gender studies graduates work in careers that have an impact on the lives of women and multiply-oppressed communities, it is especially important to assess the impact our work has on others. By internalizing the famous feminist mantra "the personal is political," women's and gender studies graduates are cognizant of putting theory into practice and of avoiding the dangerous territories of "do-gooding" or meddling (rather than supporting individuals and groups) in order to gain the tools and resources they need to succeed. Your training can help you find your niche in the world and lead you to fulfilling and meaningful work.

Self-Confidence and Empowerment

Another important internal strength is the combination of *self-confidence and empowerment*. Having self-confidence means you are able to listen to your inner voice, which tells you "you can do this" and "I want to do this"—rather than listening to the sometimes well-developed and loud self-defeating dialogue that prevents us from acting or from listening to less-than-supportive others. Self-confidence is also the ability to understand one's needs and articulate them. It means speaking up when you believe that you are right and taking an unpopular stand for something you believe in, too. We have partnered self-confidence with empowerment because they work together. A sense of feeling empowered can lead to more self-confidence. Self-confidence tends to foster healthy risk-taking. There are many jobs and careers that encourage and reward risk-taking.

A "SHOUT OUT" TO A STUDY THAT INSPIRED US: *WOMEN'S STUDIES GRADUATES: THE FIRST GENERATION*

Luebke and Reilly's (1995) groundbreaking study demonstrates that the first women's studies majors (1977–1992) credit their field of study with "increasing their self confidence and esteem, finding their voices, greater awareness, courage, self sufficiency, pride, dignity, and self worth" (Luebke and Reilly 1995: 200). In our global study, we found that many of these same themes are still salient for more recent graduates.

One graduate surveyed said, "Because of my training in women's studies, I am more willing to take risks that will enhance my professional development."

> Another life skill that I received from my women's studies major was self-confidence and self-respect. It was absolutely amazing to be learning about incredible empowered women in an environment of self-motivated women who all believed that we could do anything and how each one of them had dreams that they were going to fulfill. I feel that often times women's education is pushed under the rug and women's studies is seen as a fluff major, but even if I hadn't learned anything from a book during my time [in women's studies], the environment that I was learning in was so nurturing and encouraging, that it helped my confidence and motivation more than any other time in my life.
>   (Katelyn, 2009, UNC, Chapel Hill)

Although women's studies and gender studies attract both women and men, women students still feel that women's studies (in particular) helps them develop important internal skills in a learning environment that helps them combat living in a sexist world, specifically in terms of being confident in themselves. There were many comments that were similar to this one we received from a financial consultant for hospitals who said why confidence was important to her: "I'm not quiet, I'll speak up about issues."

Here are some responses we received:

- Women's Studies 101 was the first class where I felt comfortable jumping in and speaking my mind (at 18); it translated to all of my other classes and jobs. Thank goodness.
- Being with other smart, ambitious women in small classes really gave my confidence a huge boost and it helped me come out of my shell. I learned to speak with conviction in my women's studies classes.
- [I have gained] an awareness of my rights as a woman . . . empowering me as a person. I have gained confidence and a greater sense of self. I am aware of the workplace challenges that women face.

A reporter with a nonprofit magazine said: "I believe it [self-confidence] makes me a smarter woman, and has helped me to speak my mind and stand up for who I am in both my work and personal life." Others stated the following:

- For the first nine years of my career, I worked in the sports industry as a publicist. I think my women's studies degree gave me a huge boost of confidence just because it allowed me to study the discipline across economics, the arts, history, and yes, even sports.
- Being confident makes advocating for what I believe in for my institution easier: I'm a curatorial assistant at a university art museum. I research and help curate exhibitions. Feminism has become connected to multiculturalism for me and in terms of the museum world it helps me to evaluate/rethink inequality in terms of the art world/art historical canon.
- I am significantly more confident in my professional and personal life. I know who I am and focus on the important aspects of my life. I truly believe in helping others. With friends and co-workers, I showcase many core feminist values: non-violence, collaboration, mentoring, service and more: I learned about myself and what it actually meant to be a woman and feminist. It's the core of my identity.

Leadership

We argue that *leadership* begins internally before it is manifested in actions in the external world. Leadership is an important internal strength. In Chapter One, we discussed the learning components and philosophy that makes the women's and gender studies classroom unique. In "What is Feminist Pedagogy," Carolyn Shrewsbury (1993) identifies the core elements of feminist pedagogy or the application of feminist ideals into the teaching and learning process. According to Shrewsbury, these elements include community, empowerment, and leadership. Some of the inner strengths associated with leadership include: the development of negotiation skills not only in the professional arena but in personal relationships as well; that we, as individuals, are responsible for our actions, as well as taking responsibility for any decisions we have made that have an impact on others we supervise or who are dependent on us; and that we are responsible for the success (or failure) of our efforts. Because of the emphasis on collaborative learning and the importance of praxis, women's and gender studies classrooms are often an arena where students begin to see leadership characteristics modeled for them. Throughout your training, you may have opportunities to learn about leadership through internship and activism opportunities. In our survey research, graduates discussed how their training helped develop their capacity for leadership in both everyday situations as well as in specific leadership roles or positions:

- My coursework in women's studies, as well as the on-campus activities in which I participated, helped me develop leadership skills I never knew I had, and probably never would have developed without those classes and that environment.

- I work in politics, so a systemic understanding of gender, race and sexuality issues has been extremely helpful, especially in coordinating coalitions. It has also been personally helpful in helping me navigate workplace sexism. I've noticed that I have a level of confidence in dealing with sexist coworkers and supervisors that, unfortunately, many of my female colleagues do not.

- For one thing, I work with families and young women, and I am better aware of their challenges in terms of access to resources, repercussions in many cases of physical or sexual abuse, and gender role expectations. Many of the individuals I work with are struggling with gender and/or orientation identity, and I feel my degree has aided me in working with these issues. More importantly to me these days, as a mother, I have used my knowledge of women's rights in helping to secure the first job share at my company—this allows me to be the primary caregiver for my children and to breastfeed—a women's issue not generally covered (I think) by most academic programs.

A graduate student in social and cultural psychology credits the leadership and presentation skills she received as an undergraduate to her current success in front of groups: "I am comfortable giving presentations to peers and superiors." The director of fundraising for a nonprofit group working on the issue of human trafficking names strengths-based leadership through collaboration as one of her important skills, "I've always been able to build really strong teams—whether they were work-related teams or to gather a group of friends to participate in a volunteer project."

As another respondent stated:

> The skill of leadership provides the confidence, assertive attitude, integrity, accountability and ability to collaborate with others in order to succeed on any chosen path. As a women's studies major I was empowered to take control of my future through learning about the presence of strong women in history, and my experience working with feminist groups/Public Allies (an AmeriCorps program, which is a 10-month non-profit apprenticeship and leadership training program). The non-profit I am working with is the ACLU of Delaware.

The importance of leadership as an internal strength is also evident in the leadership opportunities that graduates often created for themselves, which we discuss in Chapter One.

Community

Inner strengths that are connected to *community* include the ability to build connections and relationships inside and outside of our workplace, family, and neighborhoods. An example would be facilitating discussion among groups in conflict. This may involve leaning toward consensus building practices rather than a stance of majority rule. It may include being the voice that calls for inclusion of a wide variety of perspectives rather than those of a select few who appear more powerful or who seemingly have the most "rational" argument. This inner skill may also draw upon your own code of morality. While our morals are shaped by our family, our social institutions, and even our disciplinary perspectives (or professional code of ethics), we often need to act in ways that support our inner sense of what is right and wrong. It may also mean stepping outside our comfort areas and becoming an advocate or an ally for a cause or group that may have been an adversary in the past.

Our survey respondents gave many examples of how their training in women's and gender studies expanded their sense of community and how they utilized the concept of community as an inner strength that is valuable in a variety of day-to-day interactions:

- The importance of listening to others, and being able to sometimes not know exactly why someone feels the way they feel, but to listen to what they have to say and show empathy [toward] their situation.

- I recognize gender power struggle in both my personal and professional life. I doubt I would be aware of such struggles without having majored in women's studies. Knowing what's going on power-wise informs my decisions professionally and personally. Knowing how to read between the lines and find out what's really going on is such a big part of working for any organization; women's studies has helped me tremendously in learning to do this. Even if there's nothing I can do about a particular situation, knowing that what's really going on involves power, and possibly gender power, means I am informed and ready to respond. It also calms me and reassures me that the situation may not be about me at all.

- One person matters. Each of us is one person until we come together for a common cause and that can evoke radical change. In addition, we can't remain stagnant—keep up the evolution of the women's movement in order to keep up with the times. Also, it's important for feminists to be vocal in the community, home, and workplace. Sometimes these big changes begin with our families and friends.

- Presently I am involved in Public Allies, an AmeriCorps program, which is focused on bringing positive social change to local communities. We work for local change through our involvement with local nonprofits, public service days in the community, and team service projects with community members. This is also the reason I am involved with Planned Parenthood's Young Advocates group. We plan and attend events to inform the local community about sexual & reproductive issues.

- It helps me remember how the public health work that I do must be tailored to the community I'm working with; it also helps me as I evaluate my own approach to healthcare, especially pre-natal care, and it gives me reason to participate in a variety of programs that I feel give other women the opportunity to explore new experiences and perspectives on life.

In this way, women's and gender studies graduates are often in a position to enact positive and effective engagement with diverse populations. In sum, several of the internal skills associated with a women's and gender studies education facilitate a broad sense of involvement and leadership by (1) engaging with how you are connected to the world as well as to other people, and (2) inspiring you to better yourself and the world through facilitating active engagement and activism in its many forms. Now we will discuss the external skills that can develop through your coursework and interest in women's and gender studies.

External Skills

External skills are learned and refined through knowledge, experience, and practice (Buckingham and Clifton 2001: 30). Often, skills are formalized into a set of steps or procedures that, through repetition and consistency, become refined (45). Here is a list of external skills that women's and gender studies students tend to possess:[38]

- thinking critically
- developing interdisciplinary dexterity
- developing critical reading and analytic skills on the variety of theoretical perspectives on sex/gender, race/ethnicity, social class, and sexuality
- developing and cultivating openness, awareness, and respect of individuals, groups, perspectives, and experiences that may differ from their own
- considering an issue from multiple perspectives
- constructing arguments with evidence obtained from research
- an ability to engage in research and analysis in order to gather information to either support or refute concepts and ideas
- locating, evaluating, and interpreting diverse sources, including statistics
- connecting knowledge and experience, theory and activism in women's studies and other courses
- communicating effectively in writing and speaking
- using gender as a category of/for analysis
- discerning the importance of interlocked oppressions
- applying cross-cultural and global awareness to "big questions" about women and gender
- applying knowledge for social transformation, citizenship.

Here is how some graduates responded to this question in our survey: *How do your skills that you developed from your education assist you in your professional and/or personal life?*

- Skill they listed as important: *Critical analysis of texts*

How it helps them:

It keeps me plugged in to what is missing/who is omitted in any discussion or dialogue, and to know to question when some people aren't included or heard from. I definitely see this come up in both my professional and personal lives (and it leads to some lively debates sometimes when others can't see who is made silent).

- Skill they listed as important: *Understanding diverse communities*

How it helps them:

As a director at a day program for developmentally disabled adults I encounter diversity among the individuals I serve on a daily basis. As a result of my minor I feel I am better able to be sensitive to their unique needs and am therefore better able to facilitate their individual goals and objectives.

- Skill they listed as important: *Critical thinking*

How it helps them:

Having a language with which to articulate my thoughts clearly has helped me achieve academic success in my post-graduate studies and has helped give weight to my perspectives and suggestions in meetings. I feel as though my input has been taken more seriously in meetings with administration and different committees, especially when I am youngest and have the least professional experience.

- Skill they listed as important: *Oral communication*

How it helps them:

Good communication skills allow me to be an active citizen who is consistently involved in questioning and challenging the systems of power as I work toward the betterment and advancement of our people.

- Skill they listed as important: *Being able to recognize the complexity of a problem or situation*

How it helps them:

> It assists me greatly in my psychosocial assessment of my female clients as a women's health nurse practitioner student. I can put their lives into context and perceive barriers to health promotion behaviors, since many of my clients are uninsured, low-income, minority women, [and] some [are] illegal immigrants. I always assess intimate partner violence, history of sexual abuse, gender orientation. I also bring a different perspective to greater policy issues such as healthcare overhaul.

How do you feel when you look at this amazing and varied list of external skills? Did you identify one or two skills that were of interest to you? If you are at the beginning of your studies, then this list may seem daunting. If you are nearing the end of your program, you might be checking off a high number of recognizable skills. But no matter where you are, there is no denying that the intellectual tradition in which you are engaged produces graduates with a sophisticated skill set that will serve them for life. Let's look at a few of these external skills more closely—specifically how you may already be developing or using several of these skills without realizing it.

External Skill 1: Thinking Critically

Many students in our research valued that women's studies training gave them technical skills, but also encouraged them to read deeply and perceptively. Here's what Katelyn, a student quoted earlier, says:

> A very concrete skill that I learned while a student, particularly in my women's studies classes, was the ability to think critically and analyze works. We employed this in every class and it was necessary to learn in order to write effective papers and get the most out of my classes. But more than simply getting good grades, this skill has translated quite well into the "real world." When reading articles in newspapers, magazines, or online I find myself using the skills that I learned as an undergraduate and questioning the authors and wondering why they did not choose to include certain facts or where they had gotten some of their information. This skill has helped my confidence in debating with people and also appearing as an intelligent person to my peers.
>
> (Katelyn, 2008, UNC, Chapel Hill)

Another graduate from our survey responds:

> My job involves working with a lot of quantitative data, which is
> very different than my undergraduate interest in qualitative
> research, including ethnography. Still, I use the skills taught to
> me by my women's studies program. I have to work within a very
> rigid system of data collection and reporting (a main part of my
> job is translating raw data into data that can be used on an
> international, statistical scale). The way I examine and critique
> hegemony in the research field is that I closely examine every
> piece of data before coding it. I make sure that a patient's true
> experiences and conditions are being reported. I monitor any
> general oversight done by the healthcare providers who are
> working with them.

*External Skill 2: Critical Reading and Analytic Skills on the Variety of
Theoretical Perspectives on Sex/Gender, Race/Ethnicity, Social Class,
and Sexuality*

While you may be predisposed or have an inner strength that makes you
interested in people of different statuses or positionalities, your women's
and gender studies courses also inform your perspective. Through dialogue
and debate with feminist theories, your women's and gender studies classes
encourage you to apply this lens to a variety of different situations. For
example, Michele asked her students to analyze or "unpack" visual
representations of African American women (see *Sidebar*). You may be
asked to do a similar assignment using Michael Kimmel's or R.W.
Connell's concept of "hegemonic masculinity," or Adrienne Rich's
"compulsory heterosexuality." You may have supported your position
through a literature review of feminist authors.

*External Skill 3: Discerning the Importance of Interlocked Oppressions
and the Ability to Apply Concepts to New Situations*

The concept of intersectionality or interlocking oppressions is a central
one in women's and gender studies. As we noted earlier in the chapter,
this was the concept that graduates ranked as a top concept. As an
undergraduate student, you began to learn that once you looked beyond
the simple classifications or heuristic devices used to understand concepts
such as gender, race, and class, your curriculum and assignments required
you to examine how these concepts impact and influence individual and

EXAMPLE: "UNPACKING" VISUAL REPRESENTATIONS

Michele teaches a course called "African American Women in the Media," which engages students to examine how African-American women have been depicted (and have depicted themselves) in twentieth- and twenty-first-century media (e.g. film, art, print, magazines, theater, and music). During the semester students read several essays in bell hooks' (1992) *Black Looks: Race and Representation* and chapters of Patricia Hill Collins' (1990) *Black Feminist Thought.* They have an opportunity to do a textual content analysis that allows them to explore the racialized images in the media. Below is a version of the assignment:

> bell hooks takes critical aim at representations of black women in advertising and fashion. You are to conduct a content analysis and discuss your findings. A textual content analysis uses cultural products and artifacts (commercials, magazines, advertisements, etc.) as a way to investigate a society's norms, values, and methods of socialization. A content analysis is a type of research method. A content analysis usually examines a wide range of materials and looks for patterns.
>
> 1. Select three items: a current women's clothing catalog (*Victoria's Secret, J. Crew*, etc.), a current mainstream women's magazine (*Glamour, Working Woman, Self*, etc.), and a current magazine that caters to African-American women (*Heart and Soul, Essence*, etc.).
> 2. Flip through all of the items. Look at every advertisement and photo/fashion layout that depicts an African-American/black woman in it.
> 3. Think about the following questions as they apply to your "sample": Observe how gender and race is represented as a theme. Who is the advertising aimed at? Or, what type of clothing is being advertised? What are the captions that go with the fashion layouts? What age(s) are represented? Is the model by herself or with others? Men or women? Is she in the foreground or background? Is the model partially dressed? If there are other models in the picture or ad, how might they be racially classified? What are the ethnicities of the other models in the picture or ad (if any)? How do the ads and photo layouts reflect notions of sexuality and class? Are traditional notions of black women represented (defined by Collins and hooks) in the ads/layouts, or are they challenged? As a viewer, how do you interpret the ad/photo layouts? What are the similarities and differences across the catalog versus the magazines (and between the two magazines)? Did you go in with certain expectations on what you might find? How were these expectations changed after doing the exercise?
> 4. Your short assignment should discuss any patterns that you find across all three items (using the questions as a starting point). It should also discuss 1–2 ads/layouts in-depth. How do your preliminary findings add strength to bell hooks' and Patricia Hill Collins' assertions, challenge, or complicate them?

group experiences in society. This concept translates into a skill through applied use in professional situations. This ability is extremely useful. For example, perhaps you are seeking a job in the real estate industry. Not only must you be familiar with laws and regulations affecting the industry, but your ability to understand the relationships or intersectionality between race, class, and gender and other social identities may enable you to help clients find housing that fits all their needs—not just square footage. Perhaps your clients are differently-abled and need access to support services or need to live close to public transport, or perhaps they need a floor plan that allows them to maximize their activities of daily living. How might housing's proximity to schools be important or the racial or age composition of the neighborhood? All of these factors play into your ability to work with your clients and their specific needs. Not only is this important for your client's well being, but if one of your inner strengths is building community, you may be very aware that a happy and engaged neighbor is a benefit for everyone.

External Skill 4: Developing and Cultivating Openness, Awareness, and Respect of Individuals, Groups, Perspectives, and Experiences that may Differ from Our Own

The ability to understand others' viewpoints while still advancing our ideas is a skill that many graduates listed as important. Many graduates reported how important this skill was in their professional and activist endeavors. This comment echoes many respondents: "I feel very flexible in my way of thinking and able to engage with many different people and approaches." Many graduates said that treating people with "respect, consideration, and understanding" was an important skill they used. Several graduates also said that being a "thoughtful listener" was an important skill.

No matter what type of employment you plan on pursuing, you will, in some way or another, interact with others. Whether working face-to-face or not, we live in a complex multicultural world, and it is essential to work with others who may differ from us. While many workplaces have some formal recognition of equal opportunity mandates and provide yearly training for employees so as to stay in compliance, your own ability to work well with others is an asset to any organization. Your women's and gender studies (and any multicultural curricula) courses, as well as any experiences you've had learning about diverse cultures may give you invaluable insight into working with others who grew up in a culture that differs from the mainstream. In fact, you may have had classes on social movements or collective action, where you were required to work together with others in a group setting despite your differences. To your professor's great delight, you probably learned to appreciate your differences and integrated these into the final product. This is a talent that can be used by you and your employer to create a just and open workplace. This brings us to one of the ethical perspectives often associated with feminism—that of "an ethic of care." Not only do we take care of ourselves, but we learn to be advocates and allies for our colleagues and to demand social justice and equal opportunities for others. One respondent listed "awareness of people's experiences" as important: "It made me able to deal with obnoxious 'good old boy networks' in a way that most feminists would have balked at, but, in the real world, you don't always get to wear a Capital F on your shirt."

Here are some comments that exemplify how people thought about and utilized this external skill:

> Within both professional and personal life, it IS important to be culturally aware of where people come from and their situations . . . even more so in a professional situation because then you are dealing with clients (in my case, social work) and do not want to be judgmental of their situations or say something offensive.

How this helps them professionally: "My office is a safe space in every aspect of the word."

Another comment was:

> That people can have different beliefs and I can still respect them, but at the same time work to preserve my beliefs.

How this helps them professionally: "Because my organization produces research on reproductive health issues, I work in a field that is emotionally charged. I have to remind myself that those that disagree with me are people too."

> One respondent, a consultant in children's mental health, university lecturer, and health data manager listed "trying to be inclusive of everyone" as one of her important skills: "I teach Psychology of Women, a course cross-listed with psychology and

women's studies. I have also used information on gender studies in my therapy." This graduate also said this skill was used in a professional context as a reminder to "use person-first language when talking to and about therapy clients."

A critical care nurse notes the importance of the skill of being able to empathize with different groups of people:

> If I'm not able to empathize I'm not able to do my job effectively and the patient then suffers. By being able to see them as individuals and accept their lives as they are, I am able to accomplish more and I have had many people come up to thank me for making their (or their family member's) experience of being in a critical care unit, bearable.

A film studies graduate student and educator says that "listening and respecting diversity" is an important skill:

> People often forget to listen to others these days; therefore, people only listen to—linear story—what they want to hear. Women's Studies encourages you to listen to others, which is becoming the most valuable action we need.

A project operations assistant and research coordinator for a nonprofit states that: "I feel very flexible in my way of thinking and able to engage with many different people and approaches." This graduate performs grant research and writing (website, newsletter, and brochure), and says this skill helps in that: "It aids interpersonal relationships and helps me adapt to any situation."

External Skill 5: Ability to Engage in Research and Analysis in Order to Gather Information Either to Support or Refute Concepts and Ideas

An ability to examine an idea from a different perspective or to challenge the prevailing collective wisdom takes strength, empowerment, and self-confidence. Challenging prevailing assumptions and authority is difficult, especially when one feels threatened (directly or indirectly). Yet as we have seen with several recent national and economic disasters, people who challenge prevailing ideas are needed not only for a democracy, but as well, it's just good business. Often it is not enough to challenge an idea, but one must back up the challenge, utilizing a variety of viewpoints, research, and standpoints. Therefore, core external skills of women's and

gender studies undergraduates include researching and gathering information from a variety of resources, standpoints, and perspectives. Also, these
skills can make your own perspective more rich and perceived by others
as more valid. Your training also helps develop your ability to see
connections between unlikely issues and develop arguments and positions
that take into account hidden or marginalized perspectives.

One graduate responded:

> I used it [research skills] regularly while coming up with a strategic
> plan for our Government Relations department at Planned
> Parenthood, and while planning the best methods for grassroots
> organizing. I am aware of the human rights critiques and power
> disparities when I discuss international human rights programs at
> my law school. I look for silent perspectives alluded to in our
> casebooks, in cases populated by and judged by wealthy white men.

Cheryl feels that she uses this external skill constantly. She teaches
about the history and theories related to HIV/AIDS. It is not enough to
be familiar with the current epidemiological and biomedical perspectives
about HIV as a retrovirus, or how it is thought to enter and interact with
the immune system. Cheryl finds that it is helpful to use metaphors of
the virus that make it more familiar and easier to understand. Cheryl also
discusses how the very metaphors we use in relation to HIV and AIDS—
plague, military metaphors (invading army), pollution (punishment for
sin or sex)—are the subjects of study by feminist scholar Susan Sontag
in her text *Illness as Metaphor and AIDS and Its Metaphors* (2001). In
addition, by referencing pop culture (e.g. films and books including
And the Band Played On, *Angels in America*) and addressing popular theories
about the origins of HIV/AIDS, the topic of HIV/AIDS becomes less
medicalized and more accessible to the general public. Its impact and
understanding can then be supported through the arts, social sciences,
journalism, etc.

Putting the Pieces Together

You might not be aware that you may have already been evaluated on your
external skills in women's and gender studies courses by your professors,
colleagues, and peers. For example, part of the process of assigning grades
to students is through exams, journal entries, quizzes, oral presentations,
papers, and other assessment tools (e.g. portfolios). These tools attempt to

capture the degree to which you are exhibiting proficiency in the standards established by your program or department's curriculum committee, the university, and even those informally mandated by the women's and gender studies scholarly community. For example, every spring Cheryl and her colleagues were asked to observe and evaluate the presentations of undergraduate students at Minnesota State University, Mankato's annual Undergraduate Research Conference (URC). She comments:

> While this evaluation did not impact the student's grade, it was a way for our department to gauge our students' core competencies in the areas of public speaking and presentation, critical analysis, and the application of feminist theory to a research issue.

She continues, "One of the requirements for gender and women's studies majors and minors was a course entitled 'Feminist Research and Action.'" In this class, students were expected to not only learn research methods, but also apply the skills and concepts learned in other core curricula to original research projects. During the semester in which Cheryl facilitated the course, students explored a variety of topics that were later presented at Mankato's Undergraduate Research Conference at Minnesota State University.

There are many places in your education to begin to assess your inner strengths and skills:

- Examining components of your study: coursework, internship/externship, honors and awards, study abroad, praxis project, honors thesis, and independent study.

SPOTLIGHT: STACY HUNTINGTON: A REFLECTION ON SKILLS LEARNED

In this spotlight, Stacy reflects on the skills she gained through her women's studies education, participating in the undergraduate research conference held at Minnesota State University, Mankato, and how it informed her thinking, research, and postgraduate life:

> The words "critical thinking" are often bandied about in academic settings, yet one person's idea of critical thinking is seldom comparable to another's. I experienced many types of academic settings, most of which prided themselves

on enhancing the student's critical thinking skills, before I encountered the feminist classroom. The feminist classroom provided me with a setting in which critical thinking was truly, in its most honest form, not only encouraged and enhanced but sincerely represented. The professors who facilitated my women's studies classes did not engage in demeaning debate with a student over a concept, but encouraged the student to explore the idea more thoroughly through a different lens, the feminist lens. This was done all while empowering the student to explore not only what they thought and felt but why that was their perception. Thus, I developed what I like to call on my cover letter and resume "a truly unique perspective" which not only identifies multiple aspects of a situation, but also allows me to analyze and discuss the implications of each. I do not always represent the most popular opinion or simplest solution, but my voice is always heard and I know that when I speak people listen.

One of the very first concepts introduced during the WOST 101 Intro to Women's Studies Course is the "invisible knapsack." Peggy McIntosh wrote the essay *White Privilege: Unpacking the Invisible Knapsack* in 1988 and it resonates just as loudly twenty-two years later as it did then.

My research project for the URC was titled, "Deconstructing the Slut" and explored the ramifications of sexually active young people in a small Midwestern university. While constructing the survey questions my professor encouraged [me to] incorporate questions that explored sexuality, gender identity, race, ethnicity, and age. While I found it difficult to adequately construct applicable questions which would provide an opportunity for each of the issues to be addressed, I feel that my research provided a reasonable representation of the demographic. The results of my research suggested that young, white, college-aged, heterosexual women who are sexually active with more than one partner are more likely to be considered sluts than young, white, heterosexual men, young, black, heterosexual men, young, white, gay women, young, black, gay women . . . and so on.

Currently, I am a church secretary and contract writer for a small town, weekly newspaper. More than anything, my women's studies education provided me with a skill set more conducive to living a meaningful, insightful, tolerable life. My feminism cost me one job but at the same time gave me the courage and empowerment to be steadfast in my opinion. My feminism does not make me popular or well-liked but it does enable my voice to be heard which is a voice that is willing and able to speak for those who cannot. My success at the URC empowered me to openly and confidently discuss those nasty "taboo" topics such as sexuality and gender in public settings. And I honestly felt people walked away happy to have listened.

(Stacy, 2008, Minnesota State University, Mankato)

- Talking with people: conversations with peers, mentors, and parents.
- Reflecting on passions, hobbies, interests, and activist history.

The exercises below will help you get started on this exciting work.

YOUR TURN: EXERCISES

1. Rate Yourself on Internal Strengths and External Skills

Below we have listed all the internal strengths discussed in this chapter and eight of the external skills based on the longer list above, each worth ten points. If you feel you have an internal strength or external skill that is just developing, give yourself five points. If you have a well-developed internal strength or external skill, give yourself eight points. If you feel that you have a fully developed internal strength or external skill, give yourself ten points. If you feel your strengths and/or skill is not developed at all, don't award any points. Tally up your points. Scores of seventy and above are in the target range—congratulations, you possess some key strengths and skills that will serve you well in work and life! Scores below seventy indicate where you might want to continue to improve or may indicate a lack of interest in this area—no worries, you now know what you need to build on and can move ahead.

Use your results to create a plan for moving forward. In other words, if you're lacking in an area, seek professors, mentors, training, or coaching to fill in your gaps or weaknesses. Most importantly, however, take pride in your internal strengths and communicate to others your external skills.

Examples of Some Internal Strengths and External Skills

- Critical self-reflection
- Confidence
- Feeling empowered
- Leadership
- Ability to build community
- Applying cross-cultural and global awareness to "big questions" about women and gender
- Considering an issue from multiple perspectives
- Thinking critically
- Locating, evaluating, and interpreting diverse sources, including statistics
- Connecting knowledge and experience, theory and activism in women's studies and other courses
- Effective verbal communication

- Discerning the importance of interlocked oppressions
- Applying knowledge for social transformation, citizenship

2. Letter of Recommendation

It is not uncommon that during your academic career you will ask someone—a professor, teaching assistant, internship advisor, or employer—for a letter of recommendation. Letters of recommendation are used to assess students for a variety of programs, jobs, honors, etc. You may have already asked someone you know who can discuss your assets to write a letter of recommendation. One technique for learning how to communicate the knowledge and skills you have gained through women's and gender studies is to craft your own "letter of recommendation." Cheryl reaped the benefits of this activity when her advisor asked her to create a letter of recommendation as a self-reflective exercise in preparation for a job application. Not only did this activity give Cheryl's advisor a better idea of her student's talents, knowledge base, and experience, but in the process of writing the letter, Cheryl had to learn how to promote herself, frame her talents in a manner that corresponded with the requirements of the position, and actively acknowledge her strengths. The act of writing often allows us the opportunity to reflect, edit, and compose our lives into scripts that we internalize and ultimately believe. You might share your letter with your mentors and people you name as references and see whether they would describe you in similar terms.

SECTION THREE

YOU'RE GRADUATING: GREAT! NOW WHAT?

5
WOMEN'S AND GENDER STUDIES GRADUATES AS CHANGE AGENTS: SIX PROFILES

In Chapter Four you took some time assessing your interest, skills, and strengths in women's and gender studies. We hope that you came away from that chapter eager to find out more about how others have used their degrees in obtaining employment and developing satisfying careers. In this chapter you'll discover the range of career pathways and employment opportunities that women's studies and gender studies students have pursued over the past fifteen years. You'll discover a diversity of pathways—some graduates pursue positions that directly utilize and apply their knowledge and understanding of gender issues, whereas others may work in environments in which a gender and women's studies degree is a benefit, yet not always actively acknowledged. There is no one model or way to use one's women's and gender studies degree! These employment paths are marked with trial and error, inspiration, passion, serendipity, creativity, and tons of hard work.

The graduates' employment profiles presented here grew out of our survey analysis and interviews with women's and gender studies graduates. Our survey demonstrates that women's and gender studies graduates go on to find fulfilling work in a variety of fields. You'll find how they talk about their path useful, not so that you can replicate that same path, but so that you can understand the process by which they got there. These profiles also provide a context for living one's ideals and values of women's and gender studies.

We also present a framework of "Sustainers, Evolvers, and Synthesizers" designed to highlight unique ways to think about how graduates have found their way in the professional world and build on our idea of women's and gender studies students as change agents. You'll read the profiles of six individuals who exemplify this framework. They are change agents in small and large ways through their paid employment and commitments outside of work. Their struggles and triumphs provide useful models for you as you think about how you will use your training after you graduate. We think you'll find yourself inspired by their commitments to gender equality and creativity in pursuing meaningful work. You may hear people say they don't know what you will do with your women's and gender studies degree. And that women's and gender studies doesn't seem to have as direct a line to a career as, say, going into accounting. We actually think that perspective does not tell the full story nor agree with the findings of our research. There actually are direct paths to several career areas with a women's and gender studies degree. Moreover, your training in women's and gender studies allows you to assess the job market in new and different ways that lead to creating opportunities that go beyond "getting a job."

Employment and Career Pathways from the Survey

Graduates have held a variety of diverse and interesting employment positions: everything from professors to stage managers. You are definitely not going to starve pursuing work in women's and gender studies! We found that there are several professional areas that graduates clustered in over the past decade and half: higher education administration, entrepreneurship, law, academe, the health professions, and nonprofit work.

Some trends we note are the high number of medical and health professionals in our survey, especially those working on issues of women's health and HIV/AIDS issues. There were many doctors and surgeons in our survey and several of them specialized in women's health. There were also a high number of nurses of different credentials (that is, registered nurse, nurse practitioner, etc.) in a variety of settings (e.g. psychiatric, operating room). Additionally, many graduates worked in the health professions through research and clinical opportunities.

We see this finding as particularly interesting in that it perhaps denotes the next cycle in the second-wave women's health movement that began in the mid-1970s, which fought for more women health practitioners and created new opportunities for women in the health professions. This US trend also mirrors the international increase in employment opportunities in the health professions.

There were many graduates who worked in the area of HIV/AIDS—specifically counseling and testing services. Moreover, there were graduates who worked in the HIV field through community-based organizations, local, state, and national government, or who are fighting for the civil rights and dignified treatment of HIV-positive people through law or nonprofit advocacy work. It stands to reason that HIV/AIDS has emerged as a prominent issue for women's and gender studies communities. Not only does the epidemic affect people across a wide spectrum of identities (gender, race/ethnicity, nationality, social class, age, and sexualities), but as it emerged, the way that state actors and public health entities addressed this epidemic was different. In large part, this was due to the activism and utilization of social movement tactics by those infected and affected by it. This pandemic also emerged in concert with the gay liberation movement, as well as second- and third-wave feminism.

Another important trend that has less to do with a specific career but is about broader intellectual and employment trajectories is the high number of graduates who have pursued advanced degrees after graduation. Over 70 percent of all graduates who completed our survey had or are pursuing advanced degrees since completing their bachelor's degree. We think that this finding signals that a few things are unique to the training that women's studies students often receive:

- Intensive and individualized mentoring: Given the structure of many programs and departments, students often receive support and outstanding mentoring during their education.
- The "interdisciplinary advantage": In Chapter One we highlighted the importance of interdisciplinary training in women's studies. This kind of intellectual dexterity and synthesis may create competitive advantages for students seeking graduate training in a wide variety of fields.
- The women's and gender studies classroom: In Chapters One and Two we discussed how the emphasis on peer-to-peer learning,

critical engagement with texts, and participation are features of many women's and gender studies classrooms. It could be that this type of training produces a student who has very strong writing and communications skills that also provide an advantage when seeking advanced degree opportunities.

Employment of Women's and Gender Studies Graduates

Here is a sense of the range of employment opportunities that graduates have pursued:[39]

- Deputy Director, Affiliate and National Programs with NARAL Pro-Choice America ("developing offline activism opportunities for pro-choice activists and organizational development support for our affiliate network")
- Manager of Reporting & Analytics ("I work for an IT media company and analyze the lead generation campaigns, lead delivery and reporting for our sales team and clients.")
- Certified Public Accountant
- Internet entrepreneur
- "I work at the Democratic National Committee doing political research."
- Health Center Assistant at Planned Parenthood in Louisiana ("an office assistant trained by the company to counsel women on birth control and STIs")
- "I am the leader of the educational division at a national domestic violence organization."
- Director of Business Development & Scrum Process Mentor ("I work with small businesses to help take them to the next level. This could mean increasing their revenue, software quality or employee satisfaction. Most of my work falls in the field of Sales, Marketing and Organizational Transformation Coach.")
- HIV Counselor/Educator/Phlebotomist ("I test individuals for HIV using a rapid finger-stick test. While the test is running I educate people on the basics of HIV, prevention, and risk reduction. I also counsel clients and link them to services if they test positive.")
- Civil rights lawyer
- Administrator at Equal Rights Advocates—a nonprofit women's rights legal organization

- Researcher ("I work with two nonprofit organizations based in Colombo, Sri Lanka. One organization works on women's rights while the other works on LGBT rights.")
- Middle school Literacy Specialist ("Reading and Writing teacher for struggling 6th–8th grade students and literacy coach")
- Project Manager, Webpublisher, and Public Relations Manager responsible at the Universities of Bern and Basel, Switzerland
- Psychiatric nurse
- Gender and Development Specialist (freelance, mostly for the United Nations and some NGOs)
- "I am an editor at a progressive women's magazine based in the southeast."
- Field representative for a member of the state assembly
- Special Projects Coordinator at the Public Education Foundation, a nonprofit that seeks to improve k–12 public education in southern Nevada ("I write grants, manage programs, assist with special events, etc.")
- "I am a novelist. I write lesbian romances. I've published two books and have two more completed and scheduled for release."
- Deputy Director for a nonprofit farmers' market working on food access and food justice issues in a low-income community
- Licensed Mental Health Counselor
- Immigrant Services Program Director at a nonprofit community-based organization
- Assistant Professor, Psychology and African Diaspora Studies
- Claims Examiner ("I examine workers' compensation claims.")
- Director of Public Relations at a unique grocery store with four locations in NY/CT
- Research Analyst for an HIV/AIDS policy and economics research group
- Stage Manager for Stage Theatre and Corporate Theatre
- Sexual Assault Victim Advocate
- Government Services Executive ("I'm a consultant/advisor to government entities that provide health and human services, namely child welfare, workforce development, and public assistance and housing.")
- Entrepreneur ("I have a small popsicle company.")

- Marketing Associate/Graphic Designer and Editor for a garden store
- Editor and Project Coordinator at a breast cancer nonprofit that provides medical and quality-of-life information for women affected by breast cancer ("I write articles and edit a newsletter.")
- Adolescent Continuing Care Case Manager
- Research Director for Office of Indigent Defense Services
- Research Manager in Hematology/Oncology and Genomic Medicine
- Cataloging Services Specialist (library cataloger) and Crisis Worker at a domestic violence service organization

Sustainers, Evolvers, and Synthesizers: Six Profiles

There are three groups around which we have categorized our six respondents. Their experiences represent a more general pattern that we have seen through interviews and survey data. The first group is called "sustainers." This group has two key features: the graduates in the group have pursued career paths that involve working on gender issues directly and in types of employment where the women's and gender studies degree is often a complementary fit for the skills required for the position. There is a well-established track record of using a women's and gender studies degree in these professional fields. The road is well traveled and there are lots of landmarks. In choosing the path of a "sustainer," you would follow the career journeys of many other women's and gender studies practitioners (such as by becoming a domestic violence counselor).

The other key feature of sustainers is the role of activism, which is central to their stories and undergirds how they find their career paths. Activism helps sustain their interest in both the paid and unpaid world.

The second group is called "evolvers." The three profiles that you'll read in this "category" share two features: (1) these individuals have taken women's and gender studies into arenas where it previously was not, either in terms of finding or creating new employment opportunities, and (2) they are highly adaptable and innovative, and are continually taking risks that support their inner vision.

"Synthesizers" move back and forth between these two categories. As with sustainers, they are connected to career paths that tend to emphasize gender issues. As with evolvers, they have high energy and passion for trying new ideas. Synthesizers have an ability to move among and between careers that involve gender issues directly and utilize their activism in both their paid and unpaid work, as well as being creative in exploring new areas for taking risks with their vision.

This framework is a heuristic tool and not meant to create mutually exclusive categories. Indeed, we invite you as you read these wonderful graduate profiles to consider similarities and differences between them that might suggest other ways of organizing them.

Sustainers

Rebecca Mann: Becoming a Paid Feminist

Michele met Rebecca during a career services night at her university. During Rebecca's presentation on how to go into community organizing, she heard Rebecca say she had learned how to become "a paid feminist." Michele had never heard that term before and was very intrigued and asked if she could hear more of Rebecca's story. Rebecca Mann is currently the director of community organizing and outreach for Equality North Carolina, a statewide group dedicated to securing equal rights and justice for lesbian, gay, bisexual, and transgender (LGBT) people.

She is a lifelong North Carolinian and holds a BA in English, with a minor in Women's and Gender Studies, from North Carolina State University and an MA in Women's and Gender Studies from the University of North Carolina at Greensboro. She graduated from college in 2000. Rebecca has worked as an advocate and organizer with the YWCA of High Point and Planned Parenthood Health Systems, and in the communications departments of IntraHealth International and the international reproductive rights organization Ipas.

Rebecca was one of the first people to minor in women's studies when it was first offered at her university, which to us makes her a "mini-pioneer." She stumbled across women's studies and she believes that she connected with it because it mirrored some of her interests developed in high school. She always believed in principles of fairness and equality: "Since the first [women's studies] class, I realized I want[ed] to do this." In her English and journalism projects, she remembers trying to infuse those assignments with women's studies interest and content.

During her first semester in her sophomore year, Rebecca became involved in a local chapter of NOW. She got involved with NOW as a manifestation of her activism. Little did she know that this involvement as a student activist was going to shape her career choices in small and large ways. She believes that it is important for students to apply what they know outside of classes:

> Coursework is great, but if you aren't connecting it to something bigger outside, I would find it hard [for] it to be meaningful. You're learning about stuff, but you're learning about systems, but seeing how that is impacting women is important.

Her parents were supportive of her minor in women's studies—it helped that she was also focused on editing and journalism. During the first year of being educated in women's studies, she also accepted a broader label for herself: "A roommate that I wasn't getting along with during an argument called me a feminist and stormed out of the room and I thought, 'Is that the worst thing you can call me?'"

She sometimes found the campus climate challenging as an activist for women's issues:

> At the time it was hard, but I think that after pushing through that for a little while, I realized it was so much better to be in that situation, because I feel like if you can stand up for what you believe in, when a lot of people around you aren't in your immediate core and even the ones who are—I definitely had a lot of friends who just didn't get it—I feel like if you can do it in that environment, then when you get out, everything else is just cake. For a while I daydreamed about transferring to [a] campus where there was a strong feminist presence. But, I'm glad that I didn't because part of the learning process is to have that opposition . . . I wouldn't have been prepared for real life activism.

Rebecca believes the challenges she faced as an activist on campus prepared her for the challenges of activism and community organizing after college. Her first job after graduation was as a technical editor for a firm that contracted with top *Fortune* 500 companies. It was extremely well paid, though not very interesting or challenging to her. She was laid off during the "dotcom" bust, and she called it a blessing, because it allowed her to stop pretending that technical writing was the work she really wanted to do. All during this time, however, she continued her activism with NOW. While she was laid off, she used her connections through NOW, who knew her and could vouch for her, to gain several nonprofit positions.

ABOUT NOW

The National Organization for Women was founded in 1966 by a small but determined group of women's rights advocates. NOW is a leading progressive US feminist organization. Feminist activists, scholars, and policymakers have been a part of its long history. NOW has devoted itself to issues of changing policy and public opinion on major issues including: reproductive rights, sexual violence, equal pay for women, gay and lesbian rights, employment discrimination, civil rights, and support for more elected women in political office. See NOW's website at www.now.org/ for more information.

Because she had been a committed volunteer and organizer for so many years, it was easy for Rebecca's friends to call potential employers (that they often knew at other nonprofits) or write compelling reference letters for her. That allowed her to get a position at Ipas, an international reproductive rights organization. She attributes her success in getting in the front door and eventually landing a position with them to her personal connections. Her friends, mentors, and fellow activists called on her behalf, which helped move her into a more competitive position to be considered for a job. The position was in the communications department, and this was a stepping stone position that led her to other positions with nonprofits, including a position at a local Planned Parenthood doing policy work and organizing.

On her resume and in job interviews she highlighted her minor in women's studies. She had devoted time to work in community organizing and advocacy, which helped compensate for the lack of skills she had in specific areas. Her activism augmented her resume although she did not have direct paid work experience. Since she had been with NOW for several years during and after college, she gained an impressive list of external skills: event planning, community organizing, data systems, phone banking, canvassing, etc.

She also credits her activism with keeping her "sane" for the times that she was not in work that she loved. While an activist at NOW she did research on timely issues, including pay equity and reproductive rights. This kept up her skills and she could show nonprofits that she was well read in a variety of areas.

When Rebecca talks to students, she tries to dispel the notion that you have to have a certain type of job with a women's and gender studies degree: "Any job you have will be a feminist job if it's done with intention, if you're being aware."

She went back and decided to pursue an MA in women's and gender studies because she wanted to deepen her work, and she also saw that positions in several areas of interest were looking for candidates who had postgraduate degrees. She chose a program that was very connected with the public policy world. The transition between being an activist and graduate student was a bit challenging at first. Despite this, she was able to deepen her knowledge of feminist theory and sociology.

Her current position continues her interest in lobbying, policy, and organizing. She looks at this position as a culmination of several of her areas of interest: Director of Community Organizing and Advocacy for Equality NC. This job opened serendipitously as she was finishing her Master's program. Equality NC works on state policy affecting lesbian, gay, bisexual, transgender, and questioning (LGBTQ) North Carolinians. The organization works with the state legislature to pass bills that positively affect the LGBTQ community and also conducts grassroots campaigns in communities across the state.

In her interview for this position, her longstanding work with NOW was noted. During her interview, she discussed how NOW had also helped her do work concerning LGBT issues. As a straight, married woman she feels incredibly privileged to do this work. She also credits her work in her Master's program, which concentrated on theory and gender and gave her a broader foundation. She believes if you are part of a majority group, "that it is an onus on you [to make sure] that other people are being treated equally."

Matt Ezzell: Radical Teacher and Scholar

You met Matt in earlier chapters. By the time he arrived at UNC's campus, he had seen his older sister struggle, at an early age, with eating disorders and also later pursue a minor in women's studies when she was at college. He had also witnessed his mother find fulfillment going back to school for a Master's degree in literature with a concentration on contemporary fiction written by African-American women. Discussing issues central to women's lives was not a foreign experience to Matt. The first semester he, like most students, looked at different majors, including business. Matt says that "Introduction to the Sociology of Gender", which he enrolled in during his first semester, changed "the course of [my] academic, professional and personal trajectory."

He was amazed at how the class was structured to emphasize co-facilitation between students and instructor, and he reveled in the small group discussions, as well as the emphasis on critical thinking and that "the material is grounded in the lived realities [of people] . . . it wasn't abstract discussions of the social world." The instructor also invited students to share their lived experiences through the prism of gender, race, and class. Situating himself in relation to the concepts he was learning was new and exciting: "I didn't know that education could be like this."

His experience in that class provided him with tools to think critically about masculinity. After that class, he went and changed his major from business to women's studies. When he told his family about his major, his mother and sister were supportive "that I had stumbled into women's studies." He was worried about what his dad would say, given that his father had been in business for most of Matt's life and was looking forward to his son following in his footsteps. He said, "Do you enjoy it?" and when Matt said he did, his father said to follow his interests.

When asked about pushback from his peers in the community after he announced his major, he said it wasn't so difficult: "Most of what I experienced was positive, partly because the deeper I got into women's studies, the more I surrounded myself with a self-identified feminist community."

As he discussed in Chapter Three, Matt had to navigate being the only male-identified person in the women's studies program. He was keenly aware of the challenges of the privileges he had as a man and the necessity of using that privilege to confront male bias. Soon after he took the class, he wanted to do an internship and work on issues of sexual assault and violence, an interest that emerged strongly for him:

> The more I started thinking about these issues and having conversations with people in my life about these issues, the more of my friends, particularly women friends, started to disclose issues of sexual violence; I was realizing very quickly that I didn't know any women who didn't have some experience of men's violence that they could connect to immediately. It was part of the

experience of being a woman. There is this shared experience of being targeted within a rape culture if you are a woman. And, I was starting to approach a realization of what that meant. And I felt like I wanted to do something about this because I knew too many people that I care about who are struggling with this . . . and I hadn't really thought about this much before and I want to be active. I felt like I got the benefits of the targeting of women just because I'm a man. So, it's our responsibility to do something.

Matt called the local rape crisis center and said, "I don't know if you have male volunteers, I understand if you don't. The last thing I would want to do is be a trigger for someone who walks in the door to get help just because I am a man . . ." The person who answered said, "We do have male volunteers. We think it's really important to have male volunteers. And, there is definitely a role here for you." He was able to volunteer at the rape crisis center, which included sixty-three hours of training; he decided to do an internship there and as part of the agreement with the agency, he also had to commit to volunteering an additional semester after he was finished with the internship. Becoming involved with the rape crisis center became a total immersion into the topic of sexual violence and working at such a center.

As a volunteer and as part of his internship he became a community educator. He did a number of training sessions in the area: ". . . a lot of material was geared toward elementary school kids," but also high schools, community colleges, four-year universities, and community organizations. His focus became how to get men involved as allies with women against sexual assault. He would make a point of speaking to any organization that wanted to learn about preventing sexual violence. He learned he loved working with groups on this issue and found it very rewarding. It gave him experience of how to talk about issues that are difficult to talk about, particular with men, without getting defensive. He did this work during his junior year and he still feels that he draws on the lessons and insights he learned about working in groups even now as a professor. During this time, he also wrote a paper drawing on his own experience and research to support the rape crisis center in conducting outreach with men. After the official internship semester ended he stayed on as a volunteer, as part of his agreement, and continued developing and honing male outreach on sexual violence.

Matt's activism on sexual violence continued to blossom on campus. He developed and co-taught a course on interpersonal violence prevention and leadership, which became a popular class (and now has been institutionalized as a service learning course). Also, noting the holes in student affairs administration regarding sexual violence, he advocated for developing a paid staff position for an interpersonal violence prevention coordinator—someone who would be responsible for helping to coordinate resources, talks, etc., on preventing sexual violence across the campus community. This has also come to fruition since he has left UNC.

The rape crisis center was where he got his first job after graduation. He saw an office manager position open up during his senior year and knew, "I had to apply and interview. Once I had the internship experience—I knew I wanted to do more work on eliminating sexual violence and getting more men involved." He felt passionate about this work. In the interview he was able to demonstrate that "I had internship experiences and the connections I made were, without question, putting the skills and lessons that I learned from my women's studies major to use." He was offered the position. As he was graduating without debt, he felt he could take an entry-level nonprofit job for a few years. Matt believed that taking an entry-level nonprofit position was a good way to use the class privilege he possessed of not having had to pay for school because of his parents' socioeconomic status and ability to pay for his college education.

Matt worked in the rape crisis center for three years and was promoted several times: office manager, administrative services coordinator, and finally, community education coordinator. He completely enjoyed working in the community and talking with a variety of audiences, but over time he grew:

> ... very frustrated—I had only 45 minutes with students to dismantle rape culture—I thought how wonderful it would be if you had a semester—you can't do everything in a semester either, but you can get to know students, you can build on discussions and I thought that was amazing.

He loved teaching and facilitating and could see pursuing the path of becoming a professor.

Early on in his undergraduate career he had found a mentor, someone he identified as a "radical feminist mentor" who encouraged his work and supported him. With her encouragement, he developed his voice through writing for local newsmagazines and with her on topics including sexist language, the role of pornography in everyday culture, and teaching gender. He was torn between choosing a graduate program in sociology or women's studies. He was, however, drawn to working with his mentor in sociology and continuing the activism that he had begun in the North Carolina community. When he was accepted into UNC's sociology program, he felt that it was a good fit.

He loved deepening the work in sociology with an emphasis on gender as a graduate student. His sense that he would excel in the classroom and enjoy working with students was confirmed. During his graduate career he earned a teaching award, as well as the first university award to recognize a person making a significant contribution to women in the campus community. Matt finished his doctorate in 2008 and took a position as an Assistant Professor in the Department of Sociology and Anthropology at James Madison College, a small, private liberal arts college. He teaches a wide variety of courses including, "The Development of Sociological Thought and Method," "Microsociology," "The Sociology of Race and Ethnicity," and "The Sociology of Gender."

James Madison has a Curriculum in Women's Studies. Matt's course on "The Sociology of Gender" counts toward the women's studies minor—and he serves on the WMST advisory board. He says, "I get more radical every day." As a relatively new professor, he is interested in mentoring students, building a feminist community, and raising his daughter.

Take Aways from Rebecca and Matt's Profiles

- If you have an interest in women's and gender studies prior to college it, may serve you throughout your academic career—Rebecca and Matt both had a longstanding interest in women's and gender studies before they entered college. Once in college, they found themselves in classes that nurtured their interest in gender equality.
- Find an internship experience that is right for you. For Matt, his experiences as an intern and work on campus on the issues of sexual violence gave him a strong advantage when applying for an entry-level position at the rape crisis center.

- Allow yourself to be mentored. Matt and Rebecca both drew on mentors (from college networks and activist networks) who helped them gain perspective in making career decisions and applying for positions.
- Don't give up if your first position is not everything you dreamed it was going to be. Cultivate interests outside of work—Rebecca's interests did not align with her first position. But she continued to pursue her interests through volunteering and community work. Her activism kept her sane while she was not in her dream job. Over time, the experiences gained as a longstanding volunteer and activist gave her the expertise to move into positions that more closely aligned with her interests.

Evolvers

Rachel Burton: Industrial Maven

Rachel first came to college interested in becoming a nutrition science major, but she took an introductory course in women's studies because of her interest in women's health issues and because someone had told her there would be information on that topic in this course. While in the course, "a big light bulb went off," and in her second semester she realized she could combine nutrition science and women's studies. She liked the idea of combining a liberal arts discipline with a science-based discipline. Rachel wound up not finishing nutrition science, but finished the women's studies major and became extremely involved in activist issues.

During her college years, Rachel was very involved in several issue-based groups on campus: an animal rights group; a variety of women's groups and organizations working on specific issues, such as sexist fraternity practices. She also undertook environmental activism off campus, including direct action with organizations such as Greenpeace, Earth First, and the Rainforest Action Network.

Her parents had questions when she dropped nutrition science, but she was so involved with activities off campus that she did not really pay attention to them. She also took a semester off (between sophomore and junior year) and lived in a collective in Detroit. This move prompted her parents to focus more on her major and how it was going to serve her in the future, and she says it became a "big question." She always felt that:

"you can do anything you want with a women's studies major, it's just a matter of how you apply yourself."

She remembers that when she was getting ready to graduate and thinking about next steps, her visit to the Career Services office was not

NEW PATHS IN FARMING, ACTIVISM, AND SUSTAINABILITY

Rachel was able to tap into a cluster of interests that have been steadily developing. There is a growing convergence among many people interested in the connections between sustainability, "food justice," sustainable agriculture, and connecting to the land in secular and spiritual ways. Over the past twenty years, farming and building community through sustainable agriculture have become attractive to graduating students. Women make up a growing percentage of farmers. According to the US Census of Agriculture, the number of women who owned farms jumped 29 percent between 2002 and 2007. Many states have seen even larger jumps in the number of women farmers. One in ten US farms is owned by women. Men still own and run farms, especially those that are large scale, but "women tend to run smaller, more specialized enterprises selling heirloom tomatoes and grass-fed beef" to smaller niche markets (Aranti 2009). Women farmers have also benefited from the upsurge in the public's interest in buying local and organic produce from farmers' markets and through community supported agricultural (CSA) programs.

Sometimes, farming communities are also places that encourage and foster spiritual growth. A former colleague of Cheryl's, Lisa Coons, is the Center Director for the Center for Earth Spirituality and Rural Ministry for the School Sisters of Notre Dame (SSND) in Mankato, Minnesota. According to the Center's website:

> The Center promotes and fosters awareness and ways of living that recognize and support the interconnection and interdependence of all life. In embracing people of all spiritual paths, the Center strives toward earth justice and sustainability through education, spirituality, sustainable agriculture, rural ministry, and political advocacy. One of the purposes of the Center is to model environmental stewardship on the SSND land itself through ecological awareness, ecosystem restoration, support of local food production, and environmentally sensitive maintenance practices.
>
> (www.ssndmankato.org/whatwedo/ministries/earth.php)

If you are interested in farming and sustainable agriculture, a good place to start would be the American Farm Bureau's "Young Farmers and Ranchers Program." See www.fb.org/index.php for more information.

very helpful. After graduation, Rachel traveled overseas and began working on organic farms, pursuing her growing interest in sustainable agriculture (in England, Wales, Ireland, and Scotland). She also traveled to small farms and communities to learn how they organized on issues of the environment.

FOR YOUR LIBRARY

Temra Costa. (2010). *Farmer Jane: Women Changing the Way We Eat.* Layton, UT: Gibbs Smith.

Rachel came back to a rural community in North Carolina and deepened her interest in sustainable farming practices. She worked with a woman who owned a small organic farm, and Rachel notes, "She became a real mentor for me." Rachel took a tremendous leap and enrolled in a one-year certificate program in sustainable agriculture from a local community college. She worked part-time on her mentor's farm and then as a waitress and tried to stay active in environmental groups.

During the sustainable agriculture program, she got to know one of the teachers, a man who also taught the automotives mechanics class, and she mentioned that she had a broken transmission on a truck she owned. He said to her, "I'll show you how to fix it, if you buy the parts." Intrigued, she went to buy the parts: "It was a totally new arena." She spent the entire day with her teacher working on her transmission. At the end of the lesson, he said, "Girl, you're not half bad at this—you should think about doing this!" He convinced her to enroll in the automotive mechanics program.

As she evaluated his suggestion to return to school in a new subject area, she engaged in some self-reflection and goal planning. She currently had an excellent informal mentor (carpenter by trade and running her own farm) demonstrating hands-on and life skills concerning what it meant to be a female farmer. She surmised that her hands-on farming knowledge combined with learning mechanical knowledge would make a strong combination. She thought that if she

> . . . wanted to pursue farming, it would be useful for the rest of my life whether I wanted to be a mechanic for the rest of my life and work on cars or if I just wanted to have the basic knowledge of engines and engine operation and maintenance [which] would be useful on farms.

She enrolled in the automotive mechanics program. Two other women were with her. One woman had a husband who was a truck driver, and she wanted to beef up her knowledge of engines and maintenance to help him. The other woman was generally interested in cars. Rachel was twenty-five at the time, and all the other members of the program were younger men. "Early on there was a proving ground time period. It felt like the first semester, there was [a sense of being questioned] how much do *you* really want to know about automotive technology? Are you just here to find a boyfriend?"

Rachel tried to cut through the hostility and suspicion: "I want to get dirty. I'm serious, not here to sit on sidelines and watch. And it was unacceptable for someone to do something for me." She tried to correct what she calls "tool grabbing" and the "let me just show you" attitude where men in the class would dominate the tools and not give her or the other women an opportunity to use them and learn on their own. She had to instruct the male students "Tell me, and then show me once." And, "I'm here to learn and I'm going to learn more than you." Luckily, the teacher was very supportive throughout the entire program, and she felt no intimidation or need to prove herself to him.

Rachel was able to pursue her training in automotive mechanics through what is now called The Carl D. Perkins Career and Technical Education Improvement Act of 2006. An earlier version, the Carl D. Perkins Vocational and Applied Technology Education Act ("Perkins"), refers to the federal law that funds vocational education programs at secondary and post-secondary institutions across the country. The Perkins Act contained provisions, dating from the 1970s, intended to help ensure that women and girls had equal access and opportunity to succeed in vocational education. A version of this grant was administered through the state of North Carolina in partnership with local community colleges. This grant supported women in pursuing training for a two-year degree in motorcycle mechanics, automotive mechanics, industrial maintenance, welding, and electric engineering. For Rachel this meant that her books and tuition were paid for and she also received a set of mechanics tools when she graduated. If you are interested in these opportunities, you should talk with either a financial aid counselor at your current institution or an administrator at your local community college to see if there are programs funded within your state.

If her parents were skeptical of her interest in women's and gender studies, they were even more skeptical of a two-year degree in automotive mechanics. After answering their questions and fixing her father's car, however (she said with a smile), it did not take long for them to see the utility of the degree. She even inspired her father, who was retired, to enroll in an automotive body program.

Her teacher and mentor helped her get her first automotive mechanic job at a local dealership for a year while she was finishing school. The move from student mechanic to the paid professional world of being an automotive mechanic was not easy for Rachel: "The transition from automotive classroom to automotive workplace was dramatically different in comfort level. The workplace was difficult to have a positive powerful learning experience."

At the two dealerships where she worked over a two-year period there were very few women. If there were women there, they worked in very different positions than Rachel—mostly secretarial. Rachel was also keenly aware that the women who did work in the office were often relatives of the men who owned the dealership. She met no other female mechanics in her first two positions.

She faced sexism and heterosexism continually on her first job. A typical question from one mechanic was, "Are you a lesbian or carpet muncher?" She went through a hazing period with many of the male employees, who used the excuse that "we're teasing you because we like you." Although she was able to prove herself with several of the technicians, there were still technicians who would not work with her. Many women experience sexual harassment in the workplace, and women in the trades often face open hostility and discrimination such as this.

Rachel found that she was able to have a more a positive effect by being an automotive instructor at the community college. She was asked to do this by her instructor and taught full time for three years—taking over his class often. Later, during this time, her first mentor also asked her to teach automotive high school classes. This was a gift for her:

> It was great; I learned even more working with him and beside him. First year was a challenge [with issues such as] not being a trained teacher, curriculum, dynamic of [being in my] late twenties and students were seventeen/eighteen and ready to get out of high school and stuck with [9] "newbie female instructor." Every year

though, more and more girls would come into the program
because they heard through other students that there was a female
instructor.

She could see a significant change as more and more women signed up
to get these skills, and she felt comfortable in her class because they felt
they would not ". . . be picked on because people think they're hanging
out with the boys." Rachel believes that paying attention to making women
as well as male students feel comfortable creates a stronger classroom.

She was invited to teach night school, working with returning adults.
Over time, as a teacher, she found more and more administrators who
were supportive of her as an instructor of automotive mechanics.
Sometimes, older male students would say "I don't want to be in her
class," but an administrator would back Rachel up.

The move to her current work in biofuels production and distribution
was a natural outgrowth of her interests—a combination of sustainable
agriculture, environmental activism, and new industrialism—and fit well
with her skill set and self-confidence in working in often male-dominated
work environments. Her interest in biofuels came from a different
perspective, asking what was in fuels for cars, and from this she started
researching alternative automotive fuels. Rachel then co-hosted a
continuing education class on "biofuels," which was the first of its kind
in the community. Every time she taught the class it got bigger, with
more people taking the class. Over time, as people began learning about
biofuels, they wanted to know how and where to get them. Rachel teamed
up with a few people to investigate, which caused this to grow into a
bigger pursuit, which led to a substantial enterprise: "Let's make biofuels
for ourselves." Her team then helped to induce demand for creating a
distribution network—one tank a time.

Rachel is co-founder of Piedmont Biofuels, a leader of biofuels in
North Carolina. Piedmont Biofuels is a worker- and member-owned
cooperative promoting and offering biodiesel fuel made from vegetable
oil. They offer classes, consultations, and have also become a hub for
issues of sustainable agriculture in the state. Her official title on her
business card just states "in charge," but she explains that she's really the
control manager for the biofuels plant and also the research director. She
handles the understanding and handling of all the fuel issues (the making
of the fuel and the quality of it in the laboratory). This brings her back

to her roots in chemistry and nutrition science. She believes, "Nothing is ever wasted in one's development." She also gives fuel quality presentations all over the world, writes grants, manages public funding, and plays a key role in the day-to-day operations.

If she had not spent time in the women's studies arena, Rachel says:

> I may not have not gone down the auto pathway, because I may have not felt: this is something women don't do . . . but here's an opportunity to do it. I think there is definitely a connection between the fact I was a women's studies major and I went to pursue a nontraditional career and to understand and further my experience of being a woman in the workplace.

OPPORTUNITIES IN TRADITIONAL AND VOCATIONAL TRADES

While your women's and gender studies education provides you with the critical thinking tools to analyze gender and oppression in the world, perhaps you have always had a gift for working with your hands and creating beauty with hair, or repairing your car, or building a cabinet to hold all your textbooks from class. Rather than pursing a graduate degree, you may be more inclined to get your journeyman's (-person's) card, your cosmetologist license, or even a pilot's license. According to Chicago Women in Trades (CWIT) website (www.chicagowomenintrades.org/artman/publish/article_252.shtml):

> Careers in the trades include carpentry, plumbing, welding, auto mechanics, and other high-wage, high-skill blue-collar careers. These careers offer women insurance benefits, pensions, career advancement and challenging careers in addition to starting average wages of $12.00 an hour and the potential of making over $30.00 an hour!

As you'll see in the next chapter, there are many ways to use what you learn in an employment situation. We want you to keep your thinking broad.

For more information see:

- Department of Labor, "Quick Facts on Nontraditional Occupations for Women" (www.dol.gov/wb/factsheets/nontra2008.htm)
- *Ms.* magazine, "Tradeswomen Unite" (www.msmagazine.com/summer2002/thom.asp)

She feels her time in the automotive mechanic workplace was "just a different arena of understanding women's roles in society." She feels like she is a model for other women who wish to pursue untraditional pathways using their degree.

Kimberly Wilson: Tranquilista and Social Entrepreneur

Kimberly Wilson is a prime example of a person who is living her passion for women's studies and empowering women as leaders in new ways. She is a yoga teacher; entrepreneur (beginning at age twenty-six); designer of eco-fashion; self-proclaimed do-gooder who runs a nonprofit that provides a space for yoga, creativity, and leadership for girls in grades nine to twelve; and lover of "all things fabulous." Although she came to women's studies toward the end of her academic career, she felt that it offered her a new way of thinking and living her life.

During her last year at the University of Oklahoma, she took her first women's studies course. The first thing she thought was: "Why did I not know about this sooner?" In her community in Oklahoma she knew very strict gender roles: "You get married, make babies and stay at home." In theory, she did not see anything wrong with that as a personal choice, it was never, however, her interest and she felt that women were not encouraged to seek other opportunities for professional and self-fulfillment outside of more traditional roles. Kimberly found that the women's studies and feminist community she discovered in her classes allowed her to think about her options as a woman. She loved the field's emphasis on activism, and this has been a recurring thread in the decisions she has made—and so has empowering women. She found it ". . . so empowering to find a course of study that comported with the way one could live life . . ."

After graduating with a degree in psychology and a strong interest in women's studies, she moved to Washington, DC, and enrolled in a paralegal program. She still did not know how she was going to use her interest in women's studies, but she kept looking for ways to make her work relevant to women. It was clear a few years into her paralegal job that she was just making it through, though it was paying the bills. She says she often thought, "There's gotta be more [to life] than to work your ass off for someone else."

She happened upon a book that helped her to ask questions about what was next. She worked through *The Artist's Way*, a famous book that promotes self-discovery through embracing one's creativity and passions in an everyday, practical way. Reflecting on things that she truly loved and loved to do planted a seed that was later to become her first business—Tranquil Space. Kimberly also did two important things that helped launch her business, her writing career, and her philanthropic work. She sought out further education and kept fine-tuning her inner vision.

Kimberly undertook a yoga teacher-training program after being a yoga practitioner for many years. She realized that there were not many yoga studios in Washington, DC, that considered busy young women who needed a space to get connected to what they needed in their life and for the opportunity to become tranquil. This demographic was not being served, and she realized that she desired to create this space to serve women. She launched her yoga studio in the living room of her small DC apartment. The demand was so great that in just a few short years she was able to launch Tranquil Space, a yoga studio listed in *travel + leisure* as one of the best in the world.

Kimberly also wanted to deepen her work in women's studies, so she searched out MA programs in women's studies and settled on the one at George Washington University. This program gave her a way to be focused on coursework, but had a lot of flexibility, and she was able to work on entrepreneurial leadership and interview many successful businesswomen. During her MA, she made it a point to study the structure of women-focused nonprofits and organizations.

 FOR YOUR LIBRARY

Julia Cameron. (2002). *The Artist's Way: A Spiritual Path to Higher Creativity.* New York: Tarcher.

Kimberly Wilson. (2006). *Hip Tranquil Chick: A Guide to Life On and Off the Yoga Mat.* Novato, CA: New World Library.

———. (2010). *Tranquilista: Mastering the Art of Enlightened Work and Mindful Play.* Novato, CA: New World Library.

Through her postgraduate work, Kimberly soon wanted to document how she had come to create her vision of women's interests, yoga, and lifestyle, which she was embodying through her yoga studio and consulting work. She knew she had a book in her, but she decided to work with a writing

THE MA IN WOMEN'S STUDIES AT GEORGE WASHINGTON UNIVERSITY

Kimberly liked the flexibility of the MA program at George Washington University, which was designed for working professionals. Students have many choices of how to structure their MA program. Evening courses are available to accommodate working students, as is part-time study (six credit hours per semester). Students have the option of working on a practicum, independent research, or the more traditional thesis.

The MA in Women's Studies with a concentration in a liberal arts discipline or a topical focus offers students the opportunity to craft an individualized program of study in close consultation with faculty advisors. Students are expected to develop intellectual depth and a degree of expertise through a four-course concentration in either (a) a specific discipline such as Anthropology, Sociology, English, History, Philosophy (other disciplines are also possible, with permission), or (b) a topical area such as women and health, women and international development, race and gender (other areas are possible). There are ample opportunities for students with policy interests to include policy courses (such as Women and Public Policy, among others) in their program of study, either as part of their chosen discipline/field or as electives.

The disciplinary concentration works well for students interested in going on to a Ph.D. in a discipline and for those whose interests fit easily within disciplinary lines. Students are encouraged to find a faculty mentor in their disciplinary concentration. Alternatively, students may choose an MA in Women's Studies because their intellectual passions and career objectives are truly interdisciplinary. The topical focus option provides academic space for students with diverse interests.
(www.gwu.edu/~wstu/programs/masters.htm)

coach to help the process. She worked for many years writing for local publications and newsletters. In 2003, she had a big "aha" moment:

> Observing the growing number of yoga books on the shelves, but realizing there were none about the city-dwelling diva living *la vida* yoga, I decided that was my story. I coined the book concept "hip yoga chick" and took a local book writing course for aspiring authors to hone my idea . . . After many months I finished my proposal, researched like-minded agents, and sent query letters to a dozen of them.
>
> (Wilson 2010: 26–27)

It took over a year, but she was able to find an agent and sold the idea:

> I had six months to write and edit the book . . . *Hip Tranquil Chick* was released in 2006. By including the word *tranquil* in the title, I was able to associate the book with my businesses: my yoga studio, Tranquil Space; clothing line, TranquilT; and nonprofit, Tranquil Space Foundation.

In starting up her business and going back to graduate school, she evolved her interests and did not get intimidated in building a business even though she did not have a business background. She focused on her "desire to create community around this idea of stimulating the body and mind," and her sense of herself as "womencentric." During this time she also facilitated women's circles, women's retreats, and mentoring women, one-on-one, who wanted to launch a business.

By following her interests through she was able to open a well–regarded yoga studio and become a nationally sought-after speaker and author. Her latest book, *Tranquilista*, lays out her guiding philosophy, which helps people who have entrepreneurial interests get started with their ideas. She outlines a three-step process: spirituality, creativity, and entrepreneurship. This makes up her *Tranquilista* philosophy, which is about unlocking a women's potential to make a difference through enlightened work and mindful play. In the next chapter, we'll learn more about how she launched her nonprofit organization.

Her advice for those seeking a creative and/or entrepreneurial path is:

> Really get clear on what it is you want, hone in on your passion. But, recognize that your passions may change, and that's OK— allow an evolution of your journey. If you're interested in a business think about what things you want in the marketplace that do not already exist. Never be shy about who you are. Never lose sight of who you are, what your passions are and make sure you have a community that does support that even if that is not at work.

Peter Stuart: Untraditional Educational Counselor

Peter Stuart describes himself as a person who came from a sheltered family, from a "suburban monoculture" without a lot of life experience before he entered Queen's College in Ontario, Canada, in 1990. He started off as a math and physics major, and he quickly discovered that, while he liked and was good at these subjects, he did not feel challenged by them.

He had heard about gender issues from his mother, and although she would not necessarily describe herself as feminist, she often talked to him about the limited job choices she and her sisters faced. His mother is a nurse, and her five sisters all work in typically female-headed professions— as nurses, teachers, and secretaries.

He found himself attracted to women's studies and English classes, hoping to find new opportunities to problem-solve other than in his science and math classes. He says this about his first women's studies class, taken toward the end of his first year at Queen's College:

> Intro to Women's Studies just blew my mind. It completely opened my mind to a whole new way of studying the world. A really big thing that women's studies gave me was the words. It gave me the words and framework to describe things that were wrong. It gave me words to look at the power dynamics, and who benefitted and who were kept down in any situation I was in. I loved it!

By the end of the second year of university, Peter had changed majors and was studying to become a teacher. Once he decided to go into the teaching program, he chose his "teachable subjects" as English and Science. Although it was not offered as a "teachable subject" through the teaching program, he continued to take a number of cross-listed women's studies courses and declared it as a "medial subject." At the time at Queen's College, women's studies was organized as a "medial subject"—halfway between a minor and major through the Institute of Women's Studies. He loved the interdisciplinary nature of women's studies.

As Peter became more engaged in women's studies, he met other men who were also pursuing women's studies and he developed friendships with them. He also experienced some of the typical things that men face when they choose women's studies as an academic interest: an assumption by some men that their interest is motivated by wanting to date women and questions of sexual identity.

Peter got asked often if he was gay: "This might have bothered me when I was younger but not by the time I was in university. We definitely talked enough about sexuality issues in class," which contributed to his comfort level. He also felt that there "... were much bigger things to worry about than whether someone thought I was gay in a women's studies class." He felt welcomed, however, by the faculty and the majority of his women peers in women's studies classes.

His mother was very supportive about his interest in women's studies, but his father was not: "My dad thought it was funny and made dumb jokes about it and still does. He never told me I shouldn't be studying it. He just thought it was a typical silly thing that one studies at university."

These issues did not deter Peter from continuing in women's studies. He became actively involved both in student government and the December 6th Memorial Committee,[40] which worked on issues of sexual violence through programming events on campus. He also became very active in *SURFACE*, the monthly progressive newsmagazine that was designed to be a voice for marginal perspectives on campus. This magazine challenged the misogyny in the main campus newsmagazine and agitated for various issues on campus. Peter was co-editor of the newsmagazine and wrote articles for three years while at Queens. Co-editing and writing provided him with an opportunity to utilize his skill sets gained through English and women's studies.

He also was able to put his women's studies training into practice as he was developing his teaching skills. He often had to make visits to schools and do observations. He credits his ". . . women's studies background in learning to teach and create an egalitarian classroom."

> I came into women's studies pretty blind and so I often used the lens about power structure—race, class, and gender and structure. No matter what type of oppression existed, we looked at who was benefitting here, [and] why? What structures were maintained and how can they be altered? In student teaching I looked at how the traditional classroom is set up with bad kids in back and good kids in front and how teachers like it that way. That structure is set up for the benefit of the teachers. A lot of structure in the [average] classroom isn't questioned . . . [Because of] women's studies I could make active choices about who to pay attention to, how to set up a class and how to focus on structural inequalities. I'd look at how the classroom was set up, who it was designed for, who it wasn't designed for, why and how could it be altered to make it work for more people.

When he graduated in 1995, he moved to Toronto where he wanted to work with troubled high school kids in an urban area. He thought this would be a good way to apply his teaching and women's studies background. It did not turn out to be as straightforward a process as Peter hoped. He was underemployed for a while, because it was hard to get a job through the Public School Board. He became a tutor and through the tutoring job he met a few parents who had their children in a private school for special needs kids. They encouraged him to apply for a teaching position at the school.

At this point Peter felt conflicted, because he did not see himself teaching in a private school. However, he was attracted to working with kids who needed particular kinds of experiences in the classroom. This was the first time he felt he had to be flexible with his broader values and goals. As it turned out, he taught at the private school for eight years. Over time, he says:

> . . . [I] found it very difficult to teach in a private school setting. A lot of these kids were getting this support because their parents could afford it. Over time it wore on me and even though I could focus on the fact that it was the kids who needed help, it was hard to overlook the money and politics and elitism.

He decided he wanted to work with adults, even though he was not sure how that was going to look. He got married and left Toronto to live in a smaller, less expensive city, near Kingston, Ontario. He briefly found a temporary position helping to retrain workers who had been laid off. He found that he did indeed really enjoy working with adults and kept his eyes open for other opportunities.

His mother-in-law had done some part-time teaching at the Federal Women's Prison in Kingston and told Peter that the school within the prison was hiring. Peter had never thought about teaching in prison or ever thought he wanted to be part of a correctional facility. He thought, though, that the position might be an opportunity to use his women's studies background, work with adults, and work in a totally new setting. He was hired on a four-month contract and the staff was very happy to hire someone who had a background in women's studies. His women's studies background was viewed as an asset and an advantage. He began teaching science and math classes to inmates. Four years later, he is on staff full-time as an Educational Counselor. He loves his work. He believes he was meant to do this work:

It's great. It's the job I was meant to do. I can use my women's studies background everyday. The philosophy of women's correction in Canada is informed from a feminist perspective. Corrections itself isn't really a feminist organization, so in practice it's sometimes difficult to make the two work together; it doesn't always succeed but at least the philosophy is there.

At any given time in the federal prison there are about 160 women. As an educational counselor, Peter's work encompasses doing an assessment of a woman's previous work and educational history, and preparing them to obtain their high school diploma. He is also an informal mentor to his clients:

People have an illusion that it [prison] is a difficult place to teach. That is an illusion. It is probably the easiest place to teach. You have got motivated students who understand the importance of education. You're working with people who want to get the most out of a horrible situation. The women really want to graduate because they know when they leave they will have to be very focused on finding a job, reconnecting with family, etc. and won't have as much time to focus on themselves.

Peter finds his work deeply fulfilling at this point in his life. He has been actively taking on informal leadership roles through the correctional facility. He looks forward to working on ways to improve school classes and facilities in the prison and provide new opportunities for his clients. He and his team of teachers share a broad vision of improving the school. He says that he never thinks, "This is as good as the school can be. There's just so much more to do."

Besides working full time, he is also a very devoted parent. Being a "pro-feminist" parent is very important to him, and he credits his training in women's studies for shaping his understanding of how to raise a child in a gender-neutral way: "I'm shocked at how many parents do not question the gendering they do to their kids right at the beginning." Feminist community and political community is important to Peter and he feels that he was very naive in thinking that he would find these easily once he graduated. He thought it would be easy to sustain intense conversations in the workplace, but he felt really "cut off" from the intellectual engagement after graduation. He has actively sought community through his work in the Green Party. He also has developed community through recreational sports and his love of hockey. He tried a few leagues looking for great sports and deep discussions and was not able to find this combination easily. So, he rejoined a hockey group that he had played in during his days in Toronto and drives an hour each way to it on the weekends:

> I rejoined the Gay Men's Hockey League in Toronto. I found that it's a great league to play hockey in but also because it's a hockey league formed from a political sensibility (and it's very accepting of straight guys) that there are more political discussions and people. I'm more politically aligned with [people in this league] than in other hockey leagues.

Peter has found a place for authentic expression in his work, home, and social life.

Take Aways from Rachel, Kimberly, and Peter's Profiles

- Evaluate your ability to take thoughtful risks: Rachel, Kimberly, and Peter all took important risks in order to follow their inner vision.
- Don't be worried if you have several interests that do not all seem to fit together easily. They all had a cluster of eclectic interests that they nurtured through work, activism, and further schooling.
- Think about the kind of community you have now as an undergraduate and in what ways you will sustain it after graduation.

Synthesizers

Diana Rhodes: Arts Promoter, Coalition Builder, and Organizer with Lots of "Nevada-tude"

Cheryl met with Diana Rhodes in a local coffee shop near the campus of UNLV to discuss her career pathway, her journey into women's studies, her advice for women's and gender studies students, as well as her recent transition from being the Educational Outreach Program Director for the Women's Research Institute of Nevada (WRIN) to graduate student in the Public Policy Program at George Washington University with a concentration in Women's Studies. Since Cheryl has known Diana, she has witnessed Diana's ability to utilize her knowledge and skills from women's studies, along with the skills she has developed through her volunteer and unpaid labor in a variety of arenas: the arts and music scene, as a columnist for *Q Vegas*, as well as in grassroots activism and public policy advocacy. Diana Rhodes graduated from the University of Nevada, Las Vegas, in 2006 with a dual Bachelor's degree in Sociology and Women's Studies.

> I have to say that the feminist "click" happened when I was an undergrad. I had already declared my major in sociology because I had taken sociology courses at my high school in the community college program. I was eighteen and I wanted to save the world and I didn't know how. I got interested in gender stuff through sociology, but I was still quiet and taking classes. At that time, [and] during my entire life, I was really quiet. I didn't like giving presentations. I never did public speaking. I just went to class and left. I took a women's studies class taught by Dr. Anita Tijerina Revilla in the Women's Studies Department at UNLV. Her classes were taught as experiential learning. It was a small class, but we sat in a circle, which was really huge [to me]. We all had to make eye contact with one another and it was less than a lecture type of environment but more of creating a dialogue and making sure everyone's voices were heard. This was a situation that I had never been in before and I realized how huge it was for me to be in that environment. I know at that time it was like pulling teeth to actually get me to talk, but I started taking women's studies courses and I had this "click" of everything I thought I knew. It actually had a name, a word, and a theoretical framework, and I was able to articulate what I felt inside. If I was angry or upset I could know why something was wrong, if a dude said something to me, I would know how to articulate why I felt like it wasn't OK. That was around my sophomore year at UNLV and then I pretty much dove deep into women's studies after that. Soon after that time, I had decided that I identified as a feminist. I took as many WMST courses [as I could] and I became close with some of the women's studies professors who helped me process things in a way that none of my other professors in any other department had done.

However, while some students may have been satisfied with this experience alone, it was the spark that ignited Diana into activism and creating community dialogue. Diana has a gift for bringing people together in a group who may not have necessarily interacted independently, ranging from academics to service industry workers, to those who work and perform in the independent arts and music scene. Whether she organizes feminist discussion groups at coffee houses, recruits members for the local "Feminist Drinking Club" or the "Feminist Drinking Caucus" (at NWSA), or facilitates meetings for Stand OUT for Equality, the Vagina Monologues, or Ladyfest, Las Vegas, Diana often initiates these groups as an outlet for her own interests and to satisfy elements of her inter-sectional identity (arts promoter, feminist, Asian-American, and self-described nerd).

After her first women's studies class, she says:

> My mind was going crazy and I was still processing all this stuff and trying to form my identity and figure out my experiences. But then it was the summer and all that rich dialogue [from class], all my peers were no longer in my life because classes were over. I didn't know what to do about it and so I decided to start my own consciousness-raising group because I had just learned about consciousness raising.

Diana says she had a deep desire to:

> ... create a community of people that actually gave a shit about what we were talking about or cared about, because a lot of my friends didn't. So I started a weekly feminist discussion group at a local, independently owned 24-hour coffee shop in China Town, which was really important to me to actually bring other people into this world that not a lot of people go into.
>
> The group started at 9 pm so people who worked retail or whatever were able to come later. I had advertised it in *City Life* [a free local Las Vegas arts scene periodical] and I My-Spaced messaged a few of my friends and fellow students and it [the feminist discussion group] was basically to talk about whatever we wanted to talk about. I wanted to get like-minded people together because I didn't want that dialogue to end [during summer break from college]. I just needed to keep it going for my own purposes, but also to create a community. I had my academic side but I also had my scene of subculture, punk rock, and independent music. Most of the people who came to the discussion group, week after week, were not academics, not actually even students [but] they were kids who worked at a record store and saw a flyer, they were young 15-year-old riot girls who had just learned about "Bikini Kill" [a group widely considered to be the pioneer of the riot grrrl movement] or they were straight Summerlin [a suburb

of Las Vegas] couples who just saw it in *City Life* and who thought the group might be interesting and [they could visit] a new coffee shop they'd never heard of.

The coffee shop's all-night atmosphere contributed to lots of arguments, debates, and chain smoking. Diana calls this her 'bonding through vices' hypothesis. "Sometimes it would get heated between the academics versus the non-academics, and [during conversations] this whole kind of privilege and breaking down the privilege and class [structures] happened." The feminist group lasted a year and Diana had "created this weird community that I really appreciated, loved."

Her exploration of arts activism began almost immediately. Through a discussion initiated in her feminist discussion group, she helped organize Ladyfest Las Vegas, a two-day music and arts festival, highlighting women in the creative arts and held at UNLV in 2006.[41]

> I learned a lot of stuff through Ladyfest. I'd never organized something like that before. I had never organized anything that big. What peaked my interest in nonprofit organizations and consensus-based decision making was how this loosely based egalitarian group who was like "we don't do anything unless everybody agrees" shifts when you are throwing an event that costs money. There's a lot of logistical things that you need to think of. We had never done it so we had to figure it out as we went. It was a huge learning experience, lots of fights, a lot of dealing with having to become more bureaucratic, having to have consensus at meetings, making sure people followed through with what they said they were going to do.
>
> During the time of Ladyfest, I did a bunch of fundraiser shows. A lot of my activism started off in the arts, so I would bring bands in and perform in shows. Most of my shows were women and/or queer bands. When I started working with bar owners and people who ran venues, it was funny in that, in my entire life before that, ever since I was thirteen, I was going to shows and local music shows and my boyfriend was in a band, my best friends were all in bands, all my friends owned record stores or worked at record stores and so I knew a lot of people. But as soon as I started doing what my other friends, guy friends, were doing, a lot of them turned their back to me.

Diana was dismayed that there were several people who did not understand the need for or value of creating and organizing a women-oriented arts and music festival. That initial lack of support, however, did not stop her and her loosely based group from putting on several very successful Ladyfest events.

Through her position at WRIN (a statewide research and education institute for women in Nevada and located at UNLV), Diana honed the skill of fundraising and deepened her interest in connecting communities. In her position, she put into practice the skills of building community she had utilized informally for the past several years. Diana actively worked at creating and maintaining relationships with community organizations, government officials, and lobbyists: "I had to go to a lot of events, corporate stuff, and I learned how to navigate all these worlds through that position." She learned how to lobby for WRIN at the state legislature (in order to receive funding) and interacted with representatives' senior staff in Carson City (Nevada's capital). The staff at WRIN is small, so she actively cross-trained in supervising, management of research projects, and events planning. Diana's entry into this line of work echoes a theme that is shared by several women's and gender studies students. Women's studies (the classroom, the concepts, and the faculty) gave Diana the encouragement she needed to voice her opinions and feel confident in doing so. She was then able to take on paid and unpaid positions that required effective communication skills.

Diana brought her women's studies knowledge, her community leadership gained working with WRIN, and her interest in public policy to activism during the monumental Proposition 8 ruling in California in the fall of 2008.[42]

> By early 2008, I had worked with the students [at the Gay and Lesbian Center of Southern Nevada]. I tutored students and helped some of the students get their GED, and that was my only involvement with the Center and with the queer community in early 2008. But when Proposition 8 happened, there were so many people who were so upset and emotional, I had to get involved. Candice Nichols, the director of the Center, put out an email . . . and said, "People are pissed, people are sad, people want to do something and people are calling me." Eight of us . . . sat in the conference room at the Center and decided we should have a rally, for people to be able to express themselves about this event. We only had three days to do it because there were many national rallies going on in response to Prop 8. We did it. We had a lot

of speakers and we sent press releases out. [We were successful] because so many of us had so many skill sets and so many different populations that we could reach. There were approximately 2,000–3,000 people who showed up for the rally and it was amazing and beautiful. It wasn't something that necessarily happened all the time in Las Vegas. It was exciting to us and that group that organized that rally—the eight of us—decided to call ourselves "Stand OUT for Equality" and we became the policy wing group of the Gay and Lesbian Center. We started having other meetings and following up rallies or whatever the community wanted to do. [Eventually] we decided that we wanted to do a bill draft request for the legislature at the time, one for domestic partnerships, one for adding sexual orientation and anti-discrimination laws. Later, we took on an idea that an organization called "Nevada Women's Lobby" [developed], which is "Grassroots Lobby Days," where we get people to go up to Carson City and participate in a citizen's lobby event. We decided we were going to have "Equality Days," which would be a similar concept, but basically an LGBT citizen lobbying event in Carson City . . . which had never been done in Nevada.

The launch of Equality Days supported several legislative successes. The group realized that, working together with other groups across the state on different political issues, they ". . . could have some success together, [and] we decided to create a coalition which meets every month for strategic planning."

The skills that Diana had developed from her women's studies background, her honors thesis research (see below), her work experiences (at the Rape Crisis Center) allowed her to flourish in her role of Educational Program Director for New Leadership Nevada (administered through WRIN), a five-day residential leadership program for undergraduate women in the state of Nevada, which has been held since 2003. Cheryl first met Diana Rhodes at this forum. In 2007, both Diana and Cheryl served as "FIRS" or Faulty in Residence for New Leadership. Previously, Diana had attended New Leadership as a participant in 2006. After their initial bonding at New Leadership, Cheryl was able to see Diana's poster presentation of her honors thesis research "Deconstructing Beauty: Experiences of Asian American Women" at the 2007 NWSA annual conference. Later, Cheryl worked for Diana as a FIR and was also invited by Diana to present at New Leadership in 2009 and 2010 on values in leadership.

Diana says of her New Leadership experience:

New Leadership is where I learned a little bit about policy and
a lot about philanthropy. There was a panel on women and
philanthropy and I had never known what philanthropy actually
was. I had no idea there were rich people who want to give
organizations money just to do something because they're rich. I
had no clue that existed. A well-known female leader was on a
panel so I talked to her afterwards. I was talking about the
Ladyfest Music festival, what we were doing and she was like
"Great . . . send me the information. I'd like to learn more." So
I went home and sent her the press release that I had written,
and I sent her all that information and she says "GREAT . . .
where do I send the check to?"

This shocked her and opened her eyes up to new possibilities:

I had worked my ass off at all these shows and different venues
and bars, and I was fighting with bar owners when they ripped
off my bands and dealing with all this crap, and then some rich
lady sent me a check for $1000.00? So that's when I started to
learn about philanthropy and this nonprofit world, which was really
interesting.

While Diana credits her click moment to her experiences in her
women's studies classroom, looking back she also realizes the influence
of her family on her feminist consciousness. "My mom always raised me
as a strong, independent person."

So my worlds have been in arts and music, policy, and all around
gender issues. I wear a lot of hats: my gay hat and my APA [Asian
Pacific Islander American] hat, punk rock hat and my arts world
hat . . . I feel like I have a lot of worlds I am involved in. I think
a lot of it shows [in] my own identity. I will never say that the
activism that I do or anything that I do is completely altruistic. I
don't do anything altruistically. There are things that satisfy parts
of me, like with WRIN I got to work with more kinds of
professional work and be that professional person and with the
Stand OUT for Equality, I got to do more policy stuff and that
was like my LGBT world and with NAPAWF (which I was on
the board), which is the National Asian Pacific American Women's
Forum [see http://napawf.org/], that fulfilled a part of me that I

had not necessarily had as much access to before. Some of our politics weren't always the same among the women who were involved in the organization, but being in a room with only APA women, working on APA issues was not something I had done before. That's huge for me and a big deal.

Diana has now set her sights on finishing her Master's degree and is loving being immersed in the study of public policy.

Take Aways from Diana's Profile

- As Diana's profile indicates, while she had an inclination toward social activism, the women's studies classroom and environment allowed her to begin questioning the world around her and encouraged her to engage with her fellow classmates and her professors.
- Diana participated in a leadership program that honed her skills. If you have an opportunity to take part in a leadership program, you might want to consider it.

TIPS FROM DIANA

Besides taking women's and gender studies courses, Diana suggests taking a business course or a finance course: "If your activism leads you to nonprofit work, or any other type of work with a business or organization, you need to be able to develop and follow a budget."

As enriching as Diana's experience has been as a synthesizer, she offers some cautionary words of advice:

If you are going into this activist world in any way you must learn to say no to things. We want to do so many different things, so we'll say yes to conducting this workshop, and sitting on this committee, helping on that fundraiser etc. All of it is great experience, but you get burned out really easily and it can lead to . . . being bitter. Say yes to the things you truly and actually believe in because otherwise you will spread yourself too thin and get burnt out and the things that you care about, the things that you want to make a difference in suddenly become too much and you stop caring about them the way you used to. It stops being fun anymore and it becomes a chore. The passion dies once you become overwhelmed.

- Diana lived an understanding of intersectionality and created ways to work with multiple communities across a range of issues.

YOUR TURN: EXERCISES

Now that you have spent some time reading the profiles, we invite you to reflect on how they can serve you as you decide what's next after graduation. Here are some questions to get you started:

1. Whose story did you identify with? Why?

2. What resources are you developing that will help you?

3. Take a moment and revisit the role of mentors in the profiles. Some were cultivated, others stumbled upon. What's the role of professional mentors in your life now?

4. Looking at Rebecca and Matt's stories, do you have interests that are being expressed through internship programs or activism that you could pursue in a career?

6

TRANSFORM YOUR WORLD: PREPARING TO GRADUATE AND LIVING YOUR FEMINIST LIFE

For many students (and even more especially their parents and family members), graduation is often synonymous with getting a job. "What are you going to do with your degree?" is the common refrain heard at gatherings and events around graduation time. Although these occasions are intended to celebrate the rite of passage from college and university life, there is often a subtle undercurrent reminding the graduate of the responsibilities and duties that lie ahead. For students of women's and gender studies, the questions of "what will you do with that degree?" tend to come up not only around graduation, but repeatedly throughout your sojourn through your studies. As we have discussed repeatedly throughout this book, women's and gender studies is one of those majors that, while incredibly personally and professionally fulfilling, is difficult to "take home for the holidays." In other words, it is one of those areas of study often thought by friends and family to be of dubious value in the "real" world.

In this final chapter, we set the record straight and provide you with some insights and ideas about how best to live a feminist life while also making a living. You might have turned to this chapter because:

- You are a first-year student and you want to get an early idea about different employment opportunities if you choose women's and gender studies as a major or minor.

- You are a junior and are imagining how you will utilize your degree once you have graduated.
- You are working in a job you have had for a while and realize you have no real opportunity for growth or advancement.
- You might be in a job that you like, but your work environment is toxic. Or, you also might be reading this chapter to think about how to get different employment than what you have now while you are still in school.
- You may be underemployed and, while you like your job, you cannot feasibly survive on what you are paid.
- Last, you are interested in living your values shaped by your education in women's and gender studies after graduation.

Some of these concerns about "what's next" are common for all college graduates, but for women's and gender studies students there is the added concern of how to find meaningful employment and engage in activities that will enable you to live out your feminist principles. Women's and gender studies students face the challenge of incorporating newly minted ideas and values into a world of commercial employment opportunities. Rather than view this as a problem or a reason not to pursue a major, minor, or concentration in women's and gender studies, we suggest that finding employment *and* living a feminist life is one of the skills you will gain from pursuing study in this area. Establishing a meaningful and financially stable life is one of the biggest challenges we all face in a contemporary capitalist society. Most people settle for one or the other, often without even knowing why. Our promise throughout this book is that women's and gender studies provides you with the tools for recognizing this social dilemma and making informed choices about how best to compose a life that transcends these tensions. In the following sections we offer some thoughts and tips about how to accomplish this.

Before we proceed, we should also note that, historically, women have faced additional challenges when entering the workforce. These challenges have been variously referred to as the "second shift," etc. On the issue of taking responsibility for yourself, Adrienne Rich in "Claiming an Education," an essay that has been a touchstone throughout the book, discusses how through socialization women (in particular) are expected to put their needs and desires after their relationships and responsibilities to others:

Responsibility to yourself means refusing to let others do your thinking, talking, and naming for you, it means learning to respect and use your own brains and instincts . . . responsibility to yourself means that you don't fall for shallow and easy solutions . . . you refuse to sell your talents and aspirations short . . . it means that we insist on a life of meaningful work, insist that work be as meaningful as love, and friendship in our lives.

(Rich 1979: 26)

The basic dilemma is that, as a society, we have never really resolved the question of who or what should be responsible for the hidden work that women traditionally take care of (childcare, house care, elderly care, etc.). Accordingly, when women enter the workforce, they are frequently subjected to feelings of guilt (both their own and from others) about responsibilities beyond their own employment and life fulfillment. Most women experience this at some point or another during their professional lives. As you read through this material, we encourage you to remember that one of the greatest assets of a degree in women's and gender studies is that you have the tools for thinking critically about this socially imposed sense of responsibility.

Sometimes when we are searching for our professional lives, we listen to others rather than ourselves, we narrow our vision of ourselves due to fear of economic or family pressures, and/or we look to conventional methods for looking for jobs, because it seems easier or more accepted rather than utilizing our critical thinking skills and thinking outside the norm for career opportunities. We encourage you to take responsibility for yourself in setting aside time to think about your long-term goals about what you would really most like to experience or accomplish as part of the working world.

We think it is important for women's studies graduates to take the very critical thinking and creative skills that are so necessary in this interdisciplinary field of study and apply them to finding or creating job opportunities. This chapter focuses on supporting students to think creatively and broadly when assessing their options for pursuing their next employment, career, and/or educational pathways. The other aim of this chapter is to stimulate your thinking about what broader resources you can cultivate to continue lifelong learning and leadership after you obtain your degree. We want to encourage you no matter where you are in your academic career to take ownership and responsibility for pursuing your interests.

Minimally, we hope you will remember—as the airlines always remind us in their message that we must put on our own air mask before helping others—that in order to transform the world, you must first respect the process of taking care of and transforming yourself.

Considering Your Desires, Skills, and Goals

Looking for a new or different job allows a person to step outside their current situation and imagine original possibilities for personal and intellectual growth. Taking an alternative career path also allows for the development of new social networks and the potential for an increase in income. Conversely, looking for a new job makes one really assess one's toolkit, those resources that need to be developed. It also takes time, patience, and some resources.

Many students find entering the professional job market to be daunting, but just like any other project it is actually quite manageable through time management and organization. In fact, most of us have been employed in one way or another before we first entered the "formal" job market.

In this section we would like you to think about how to align what you care about, hope to accomplish in the workplace, and what you can do. As we discussed in Chapter Four, a skill set that women's and gender studies majors possess is the ability to do research and critically assess complex social issues. We recommend that you pair these skills with your own talents and through creative thinking adjust them to what works best for you. In Chapter Four we explored some of the unique skills and perspectives you, as a women's and gender studies graduate, possess. While this book specifically addresses the knowledge, talents, and characteristics women's and gender studies graduates possess, we recommend spending a little time reflecting on yourself by thinking critically about what skills set you apart from other recent graduates entering the job market for the first time.

There are many publications available in the mass market that may be useful for you in researching career pathways. Two recent publications that we believe are extremely helpful and useful include: Richard N. Bolles' updated (2010) *What Color is Your Parachute? 2010. A Practical Manual for Job-Hunters and Career Changers* and Katharine Brooks' (2009) *You Majored in What? Mapping your Path from Chaos to Career.* Bolles' text is the classic reference for job searchers. Brooks' text stands out as a paradigmatic shift. Her book argues for the shift from a deficit model to one of strengths and experiences in searching for employment and assessing educational experiences.

What Color is Your Parachute? is a standard guide about finding a fulfilling career and is an extremely accessible and easy-to-read resource chock full of helpful advice and development activities. Cheryl appreciates the author's guiding idea that job seekers need hope and tools for developing their own ideas for their professional lives. Bolles also addresses job seekers' positionality and how who we are (age, race or ethnicity, class background) may impact our job search, and he acknowledges social inequalities in the marketplace. Yet Bolles also encourages readers to focus less on positionalities as factors in limiting your ability to get hired. Instead, Bolles recommends developing a list of transferable/functional skills that you possess and promoting these to potential employers. His book uses an inspirational message to convey his concerns.

Another resource that you may want to check out is Brooks' *You Majored in What? Mapping your Path from Chaos to Career* (2009). Brooks, who is the director of the Liberal Arts Career Services at the University of Texas, Austin, challenges traditional ideas that one's major has a linear relationship to the occupation or field one will obtain work in. Utilizing her degree in Educational Psychology, Brooks maintains that vocational researchers of the early twentieth century sought methods to link individual skills, interests, and talents with possible occupations. They developed a variety of tests and measures for these purposes, which reflected the epistemology and social context of the time—including institutional access and the power structure of academia. As women's and gender studies students know, theories for explaining the world change over time. In order to address the needs of students completing their education in the twenty-first century, Brooks' text utilizes a more contemporary theory to assist students in assessing their skills and talents: chaos theory. A major idea within chaos theory is the so called "butterfly effect." The butterfly effect contends that seemingly unrelated events can produce a complex outcome affected by often unrelated but interconnected variables. Brooks believes that your career path can be analyzed in much the same way complex mathematical formulas or weather events can be (2009: 11).

As with *What Color is Your Parachute?*, *You Majored in What?* offers
readers exercises and activities in order to assess individual talents,
interests, and skills. Cheryl likes that the book gives space for readers to
assess their talents. Brooks also has readers consider areas or qualities,
in which they already are strong or well developed, that can be marketed
to employers. Brooks' examples tend to reflect traditional liberal arts
majors (e.g. English, Anthropology, History), but women's and gender
studies majors/minors can certainly draw a connection between women's
and gender studies and liberal arts.

Now that you have located some resources, the ones we suggest as well
as others, you may want to take some time assessing what your overall
goals are. Dr. Robert Pleasants, whom you met in Chapter One, provides
a powerful way for you to reflect on how to approach important questions
of "What's next for me?":

> Women's Studies departments are often safe spaces for personal
> exploration, for political awareness, and for figuring out an exciting
> nexus between the two. But what happens after graduation, when
> majors emerge from the college bubble and reenter the real world?
> For many, the prospect is intimidating: it can be difficult to sustain
> feminist awareness and find fulfilling employment. In helping my
> students navigate this transition, I encourage them to reflect—
> starting with themselves and working outward. Specifically, I ask
> my students four simple questions when they graduate:
>
> 1. Who do you want to be? If you're graduating, take some
> time to ask yourself this important question. Chances are, you
> have probably asked it dozens of times during the last four years,
> likely with dozens of answers. But graduation can offer a unique
> opportunity for determining who you want to be for the rest of
> your life. Depending on where you move or what you do after
> graduation, you could face a brand new beginning, which can be
> exciting, terrifying, and confusing all at once. And if you're a
> feminist in a non-feminist world, it can be particularly tough. To
> hold on to what you have learned and live up to your ideals can
> take effort, but the rewards are worth it. If you want to be a
> feminist, I encourage you to commit and keep seeking out feminist
> knowledge. But you can't sustain this commitment alone, which
> brings me to my next question:
>
> 2. Who do you want to be *with*? The first years after college
> are an interesting time of re-evaluating friendships and forming
> new ones, so what better opportunity to surround yourself with

people who are interested in gender and social justice issues? I shudder to think who I would be if I hadn't begun a relationship (literally on graduation day) with a feminist woman. We've been together ever since. An important part of our relationship has always been challenging ourselves, inspiring one another, and holding each other accountable. I encourage you to find people you like and who are like you, but also seek out people who are different in ways that challenge you. Find people who *inspire* you.

3. What will you do? The previous question might leave you wondering, *How do I meet people who care as much as I do about gender equality?* Simple: volunteer. There are feminist organizations almost everywhere in need of volunteers. In addition to doing rich, fulfilling work at these organizations, I guarantee you'll have fun and meet new friends. Oftentimes, the organizations with the most intense training can provide the most enlightening and fulfilling experiences, giving you a perspective you simply can't get in a classroom. Volunteering is also a great way to explore career options if you're still wondering what you want to do with your life.

4. How can you change the world? Yes, I know. This is the big, tough question. In addition to the ideas listed above, there are ways to work for social change by looking at the bigger picture. You can find a career at a grass-roots feminist organization, work at a local women's center, or work or volunteer at an organization focused specifically on societal-level women's rights—NOW, Ipas, National Abortion Rights Action League (NARAL), Amnesty International are just a few of the more prominent organizations that come to mind. Or if you decide on graduate school, you can study gender issues and advocate for equity in almost any discipline. Even if your career itself isn't explicitly feminist, any of the actions listed in the questions contribute to a better society, because all social change begins with individuals. What will your role be?

Researching Employment Opportunities

When thinking about what employment opportunities are out there, we encourage you to think broadly. We believe that our research demonstrates that women's and gender studies graduates have many options for finding fulfilling employment. It is important to be creative in thinking about how to make a living, and to realize that often it is by trial and error that we learn how to apply our inner strengths and external

LABOR MARKET FACTS

According to the US Department of Labor, of the 3.2 million youth who graduated from high school from October 2007 to October 2008, 2.2 million (68.6 percent) attended college in the fall of 2008. While more women are enrolled in college than men in the US (71.5 percent for young women and 65.9 percent for young men), women also have higher rates of participation in the labor force while seeking their degrees (46.1 percent) than for their male counterparts (36.0 percent). While there are definite gender differences in the working world, your work status may also reflect your social class. Among recent high school graduates enrolled in college in the fall of 2008, 93.2 percent were full-time students. The labor force participation rate was 38.5 percent for full-time students and 75.9 percent for part-time students. About six in ten recent high school graduates who were enrolled in college attended four-year institutions. Of these students, 31.0 percent participated in the labor force, while 55.9 percent of recent graduates enrolled in two-year colleges were in the labor force. As community colleges continue to offer educational pathways to people who have been either traditionally underrepresented or lacked access to higher education, it is possible that workplace participation during a degree is higher at a two-year versus a four-year institution (US Dept. of Labor 2009).

skills in the workplace. We think the journey of how to apply your women's studies training in the workplace is interesting and unique. The temptation when seeking employment is to think of shooting an arrow out toward one's dream position. And sometimes graduates do find the perfect position their first time out. For most, however, finding out what one enjoys doing and is good at is more of a process of knocking on doors, establishing relationships, and being flexible and creative in employing self-assessment tools rather than a one-time experience.

Women's and gender studies students work in a variety of fields and occupations. According to Silius (2005), the women's studies graduates who participated in the project Employment and Women's Studies: The Impact of Women's Studies Training on Women's Employment in Europe (EWSI), who came from nine countries (Finland, France, Germany, Hungary, Italy, the Netherlands, Slovenia, Spain, and the United Kingdom) were predominately employed in five employment sectors: research and education, government, journalism and media, health and human services, and diversity/equal opportunity initiatives (2005: 118). Yet there are women's and gender studies graduates, as indicated from our survey, who have a variety of different career aspirations and pathways.

There are many "worlds," so to speak, of employment. Below, we list brief descriptions of the several categories. We then focus on a few of these worlds in depth. As you do research you will find what careers provide entry-level positions and which would require additional training, certification, or degrees. Keep in mind that this list is *not* exhaustive!

The Corporate World

Working in the corporate world includes entry-level and management positions in a small or large company that makes and sells goods or services designed to produce a profit for shareholders.

The Health and Medical World

Positions in medicine and health include becoming a doctor, physician's assistant, nurse (e.g. registered nurse, nurse's aid, etc.). Dietician and sports medic are also possible careers in this field. There are also a variety of medical administrative positions in clinics and hospitals available (e.g. medical informatics technician, medical assistant). The rise of integrative medicine has also created several positions under the label of "alternative health practitioner" including massage therapist, acupuncturist, biofeedback specialist, and homeopath. One should also not forget about veterinarian and veterinarian assistant positions.

The Legal World

There are a variety of positions in the legal field including: lawyer, legal assistant, stenographer, legal secretaries, mediators, consultants, and judges.

The Science and Technology World

Careers that can be categorized through science and technology are numerous. This world includes computer software engineers (these are the people who often create very popular "apps"). Computer systems analysts help businesses stay on the cutting edge of technological development.

The researching, tracking, and storing of information is part of the skill set someone uses when they work with information technology.

Depending on your interest in information technology, you could find yourself working on issues of bioinformatics in the field of medicine or using information technology in tracking climate change.

The Government and Politics World

Positions in the world of government and politics include working for federal, state, local/legislative, executive agency, and local councils. A career in this world could encompass international work in diplomacy, nongovernmental organizations (NGOs), and foreign service. These positions can vary from working as an assistant town manager to grant-writing for the US Agency for International Development (USAID).

The Nonprofit World

The nonprofit world—as with the corporate world—is a career world that people often make assumptions about. Nonprofits can be categorized in a broad range of organizations, from churches to foundations (e.g. the Kellogg Foundation, the Bill and Melinda Gates Foundation) to arts organizations. Although we stratify academe and government work, they could also fall into this category. The engine that drives the mission of nonprofits usually relates to serving a specific community or cluster of interests rather than a community of shareholders. Despite what you might have heard, the nonprofit world can often pay salaries for employees close to what private firms can pay, especially beyond entry-level positions. Positions in this world include utilizing the specialized skills of musicians and artists, as well as employees who perform functions such as fund-raising, research, proposal writing, finance, community outreach, website development, marketing, and accounting.

The Journalism/News Media/New Media Online World

Positions in this world can include blogging for a company, working as a radio producer, or working as a proofreader for a book publishing company.

The Small Business/Entrepreneurial World

An entrepreneur is someone who creates a business that they own. A small business can be a "brick and mortar" store or be run online from the comfort of one's own home.

The Academic World

Positions in the academic world include teaching at the K–12 (public or private school) or college level. There are numerous administrative positions in the academic world including in admissions and enrollment, career services, student affairs, and women's services.

The Corporate World—In-depth

There were a number of graduates who worked in "corporate America" in their careers. A standard definition of a corporation is that it is a legal entity of structure created and empowered through laws of a state. Corporations typically have a group of people called shareholders who benefit directly from the success of a corporation's actions. A corporation has rights and privileges that are separate from its members—shareholders and founders of the company. Here we use "corporation" to refer to large-scale businesses.

Corporate America means different things to different people. It can conjure up images of complex global entities or a brutish work environment that includes high competition and eighty-hour work weeks. Images are different from reality and you probably don't want to write off this "world" without a fair shake. Working in corporations can be meaningful, financially remunerative, include a wide variety of benefits and/or incentives, and help you develop a broad range of skills. Corporations come in a wide variety of sizes, from those that employ over 100,000 people inside the US (e.g. Starbucks Coffee) to those that employ 8,000 people in the US (e.g. Qualcomm, a company specializing in technology innovation).

The environment for women and underrepresented groups in corporate America has been slowly changing. As corporations see themselves vying for capable and desirable workers, they have been pushed (through activism by workers) to think about creating an environment that supports and values diversity, women's experiences in the workplace, and health and wellness issues. You may be attracted to a corporate environment for these reasons and because you are interested in the services and products that a company provides to the general public. Our graduates have worked in corporate America in a wide variety of positions including: marketing director, research and design staff, consultant, and manager of reporting and analytics for a sales team. We also have seen that, in several cases,

SPOTLIGHT: JENNIFER PRITCHETT AND THE MAKING OF THE SMITTEN KITTEN

The Smitten Kitten, a feminist sex-toy store based in Minneapolis, is one example of how women's and gender studies students have become entrepreneurs. According to Jennifer Pritchett, the idea of the store resulted from a combination of factors: an unfulfilling work experience exacerbated by a hostile work environment in a university student services office, knowledge gained from courses (such as ones on collective action, feminist research, and feminist theory), and experience working in a variety of university offices and organizations during undergraduate and graduate school (e.g. Minnesota State University, Mankato's LGBT Center & Women's Center).

The Smitten Kitten was conceived and eventually opened as a feminist-oriented sex-toy store in 2003. The store advocates a sex-positive approach, as well as raising awareness about sexual health and environment, as evidenced through their Campaign Against Toxic Toys (CATT). Currently, the Smitten Kitten employs both full- and part-time workers, has physical locations in both Minneapolis and Denver, and also has a strong presence on the web (see www.smittenkittenonline.com/).

Besides serving the sexual health needs of its clients, the Smitten Kitten also gives back to the community through its support of LGBT youth programs and intimate partner violence prevention and care efforts, as well as being the sponsor of a Gender and Women's Studies scholarship at MSU Mankato. While the end result of this feminist-inspired business relationship is a success, Jennifer Pritchett is quite open about the challenges she and the business faced prior to opening. These ranged from long hours, raising funds for start-up costs and working with the available resources, negotiating with distributors, little-to-no real income for a few years, as well as some resistance from the community, which was concerned about sexually oriented businesses. An important insight that Jennifer Pritchett has for feminist entrepreneurs is to follow:

> . . . a "one step at a time" approach . . . don't dream up the perfect business, just go with what you have. I started with $33,000 initially and went from there. Rather than dream an amount, start with what you have . . . and go from there.

Jennifer also believes her experience as a graduate assistant gave her applied and practical experience and knowledge that she could translate into her business: "I learned to make do when you don't have that much in terms of resources . . . making do with what you have and utilizing your resourcefulness, it is women's work." Jennifer's applied work experiences have also influenced her decisions in regards to hiring practices: "As a person who hires folks with WMST degrees, specifically what you do (and have done) makes a difference." Jennifer also believes in the importance of mentoring. A major influence on her, besides Deirdre Rosenfeld, Associate Dean of Students for Gustavus Adolphus College (and former director of MSU's Women's Center), was Megan Hooglan, the owner of Cactus Tattoo in Mankato, Minnesota, a successful woman working in a male dominated field (see www.cactustattoo.com/cactustattoo.html). Not only has Jennifer benefitted from mentoring, but she believes reciprocity is an important aspect of feminist mentoring: "Part of the mission of the store is to help people start feminist businesses." In fact, Jennifer has welcomed the opportunity to be available as feminist advisor/feminist consultant:

> I work from a philosophy of abundance. The Smitten Kitten makes new clientele as we go. I give advice and welcome people to call and ask questions. It can be hard to be taken seriously, especially as a young woman in business. I always take people seriously and am always willing to help as part of my feminist mission.

The Smitten Kitten is but one model of entrepreneurship for women's and gender studies students. If you produce products, there are a host of different physical and virtual areas in which you can advertise and sell your goods or services. You might also consider becoming an independent contractor. However you decide to pursue your goals, we recommend seeking assistance and guidance with representatives at organizations that support women-owned businesses, including The National Association of Women Business Owners (for local chapters see www.nawbo.org/) and The US Small Business Administration, which sponsors a national network of Women's Business Centers (for local chapters see www.sba.gov/idc/groups/public/documents/sba_program_office/sba_ro_do_wbc.pdf?cm_sp=ExternalLink-_-Federal-_-SBA). These organizations can illuminate some of the opportunities for being an independent business owner, helping you design a business plan as well as helping with tax and legal considerations.

women's and gender studies students have found themselves in corporate environments in positions that support creating a more inclusive and diverse workplace, including those that involve human resources. If you do find a position in a company and would like to continue to grow there, we highly recommend that you find on-the-job mentors to help you successfully advance in your career.

 ## FOR YOUR LIBRARY

Trudy Bourgeois. (2007). *Her Corner Office: A Guide to Help Women Find a Place and a Voice in Corporate America.* 2nd edn. Dallas: Brown Books.

Jessica Faye Carter. (2007). *Double Outsiders: How Women of Color Can Succeed in Corporate America.* St Paul, MN: JIST Books.

The Small Business/Entrepreneur World—In-depth

Have you ever dreamed of running your own business? Starting or owning a business is a dream for many individuals. Whether one is challenged by the constraints of a structured, formalized workplace, intrigued by the possibility of "giving birth" to an opportunity, or is encouraged to start a business by friends or family, entrepreneurship has been a growing trend, not only in the United States but throughout the world. According to the Business and Professional Women's Foundation, in 2004 there were 10.6 million privately held, women-owned businesses, 3.4 million businesses were owned jointly by men and women, and women of color owned 1.2 million businesses in the United States (Business and Professional Women's Foundation 2007).[43] We think women's studies helps prepare graduates to work for themselves—at some point in their lives—given the confidence, support, mentoring, and creativity that the training fosters.

In the Spotlight on page 228, we profile how a former women's and gender studies student went into business for herself.

The Academic World—In-depth

For many of us, we like college so much we never want to leave the environment. You may choose to continue your education with a Master's Degree, Ph.D., JD, or some other type of professional degree. If you are considering graduate school, discussing the process with a mentor will be very helpful, especially if that mentor has a degree in the field that you wish to explore.

For others, you may like the college environment, but want to work with students in another way outside of the formal classroom. For example, if you have a Bachelor's degree and some experience working for different on-campus organizations or offices, you may want to consider a career as a professional staff member for a college or university. You may want to explore HigherEdJobs.com and look at some of the positions available. For example, many universities have academic advising positions available. In this job, your experience successfully navigating your own process can be a source of information (and inspiration) for others. Plus, your life experiences may come in handy for these positions. For example, if the advising position targets international students, your double major in

Women's Studies and Slavic Studies may be extremely useful for a college that does a lot of recruiting in Eastern Europe. Plus, if you are an international student yourself, you may know the process for securing and maintaining your student visa and can advise other international students about acclimating to life in an American context. In addition, as this is a university setting, your potential employer may be familiar with women's and gender studies and the skills that this major brings to their position. There are many areas in which you may consider looking for a campus position that may welcome a background in women's and gender studies, including admissions and/or enrollment, adult and/or continuing education, alumni relations, assessment/accreditation/compliance, athletics, bursar and student accounts, business and financial management, campus safety and police, career counseling, placement, conference and events administration, development and fund raising, disability services, women's centers, LGBT offices, extension and outreach, human resources, and institutional research and planning (see www.higheredjobs.com/admin/).

Besides allowing you to remain a perpetual student who can take classes at a reduced rate, the benefit of working on a college campus includes decent pay, some built-in perks (such as tuition reimbursement), health benefits, and other workplace protections (such as representation by a union for some positions).

Job Protections: Know Your Rights/Workplace Issues

One of the areas that feminism has been associated with publicly is that of workplace justice, economic equality, and work/home balance issues. As you think about current and future employment it is important that you know what your rights are in the workplace. In *Taking on the Big Boys: or Why Feminism is Good for Families, Business, and the Nation* (2007), Ellen Bravo, the director of the film *9 to 5*, discusses a host of issues in which feminism is intricately involved in both our public and private lives. From pay equality and access to gender-dominated occupations, to part-time and temporary employment, Bravo reminds gender and women's studies students of two major areas in which we need to remain aware and vigilant while on the job: sexual harassment and the right to organize. Not only do these issues affect us personally—as many readers may be survivors of workplace harassment or may be scared to report labor violations due to fear of termination—but these issues collectively allow larger systems of oppression to continue.

Sexual Harassment

According to federal statutes, sexual harassment is defined as:

> ... unwelcome sexual advances, requests for sexual favors, and other verbal and physical conduct of a sexual nature will constitute harassment when: submission to such conduct is made either explicitly or implicitly a term or conditions of a person's employment; submission to or rejection of such conduct by an individual is used as a basis for academic or employment decisions affecting that individual; such conduct has the purpose or effect of unreasonably interfering with an individual's academic or work performance or creating an intimidating, hostile, or offensive academic or work environment.
> (Federal Register 74,677, November 10, 1980, codified in 29 Code of Federal Regulations (CFR) Section 1604.11s)

Unfortunately, we may have been exposed to these systems of oppression throughout our educational career. Some of the major findings of the 2006 AAUW Report: *Drawing the Line: Sexual Harassment on Campus* include:

- Sexual harassment is common on college campuses and is most common at large universities, four-year institutions, and private colleges.
- Men and women are equally likely to be harassed, but in different ways with different responses. Female students are more likely to be the target of sexual jokes, comments, gestures, or looks. Male students are more likely to be called gay or a homophobic name.
- Lesbian, gay, bisexual, and transgender are more likely to be harassed.
- Different racial and ethnic groups experience sexual harassment in similar, but not identical ways.
- Men are more likely than women to harass. Both male and female students are more likely to be harassed by a man than a woman.
- For many students, sexual harassment is a normal part of college life.

- For many students, their attitude about their college experience is negatively affected by the harassment.
- Experiences in college shape lifelong behaviors and attitudes that are continued in the workplace and larger society.
- Sexual harassment will continue as long as it is not taken seriously.

This report suggested that while sexual harassment may have been learned and perpetuated throughout our educational experiences, it is little wonder then that sexual harassment continues into other institutional settings, such as the military, the workplace, and religious institutions. As with myths about gender and women's studies, many myths exist about sexual harassment. According to Bravo (2007: 101), they include:

- Sexual harassment is a thing of the past.
- Sexual harassment is subjective.
- Often, sexual harassment is trivialized as an issue of taste or of someone "not being able to take a joke" rather than behavior of a sexual nature at school [or] at work that is unwanted, unwarranted, offensive, creates a hostile or uncomfortable work environment and makes it difficult for employees to effectively do their work.

Unions

As for labor organization and unionizing, there are a lot of myths and stereotypes that Bravo believes exist about workplace justice causes and organizations. You and your family may have already participated in an organized labor environment, or you may be interested but have not yet had the opportunity to join. Conversely, you may have been approached and decided not to join a union at your current job due to costs, questions about union benefits and participation, or for other reasons. While union organization has illuminated class issues across the globe, the role and impact of women and minorities in demanding access to better wages and safe, non-exploitative workplaces is often minimized. For example, Bravo points out how black laundresses organized a union in 1866 in Jackson, Mississippi, for better wages shortly after emancipation. She also discusses how issues of maternity leave benefits and childcare resources were voiced for working women by unions (the AFL and CIO) decades before the US enacted federal policies on these matters. Currently, recent workplace justice activism has in large part been enacted around issues ranging from the informal economy, home healthcare, welfare and workfare, and female immigrants (Cobble 2007). As gender and women's studies practitioners, issues of gender, race/ethnicity, sexuality, age, and ability are at the very core of our economic lives as well as for those who champion better working/living conditions. In addition, many women's and gender students apply their women's studies degree working for unions and for other local, state, and federal organizations that ensure worker safety and protections. Some of the myths that are often associated with collective action and worker activism include:

- Unions are not for women and minorities.
- Union membership takes worker's wages rather than fighting for them.
- Unions are obsolete in current professionalized business environments.
- Unions limit businesses' ability to be competitive and offer low prices for customers.
- Union membership has been decreasing due to rejection from workers.

Preparing: Getting the Help You Need

So now that you have seen and considered some pathways for employment and have raised your awareness about your rights in the workplace, it's time to talk about preparing to meet the workplace in a competent way. We think preparing for the workplace (or moving to another position) involves two key actions. The first is recognizing your skills. The second set of actions is to learn skills that will create a good fit for the workplace. You started this process in Chapter Four, and here we make additional suggestions in each of these areas. And finally, we suggest that you mobilize helpers in this process. In setting the groundwork for preparing for employment, it is important to gather helpers along the way. People that you might consider asking for help and support include mentors, advisors in formal academic advising programs, internship supervisors, co-workers, and peers. If you are actively involved in a community organization, you may be able to ask the members for help. We revisit the role of mentors as begun in Chapter Two.

Recognizing and Assessing Your Skills

You will need to begin the process of recognizing and accessing your skills. Some women's and gender studies departments and programs provide specific career and job fair events during the semester. This is an excellent place to network and gain professionalization skills.

A natural place to seek help after checking with your program is your college or university career services office. Your career services office can be an incredible resource for helping you with the basics of navigating online resources, developing resumes, and connecting you to alumni who may be interested in assisting you. Many universities (or the larger educational systems they are organized and administered under) pay for e-folio resources (to develop online resumes, portfolios, etc.) so that you can use this long after you graduate.

Your career services office may direct you to professional association websites to check for information on employment in the field. They may also direct you to blogs, depending on your interest. There are blogs for medical students, nursing students, law students, non-traditional students, and many more—many universities have their own student blogs set up. You can search through Blogfinders.com to find out what others are saying about their experiences in a particular profession.

Your career services office may also offer coaching services that provide a one-on-one connection. A coach may help you review your strengths and skills, offer feedback on goals, and help you develop an individual plan for meeting your goals. Coaching may be useful for students who already have professional jobs or are making major job changes.

More than 40 percent of survey participants primarily utilized their career services office to help them with employment options. This was a good first step for many women's and gender studies graduates. However, for a majority of students, they needed to think "outside the box" in applying and looking for jobs.

Understanding Employment Tests, Career Assessment, Aptitude, and Personality Tests

We live in a culture where we take fun career aptitude tests all the time online. You've probably been tempted more than once to find out what kind of "rock star" you are on Facebook. There are a number of career assessments and aptitude tests that you may want to investigate to see what types of jobs are out there, and which ones may match your personality type, your skills, and/or your interests.

According to Susan Doyle (2010) (Doyle is also author of the 2009 *Internet Your Way to a New Job: How to Really Find a Job On-line* and 2006 About.com's *Guide to Job Searching*), you should:

> . . . spend some time taking a career test or two, conduct a career assessment, review career options and consider how they may fit with your personality. Evaluating your goals and life style can provide insight into what types of jobs you are best suited for. You may also get some information on career options that you hadn't even thought of before. Also some of the tests are actually fun to take. If nothing else, you will gain information on potential careers that you can explore to see if they really are a good fit.

The level of complexity, engagement, and cost of the tests ranges from free and easy (with little to no time commitments) to more difficult. Some tests are free and others require a fee for use. You can take many of these tests online or you might be able to utilize your campus office of career services for access to these tests.

Some tests that Doyle suggests you may want to explore include: Myers-Briggs (MBTI)®, Career Key®, Keirsey Temperament Sorter®, Discover your Perfect Career Quiz®, and the Princeton Review Career Quiz®. The first three fee-based instruments ask questions to gain an idea of your personality type or temperament and may link these to characteristics of others in certain occupations. The last two quizzes assess the answers you provide to their questionnaires and generate the best career path for you based on their findings.

Just remember, even though these personality assessments and career quizzes may be well regarded (that is, seen as being methodologically sound), you should not take their findings as absolute. These instruments are meant to be guides in your career-seeking process and may provide some further awareness of who you are and in what situations you thrive best.

Increasingly, employers use a variety of employment tests either as part of a pre-screening process or to examine a sense of fit between the candidate and the position. Some of these tests directly assess your potential fit with the job (including measures to predict your performance and your longevity) and your personality, whereas others examine your cognitive abilities, emotional intelligence, your legal and financial background, or your health (physical, mental, substance-use history, etc.) (Doyle 2010). While the scope of questions that you may be asked may seem intrusive or excessive (harder than the GRE®, LSAT®, MCAT®) these tests are generally accepted as long as they are properly administered in a non-discriminatory way. Moreover, after you land your position, you may find yourself being asked to take a test for consideration of advancing to a new position. Employment tests are also used in some employment situations to assess leadership potential. If you find yourself in an applicant pool in which you are asked to take one (or all) of these types of tests even before being considered for a position, you must weigh the emotional, mental, legal, and time costs of these tests. While some tests may be good indicators that an organization or business wants to match the talents and personalities of their workers with the demands of the job and the work environment, other pre/post employment screening practices may seem unnecessary and conflict with your beliefs. They might also be a strong indicator of an environment with which you may ultimately be uncomfortable. Because of this, you may want to discuss these issues with current employees, your career advising center, your professors, and your peers.

Cheryl says:

> One of the best opportunities I had was to take the Strength Finders® personality assessment while I was enrolled in a Women's Leadership Institute offered by the Mankato YWCA. This test was different from others. Rather than pointing out weaknesses it analyzes strengths and gives you an idea of what you can bring to an organization. Other tests such as the Myers Briggs can also give you some personal insight into your inner motivations as well as the types of environments and management styles that work best for you. This self-knowledge and the ability to convey this to employers will set you apart from other applicants in the competitive job market.
>
> When I applied for my current position, I experienced the world of pre-employment screening tests. When I first received the phone call from Human Resources that I had been selected to continue in the search process, I was ecstatic. Because I had been working in higher education for almost ten years at that point, I expected a series of conversational interviews with supervisors and HR staff. Instead, I was informed that I would be taking a

standardized test with other applicants and that my score on the test would determine whether or not I would be selected for a formal interview. Walking into the testing room, I was reminded of my anxiety when I took standardized tests to evaluate my aptitude as part of the process for applying to undergraduate and graduate degree programs (SAT®, ACT®, GRE®). The CPS Human Resources Professional and Paraprofessional Entry Level Analyst exam is a time-limited test divided up into four sections: reasoning/analytical ability, math and statistics knowledge, written communication, and interpersonal skills. Going into the test, I felt fairly confident of my knowledge in these areas. Afterward, I was amazed that I made it into interview group due to my rather poor performance in the math and statistics section. I also wished I would have had some time to prepare for the exam rather than take it cold. After I was hired, I was required to take some additional tests such as medical screening (tuberculosis tests) and an assessment of my general medical health to secure my employment.

For more information on the test Cheryl was given, see www.cps.ca.gov/ExaminationServices/TestRental/Professional/pp_EntryAnalyst.asp.

Lessons from Cheryl's Experience

If you are selected to interview for a job, ask if there are any pre-employment tests required. Your Human Resources liaison might be able to give you the name of the exam. If so, see if there are any study guides or practice tests available online or in your local public library or campus career services office.

Aptitude and pre-employment screening tests are only one part of the screening process. Remember to take care of yourself and mentally, physically, and emotionally prepare for the interview. As women's and gender studies students are often asked to utilize their critical thinking skills in the classroom, be prepared to apply your knowledge in an interview situation. You may be interviewed by a hiring committee, which means that you need to focus, adequately answer multiple questions, and hopefully remember the names of the committee members. Or you may have a one-on-one interview. Either way, you may want to practice and pre-script answers to possible questions, pace yourself, and remember that you have practiced many of these skills in the classroom.

Learning Your Skills

Internship and Externships

As discussed in Chapter Two, internships are often a common feature of women's studies programs and undergraduate education in general. Approximately 45 percent of our survey respondents replied that they completed an internship during the course of their undergraduate degree program in women's and gender studies. This percentage is close to the data collected from a 2008 survey by the National Association of Colleges and Employers (NACE). The NACE survey found that 50 percent of graduating students had participated in internships (Greenhouse 2010). Of the more than 400 respondents who answered the question of whether they received college credit for their internships, almost 60 percent answered yes. Many of the survey respondents interned at social justice organizations, such as domestic violence shelters and women's health organizations, but others completed internships for museums and archives, state and local government departments (e.g. Department of Transportation), market research and lobbying firms, high schools, and symphonies and philharmonics. One of the best ways to find out what job areas interest you is through an internship or externship. Internships can help you to find out what you want from a job and what you do not want. This is also a great time for one to gain skills and build their resumes with vital information that can set a person apart from other applicants out in the job market. Internships can also introduce you to mentors and social networks. If you are unable to get a position with the organization you interned with, your new colleagues often remember you and can be great resources for recommending you for other positions, forwarding job announcements, or getting you in touch with important gatekeepers.

Our survey respondents indicated many benefits of completing an internship:

- I developed a close and important relationship with my supervisor, who continued to mentor me after the internship ended . . .
- [I] learned how to present at conferences, many topics [on] sexuality and gender, peaceful alternatives, counseling, networking skills, and much more.

- I learned a ton about the type of work that interested me and also discovered there are areas of women's health and rights that are less interesting to me.
- [I] learned the intricacies of working in a nonprofit organization. Gained confidence and broadened my horizons . . .

Michele notes of her own experience:

During the summer between my sophomore year and junior year in college, I participated in a program called the Minority Leaders Fellowship Program. Through that program I had an opportunity to undertake a summer long internship at the main office of the National Organization for Women in Washington, DC. I was thrilled to work in this historic feminist organization. I remember soaking in everything about the organization. I worked on two projects. One was documenting and disseminating the work by

INTERNSHIP CONSIDERATIONS

While internships can be wonderful learning experiences that allow students to apply their feminist theory to practice, you should also be aware that some organizations view interns as "free labor." Some organizations may not have the commitment to deepening your learning experience while you are an intern. To a degree, you may be asked to assist your internship colleagues with menial tasks and labor. But, if your "dream" internship makes promises of vocational experience and an insider perspective on organizations policies, procedures, and politics, yet all you do is help with mailings alone in a room, you may want to speak with your internship coordinator (at the organization or the faculty liaison) about the placement. Not only will this save other women's and gender studies students from a similar experience, but it will allow you to exit a potentially problematic situation.

We also offer a word of caution about internships: if you do not take your internship seriously or fail to perform to the standards set by your department and/or the agency you are working with, this can have major negative ramifications. Not only may poor performance problematize relations between community associates and university/ college personnel and damage the department's reputation for later students, but it could mean the difference between an interview and a polite rejection at this organization if you were to apply for a position at a later date.

Southeast Asian women in the US who were working on issues of reproductive rights, domestic violence, and literacy in their communities. This task provided me an opportunity to become more familiar with the work of these communities in the US and globally. The second project was assisting the staff on the various projects they undertook on reproductive rights campaigns. This included working on press releases, preparing materials for fundraising events, reviewing legal cases happening around the country, and preparing materials to distribute at various events. These were all skills that I would draw on for research in college and later graduate school. It was one of my first professional positions, so I learned a lot about the social norms that govern offices. An internship experience can provide skill development, but it can also provide a sense of community. Being in that environment solidified my feminist identity at the time, helped me to feel less isolated at college, and helped me hone my research and writing skills. These laid the foundation for my later work on my senior project (see the Introduction) and graduate school. Although I wound up going to graduate school rather than the nonprofit world, I had a sense that I could also enjoy working for a nonprofit organization whose mission I valued.

FOR YOUR LIBRARY

See Stephen Greenhouse (2010) "The Unpaid Intern, Legal or Not," *New York Times*, April 2.

In this article, Greenhouse explores recent state and federal allegations that some unpaid internships at for-profit employers violate labor laws. The regulations regarding internships at nonprofit organizations differ, as volunteer work is allowed.

Besides interning for a local nonprofit, or securing a summer, fall, or spring semester internship with a national organization, you may also want to consider doing an international internship. If you are unable to participate in an education abroad experience, an internship for an international company or non-governmental agency may not only give you the work experience you seek in a field you are interested in, but also allow you to practice one of the language skills you gained during the course of your education.

You may also want to explore externships as a way to develop your foundation of skills. While the concept of an internship may be quite familiar to you, the term "externship" may not. According to the Career Development Center at the University of Arkansas website, an externship might be described as an "internship lite" (http://career.uark.edu/template/). Rather than lasting the course of a semester, an externship may only last for a few days and is more informational than experiential. While internships are done during the formal education process, some externships are conducted after graduation.

Externs may observe and interview professionals in the organizations whose careers interest them, but rarely do these opportunities offer academic credit or pay. Yet externships are a great way to get some insight into a career pathway without committing an extensive amount of time, labor, or even relocation. Externships not only afford students the opportunity to consider a career, but may be the deciding factor on whether to apply for a competitive internship or find another career field altogether.

Cheryl notes of her own experience with externships:

> I took this route after I finished my undergraduate degree. While browsing the career services at a university (not my own) near my family's home, I found an ad announcing an externship at the Children's Museum of Indianapolis. While the experience illuminated the fascinating world of working for a museum, it also made me realize this was not the field for me. But it did answer my question of whether or not I had the potential to educate others. The opportunities I had to lead tours of school age kids and keep their attention were turning points for me for continuing my education and wanting to teach.

Mentors

Mentors can play an important role in this process. We discussed mentoring briefly in Chapter Two, and here we emphasize that if you have not sought help from a mentor, this is a time to do so. Mentors can provide a good sounding board for bouncing off ideas about employment. They can ask adept questions that might help you see your skills in a new light. For example, when Cheryl was first going on the academic job market while finishing her Ph.D., she was able to learn the culture of this process through discussions with her formal advisor and her colleagues, as well as utilizing the resources of her university and professional association. Your mentor is an excellent person to ask for support, help, and guidance during this process. If you are considering asking them to be a reference or write a letter of recommendation, it is useful to start by asking, "Can you recommend me strongly?"

Thinking ahead about the timing of when you ask for a letter of reference is very important. Professors typically are swamped with requests from students beginning in October through early January because of the deadlines of graduate, law, and other distinguished scholarship applications. It won't always be possible to provide a month's notice for a letter of reference, but we encourage you to be organized and polite when you ask a faculty member or former employer for a letter for reference.

ETIQUETTE FOR A LETTER OF RECOMMENDATION FROM YOUR MENTOR, FORMER EMPLOYER, A PROFESSOR, OR GRADUATE STUDENT

- Try to provide all important information succinctly in one email.
- Give specific time frames about when the reference is due, the address and proper contact info, or the appropriate link for an online form.
- Send a current resume and even a few sentences about why this employment opportunity is of particular interest.
- Remind your recommender of the courses you took with them, the semester and year, any outstanding course work (tests, research papers, etc.).
- Remind your former employer of the kinds of skills your job entailed.
- Send a copy of the job description.
- Give at least four weeks between your request and the deadline.
- If the letter of recommendation cannot be submitted online, please give a pre-addressed stamped envelope to your professor. Not only does it save time for your recommender, but it saves the cost of postage.
- Send a thank you email or hand-written note to your recommender.
- Let them know if you wind up getting the position! They'll enjoy knowing they played a role in your success. Also, you may be asked by your advisor (or the department) to serve as a role model or a resource for other students. This may include speaking in classes or on panels, or serving as a mentor.

Financial Considerations

It's time to talk about money. Thinking and talking about money as graduation approaches can feel challenging. In this section we encourage you to think about your future in fiscally responsible ways. Walking along the journey to our ideal situation takes time and strategic planning. We highlight some key areas that will be useful for you to consider as you think about the role of resources and graduation (or changing positions).

There is the assumption by many that college is a time for young adults to extend adolescence, and sow their wild oats by indulging themselves— feeding their heads during the day (through reading theoretical treatises or sitting in lectures/seminars) and engaging in hedonistic pleasures at night. It is often perceived that students do not work or, if they do work, it is temporary until one achieves the career position their college degree has prepared them for. This, however, is not the reality. Many students work either on-campus or off-campus jobs or work during the summer in order to help with some of the expenses of attending college. Others obtain loans, scholarships, or other sources of funding that may require time or service after finishing one's degree. Many students may offset these costs with military or other types of service (AmeriCorps or Peace Corps). Americans are working longer and later than previous generations due to structural constraints (such as changes in Social Security eligibility and rising retirement ages), as well as through a desire to stay in the workforce for social, personal, and economic reasons.

Also, many of us have jobs that, while they are highly needed, are not always respected or given the credit they should have—this includes double-shift work as either parents or caregivers. There has been an emerging paradigm shift about having one "career" versus having multiple jobs, along with balancing work and home demands.

Increasingly, the pressure of life after college is affected by the amount of debt students amass through the course of their education. Debt may not only influence the type of employment you seek, but affects your life experiences and changes for years to come. Your student loan debt may be influenced by the type of institution you attend (private or public, community college, or Research I-type university), your institution's tuition and fees, and the type of loan you obtain. Almost two-thirds of four-year undergraduate students graduate with debt. Student loans average in the tens of thousands of dollars and upwards (Kantrowitz 2010).

Below we explore some options that students take.

AmeriCorps and Peace Corps

Both service in AmeriCorps and the US Peace Corps can defer student loan payment. According to the US AmeriCorps website (www.americorps. gov/for_individuals/benefits/benefits_ed_award.asp):

> The amount is now tied to the maximum amount of the US Department of Education's Pell Grant. For terms of service that are approved using 2009 funds (or earlier funds) the award continues to be $4,725 for a year of full-time service, and is pro-rated for part-time service based on the full-time amount. For terms of service that are supported with 2010 funds the award value increases to $5,350.00.

According to its website, besides offering payment deferment, the US Peace Corp offers a partial cancellation of student loan debt for students (www.peacecorps.gov/index.cfm?shell=learn.whyvol.finben):

> Fifteen percent of your Perkins loans can be cancelled upon the completion of each 365 days of service during your first two years of service, and 20 percent can be cancelled upon completion of each of the third and fourth years. Therefore, four full years of service would equal a 70 percent cancellation of your existing loan.

Be All That You Can Be: Student Soldier or Soldier Student?

One way not only to offset the costs of college, but gain some valuable skills and possibly find a career is through military service. Also, military service may be a requirement of citizenship in certain nations of the world. According to the US Bureau for Labor Statistics (2010), "more than 1.4 million people serve in the active Army, Navy, Marine Corps, and Air Force, and more than 1.0 million serve in their Reserve components and the Air and Army National Guard." Some students balance their education with their military service through reserve officer training corps (ROTC) and reserve memberships. Others may enlist after high school graduation and take college courses while fulfilling their duties. In fact, many military students can finish their degrees through a combination of courses offered onbase, online, or even after duty at local colleges and universities. The military continues to be an option for many men and women from under-resourced communities as a means to escape poverty.

You may check with your recruiter (or someone on base) for these options and methods, which may make college both affordable and do-able. While degree requirements vary by the branch of military service, usually enlisted personnel are required to have a high school diploma or its equivalent, while officers need Bachelor's or graduate degrees. Yet, like many other jobs, the various branches of the military often offer educational opportunities for personnel who want to advance in their careers or to improve or specialize their training. Some of the employment areas that are available through the military for either enlisted personnel or officers include: combat specialty occupations; construction occupations; electronic and electrical equipment repair personnel; engineering, science, and technical personnel; healthcare personnel; human resources development specialists; machine operator and production personnel; media and public affairs personnel; protective service personnel; support service personnel; transportation and material-handling specialists; vehicle and machinery mechanics; executive, administrative, and managerial officers; and human resource development officers (Bureau of Labor Statistics 2010).

After serving in the military, veterans are not only eligible for preference in hiring for many types of civil service jobs, but can also utilize other resources accorded to the military, such as healthcare, housing loans, and educational benefits through the US Veteran's Administration. As a women's and gender studies student, ideally your knowledge and talents can be well utilized. While issues of discrimination have a long and varied history in the United States military (e.g. from desegregation of the military to recent widespread allegations of sexual assault of women in the military), social issues dealing with gender discrimination and sexual harassment, the "don't ask, don't tell" policy, as well as larger foreign policy issues are part of the everyday fabric of this institution. As someone trained in women's studies, you not only may have the opportunity to have an impact on the day-to-day interactions of your colleagues and your unit or office, but you may have the opportunity to effect change for your military colleagues and for others through your involvement in this institution.

Transform Your World

There are a multitude of ways that graduates in women's and gender studies try to live their vision and enact social change. In the sections that follow, we explore some ways that graduates have created meaning in their personal and professional lives that extend their commitment to gender issues.

It's OK to Shift Gears

We think it is important not to get into a trap about thinking what might be a "good feminist" job, as sometimes happens to graduates. As Rebecca Mann stated in the last chapter—any job can be a feminist job depending on the mindset that you bring to it. For some people, a feminist job means working face-to-face with women and/or girls in a direct service capacity. For others, a feminist job means working in a feminist organization, and for others still, it means making a difference through daily interactions in which we seek change regarding issues of oppression. Our study suggests that graduates find themselves living their ideals in a myriad of ways. Yet in your journey to find an applied and or meaningful work environment, you may encounter situations in which your boss or your colleagues are not as supportive as you would expect them to be. Feminism, as we have previously explored, conceptually means a lot of different things to different people. Therefore, you may practice or believe in a different type of feminism than others. Unfortunately, this also means that the "enlightened" and progressive workplace you envisioned possibly varies greatly from your day-to-day experience. For example, in *Fast Girls, or Teenage Tribes and the Myth of the Slut*, Emily White (2003) shares her perspective of being hired at what she thought would be an empowering and progressive organization, and instead experienced a hostile workplace in which internalized sexism abounded.

This experience of working in an uncomfortable workplace was echoed by Judi Brown, a 2007 Political Science and Women's Studies graduate of UNLV.

> I worked for a health information technology organization for about a year. I thought the experience would be great, but the CEO and the woman who ran my department were sexist. I knew I had to leave the job after working there for three months. Plus the job wasn't challenging, but I was paid a lot of money to do that.

While Judi continued to work for the organization in order to make ends meet and support her partner, a graduate student at the time, she was actively looking for other opportunities to fuse her feminist ideals and activist principles. One of the resources that ultimately helped her find her current job was a conversation with one of her mentors:

> I called my mentor in tears (5th time) asking about job possibilities. He [had] heard that my current employer was looking for an assistant. I wasn't really excited about being an assistant; I was really disheartened with having my dual baccalaureate and not [being] able to utilize my education and talent on the job. I met with the President and CPO and she spoke with me for about 20 minutes. She told me that even if the position was open, I had more to offer than the position entailed. She valued my community involvement and my artistic abilities. I was eventually brought into the organization in January 2010 for a position as "Special Projects Coordinator." Primarily this job involves grant writing, events, and program management. The job is challenging and I have to make things up as I go along, but it fits with the organization. The CPO/President prides herself in running the foundation like a think tank. She has a strong personality and she took a chance on me, gave me an office, and even a Mac Book Pro. Everyday something is different and at the end of the day I know I am working to impact and change the lives of children in our community. If you feel good about the work you are doing, you don't mind doing the 10 to 15 hour days.

As Judi's experience shows, through time, diligence, and social networking you can change jobs or careers. Our suggestion upon encountering such an institution as your first place of employment is to weigh your options and have an escape plan at the ready. You may find that you can enact changes and create dialogue in your organization due to your gender and women's studies training. If not, you may have to come to the realization, after some difficult internal dialogues and consultations with friends and family, that either you are not the right fit for the job at this time, or that you may have to accept the situation as it is and move on to another opportunity either of your own creation (see Jennifer Pritchett's story) or for another organization or entity.

Building and Sustaining Feminist Communities

For Matt Ezzell, building (and sustaining) feminist community has been a high priority since finishing graduate school. He worked very hard as an undergraduate and graduate student at building a strong feminist community and set of allies. Now that he is a new professor, he acknowledges that building feminist community is more challenging, given his often seventy-hour-a-week job as a professor. Still, he sees it as essential:

> . . . feminism is a process, not an endpoint. It is an ongoing exercise struggle and process of self engagement and practice self reflexivity. I think for a lot of folks, if you don't have feminist community it is so difficult to sustain this critique. It's not an academic exercise for me.
>
> If you want to do this [feminist] work it's incredibly rewarding, [and] if you do this in an organized way, you will find feminist community. You can't do this by yourself.

Stay Involved: Clubs, Networks, Organizations

You may find yourself after graduation staying near your former institution, or, conversely you may move away. If you are staying in the same area, we suggest that you really push yourself to move beyond the college and/or university contacts that you may have developed. While it is very important to keep these ties, we think it is also useful to find other anchors that will help begin your professional and broader social network.

Conversely, moving to a new city can feel both exhilarating and daunting. You will also need to develop your networks there. There are several excellent organizations that help fill that gap, and these are places where you can meet people committed to empowering women and girls in various ways. If you did an internship for a nonprofit, for example, you may decide to find a chapter of that nonprofit where you are moving and decide to volunteer in your new place of residence.

The graduates surveyed are an actively engaged group in global civil society. They are involved in professional, social, and political organizations. They are also involved in clubs, loose affiliations, collectives, networks, and informal groups. Their interests span a wide array of interests, causes, and concerns. The top organizations that most graduates belong to are: professional, (explicitly) feminist, and women's organizations. The diversity of organizations and causes is quite breathtaking, ranging from Volunteer Simplicity Groups to the Human Rights Campaign. Graduates were not only active in well-defined organizations but, continuing the trend they showed as undergraduates, they have often created groups, clubs, and organizations to meet their needs. Many respondents indicated that they belonged to a variety of clubs, groups, and organizations. Membership and affiliation continues graduates' commitment to improving society and applying what they know outside of a formal classroom. In our survey, we created some basic categories that tried to capture the range of organizations a person might belong to or be active in. Below we highlight a few of our findings on membership and belonging by graduates:

- 57.8 percent of all graduates were active in a professional or work-related organization (e.g. American Bar Association).
- 21.9 percent of all graduates were active in a women's organization (e.g. American Association of University Women).
- 27 percent of all graduates were active in explicitly feminist identified organizations (e.g. National Organization for Women).
- 10 percent of all graduates were active in social networking organizations (e.g. Jaycees).
- 24 percent of all graduates were active in health and/or fitness-related clubs, leagues, and organizations (e.g. softball league).
- 12 percent of all graduates were active in faith-based organizations (e.g. Salvation Army).
- 7 percent of all graduates were active in family-related organizations (e.g. Parents, Families and Friends of Lesbian and Gays, P-FLAG).
- 20 percent of all graduates were active in social clubs (e.g. Stitch 'n' Bitch).
- 27 percent of all graduates were active in other groups, clubs, associations, organizations, and networks not indicated by our survey categories (e.g. a theater collective or the ACLU).

Joining networks, organizations, and clubs provides the potential for support, mentoring, skill-building, and sometimes just plain fun and relaxation! Deciding if you would like to become a member of organizations, groups, or clubs will be an important decision as you navigate life post-graduation.

Give Back

After graduation you might consider how closely you want to stay affiliated with your program. We would encourage you to think about the multiple ways that you might support your program, either through making a donation, mentoring current students, or coming back to share your story of success.

Once you graduate with your interest in women's and gender studies, consider supporting your institution, specifically your women's and gender studies unit. It is never too late to start a tradition of giving, and you can start out by committing to as little as $10 a year.

Keep in touch and make sure that they have your email address.

Letter-Writing on Behalf of Women's and Gender Studies Programs

As we've explore throughout this book, although women's studies is globally flourishing it still has its fair share of critics and detractors. So, the other reason why it is important that you stay connected is that you can lend your voice to support the unit if it comes under institutional or external threats. During the fall of 2009, we were shocked to hear that the UNLV Women's Studies department was threatened with being dismantled. Cheryl received her Ph.D. in sociology and taught in the Women's Studies program while a graduate student and considered WMST an important intellectual home. Michele had her first faculty position at UNLV. She was in the political science department and the first person to be hired for an appointment in women's studies.

A massive letter-writing campaign began to save the program. Scholars from around the country wrote on behalf of the unit. The factor that made the biggest difference, however, is the number of passionate students who received a major or minor from the program who wrote in to describe the excellent training. The decision to dismantle the department was reversed due to the outpouring of these letters. Small actions can lead to important changes!

We include Judi Brown's letter as one example of the ways you, as a graduate, may be called on to support your program.

Dr. Smatresk,

I am writing this letter to voice my support for the Women's Studies Department at the University of Nevada, Las Vegas. I am a UNLV graduate (2007) with a Dual Bachelor's degree in Women's Studies and Political Science. My education in Women's Studies has served me well in my post-graduate work and has been considered an asset by employers. The Department also inspired me to get involved in my community, while encouraging others to do so. If the Department is eliminated, the University's commitment to diversity and inclusion will surely suffer, as well as its ability to remain a competitive institution of higher education.

The growing demand for individuals who are armed with the rhetorical prowess to defend concepts relating to diversity and inclusion transcends private and public sectors. I have experienced this firsthand, having received an internship with Harrah's Entertainment in Community and Government Relations right out of college, where I worked closely with the VP of Diversity. My Women's Studies background helped me understand, articulate and convey diversity initiatives the company was promoting. Currently, I work in the non-profit sector. The volunteerism and scale of community involvement that I have participated in as a result of my Women's Studies education made me an attractive candidate to the organization. Additionally, students of other majors benefit from the Women's Studies Department, as well. Just one Women's Studies 113 class has the ability to open students' minds, foster civic and community engagement, and advocate tolerance and critical thinking, all of which are valuable twenty-first century skills.

In today's globalized economy, the value of a Women's Studies education is virtually limitless. Universities, employers, non-profit agencies and government entities all have missions that reflect commitments to diversity. Community reinvestment and corporate social responsibility departments and programs thrive in various industries, and Women's Studies graduates are fitting into new and emerging roles across sectors. UNLV would be eliminating decades of progress and reducing its ability to produce competitive graduates if Women's Studies is cut.

I hope this testimony helps you understand how immensely important this Department is to UNLV's reputation and the quality of students graduating with the skills to compete in a globalized world. Thank you for your time.

Judi Brown

Start a Nonprofit Organization

We met Kimberly Wilson in the last chapter. She began her yoga studio on a shoe-string budget and turned her passions for empowering women into a successful career as yoga teacher, motivational speaker, and author. She is always looking for ways to serve women and girls that highlight issues of creativity and leadership. After several successful years as a business owner, she wanted to do more for the community. At first she and her team began a program for at-risk teenage girls to come to her yoga studio for weekend workshops. She and her team, however, wanted to create more structure and visibility for empowering women. Over several years, she created a foundation, the Tranquil Space Foundation, to do more work in the community than her for-profit-based business could.

Tranquil Space Foundation focuses on expanding opportunities for girls and women to develop their inner voice through yoga, creativity, and leadership activities. Its signature program, TranquilTeens, provides workshops for girls in grades nine through twelve through partnerships with schools and community organizations. The foundation has also recently added Tranquil Women to support women in the DC area.

STAY CONNECTED: FEMINIST MEDIA: MAGAZINES, BLOGS, WEBSITES, OH, MY!

How will you continue to stay active and abreast of issues once you graduate? Once you leave college you will not have the luxury of finding out about the latest feminist-inspired play or women's activism happening in Peru. You also will find that your friends will be busy with their lives, and you may find yourself separated. If your institution does not have an alumni network, offer to start one. There is a wealth of feminist magazines (*Ms.*, *Bitch*, and *Bust*, for instance) and many feminist blogs to choose from to stay informed. There is no reason not to stay connected to your interests.

Tranquil Space also gives money to women-focused organizations that resonate and align with its overall mission.

After graduation (or even while in school), you may have a desire to put your interests into action through creating a nonprofit organization/foundation. It can sound daunting, but remember, nonprofit organizations can dramatically range in size from two people to 2,000. See Kimberly's *Tranquilista* (2010) for an excellent overview on starting a nonprofit.

Conclusion

It has been our pleasure to travel with you on the wonderful journey that you have taken with this book. We hope you now can fully imagine what we always say to students interested in women's and gender studies—women's studies can go anywhere and belongs everywhere!

We have tried to provide many of the tools, skills, and resources that will support you to take your place in a long line of women's and gender studies graduates who have traveled the same path. There is so much opportunity that awaits you. We believe that the world needs your courage, vitality, insights, and creativity in order to make many of the changes that you have thought about in your classes. Stay true to your values, affirm your truth, and know your contribution is important.

YOUR TURN

Seek Out Exemplars

Select women and men whose careers you admire and research their trajectory. Some of them may have had opportunities and resources not available to you (e.g. family money/social connections, living in a specific historical moment, etc.), but use your best critical analytical skills to map out what aspects of these careers are replicable and set some goals of your own—and tell your family and friends about it!

Researching Your Rights

It is important for us to know our rights when we feel threatened or vulnerable on the job. Unfortunately, it is one thing to know you have rights, but another to know where to go for help and resources (people and organizations) that may be able to provide assistance. Hopefully, you will never need to use the information from this assignment, but it could help you, your colleagues, or your family in the future. Consider this exercise an important part of your preparation for employment opportunities. Below we have posed pertinent questions about what your rights are in the workplace. You can use some of the websites and books listed in this chapter and/or the references to help guide you.

- What is legal and not legal for potential employers to ask you during an interview?

- What are your basic rights in terms of sexual harassment and labor organizing?

- Who do you contact if you feel you have experienced sexual harassment, a hostile workplace, or discrimination based on union membership?

- Do you live in a right-to-work state? If so, what does that mean?

- Where might you go for more information?

- What are the local, state, and national organizations that can help?

- If you are not living in your country of origin, what are your rights in the country in which you work?

APPENDIX
A RESEARCH NOTE

In order to gain information about the types of career and employment paths people who graduate with a concentration in women's and gender studies have pursued during the past fifteen years (1995–2010), we employed a multiple-method approach for data collection. Prior to initiating the research, Institutional Review Board approval was obtained concurrently through UNC, Chapel Hill (Study #10–0107) and Minnesota State University, Mankato (Study #5504). Research participants consisted of adults (eighteen years of age or older) who graduated with a major, minor, or concentration in women's or gender studies from a college or university either in the United States or internationally. Those who participated in the study were informed on the research mandates of confidentiality, voluntary participation, and the ability to exit the study at any point through the webpage prior to beginning the survey questionnaire. Participants implied consent by proceeding to the survey.

The Survey

Data about women's and gender studies undergraduates was obtained through the use of two research methodologies. The first research method employed was an online survey using Survey Monkey™. The survey was launched on February 9, 2010 and was closed on August 21, 2010.

Participants were selected through a convenience or snowball sampling approach. Respondents either were informed of the survey through an email that was sent to the undergraduate department and program heads of active women's and gender studies departments and programs from which they graduated, or through notices posted on our behalf through various organizations and individuals on the social networking site Facebook.

There is no one standardized list of all women's and gender programs and departments globally. We primarily relied on the lists of programs and departments maintained through NWSA's website, which are all located in the United States. We sent an email to every institution listed that offered any women's and gender studies curricula at the undergraduate level. We also had our research assistant conduct multiple online searches of women's and gender studies programs outside of the US. She heavily relied on the Women's Studies Programs, Departments, & Research Centers' website: http://userpages.umbc.edu/~korenman/wmst/programs. html. This website is maintained by Joan Korenman, Professor Emerita of English, and Affiliate Professor Emerita of Women's Studies at the University of Maryland, Baltimore County (UMBC).

Because it was important to us to represent as many non-US schools as possible, we also asked programs, centers, and departments outside the US to send information about their program and their students. Department chairs and program heads received a letter that explained our research, included our IRB numbers and contained information to send to their alumni. By contacting all active programs and departments, a purposive non-random sample was obtained.

Department chairs and program heads were asked to send an email with the survey (as a link), with a brief note from us, to the alumni of the program. Besides the survey link, participants also received information about the opportunity to be invited to a Facebook group called "Women's Studies Students: School and Career."

Multiple emails were sent (if we received no response) and many phone calls were made to programs and departments to encourage as wide a participation rate of institutions as possible. We received many emails from faculty and staff members that said one of following three things: (1) the major or minor was no longer offered, (2) the department or unit had no working alumni list and was not able to create one in a timely manner, (3) the information that they ever offered a program was incorrect. As we went through the process, institutions were marked off our list as unable to participate. Occasionally, in the case of reason (2), the director or program head was able to send a request to the college or university's development director to ask that our material be forwarded through whatever alumni lists the development office might have on file. We frequently asked former students, colleagues, and associates if they would directly post our link to the survey on their personal Facebook pages. We also asked colleagues to help us spread the word to programs and departments that were unresponsive.

Ultimately, more than 1,000 participants initiated the study, and more than 900 completed it. Graduates in this survey represent over 125 institutions. The major areas of the survey included general demographic questions (e.g. age, sex, gender, racial/ethnic identity, country of origin, religious background and current practices, parental education, current marital and family status, mentors), the characteristics of the participant's undergraduate degree experience (highest degree, year that undergraduate degree was completed, age at beginning and end of degree, other degrees obtained, type of degree—major, minor, concentration—name and location of college or university for the women's and gender studies degree, international educational opportunities, internships, and involvement with on/off campus activism activities), and life after graduation (contact with department or program, involvement with organizations and or activism, opinion of preparation for the job market, assessment of the top skills and concepts learned as part of the degree, as well as any advice for potential women's and gender studies students).

The Interviews

The second research method employed was a short open-ended interview (either face to face or via telephone) with survey participants who contacted the authors of this study through the email address posted at the end of the survey. At the end of the online survey, respondents were given the opportunity to contact the principal investigators if they were interested in being interviewed about their experiences of being a women's and gender studies graduate. The email address listed was to our research assistant. The research assistant would then forward names of potential interviewees to us. Interested participants were sent a letter electronically regarding their participation in the study, their time availability, as well as a request for the participant to indicate three topic areas they were interested in providing more information about than was provided in the survey. The respondents were then asked to provide in the subject line of their response email "Women's and Gender Studies Graduate Interview." As the survey is anonymous, these respondents were asked to provide the authors some demographic and locating information, such as name, the name of the institution in which they graduated with their women's and gender studies degree, and their current employment position.

During the course of the interview, respondents were also asked to elaborate on one or several subject areas from the survey. Women's and gender studies students may have been asked questions ranging from tips for faculty about advising, mentoring, or providing career advice to women's and gender studies students; social networks and other information important for the respondent's first position that utilized their women's and gender studies major or minor; what was special and unique about their women's studies classroom experience; what information did the respondent wish they knew or planned for prior to graduation; what had changed in the participant's viewpoint of living their feminism/ women's studies ideals since leaving school; what insight or "ahas" were gained from the respondent's internship or service learning opportunities; how had the respondent applied skills and concepts from their degree into any research projects or career experiences; and who were the participant's mentors and unexpected allies since graduation. We used these interviews to select the graduate profiles highlighted in Chapter Five.

The Facebook Page and Informal Interviews

Our intention for the Facebook group was to create an online community for people interested in feminism, women's issues, and former women's and gender studies students. We created it as a space for discussion, networking, and general camaraderie. So the group consists of many people who took our survey, people who did not meet our graduation requirement (graduated too early—before 1995—to take the survey), and some faculty and staff members who were interested in our research. Before long, as we were writing drafts of several chapters, we found ourselves asking this agreeable group questions about themes in the book (e.g. "What's unique about the women's studies classroom?") and receiving prompt feedback on our ideas. We found this experience facilitated a novel and engaging way to solicit advice and support from a community of experts while writing. They kept us inspired!

Besides survey participants and the Facebook group, we both actively contacted colleagues and former students for comments and information regarding international education, business ownership, civic education, and human resource issues. Prior to being interviewed, participants gave verbal consent. We also spoke informally to employers and women's and gender studies program and department heads.

NOTES

1 Some of the related fields include Africana Women's Studies; Ethnic and Women's Studies; Feminist Gender Studies; Feminist, Gender, and Sexuality Studies; Feminist Studies; Gender Studies; Gender and Sexuality Studies; Gender and Women's Studies; Multicultural and Gender Studies; Study of Women and Gender; Women and Ethnic Studies; Women and Gender Studies; and Women, Gender, and Sexuality Studies (Kimmich 2009). Throughout the book we use "women's and gender studies" as an inclusive term where possible and to note the historical development of this interdisciplinary field. We also address the evolution of women's and gender studies in Chapter One.

2 Emotion management and emotion labor are sociological concepts largely developed by Arlie Hochschild (1979, 1983). Drawing upon Irving Goffman's concept of "impression management," Hochschild explored how emotions may be manipulated or invoked to either suit the situation at hand or to intentionally change one's own perspective. Emotion labor is often expected based on one's positionality (i.e., gender, age, sexuality, race/ethnicity, and parent status). For more information, see Irving Goffman (1959) *Presentation of Self in Everyday Life;* Arlie Hochschild (1979) *Emotion Work, Feeling Rules, and Social Structure* and (1983) *The Managed Heart: Commercialization of Human Feeling.* You may find yourself having to manage and respond to other people's perceptions of you because of your interest in women's and gender studies. You may find that people make assumptions about your sexual identity and political beliefs. We discuss these issues in depth in Chapter Three.

3 A senior project at Bard is the equivalent of an honors thesis at other institutions.

4 The abortion wars of the late 1980s and early 1990s were a time of public activism on a national, state, and local level in the US over the continued legality of abortion. In 1973, the US Supreme Court affirmed women's access to legal abortion in *Roe*

v. Wade. Ever since that decision, pro-life (or anti-choice) activists have mobilized in order to challenge this verdict. Organizations such as Operation Life helped stage protests ranging from blockades of abortion and reproductive health clinics to large-scale demonstrations in Washington. Conversely, pro-choice (or anti-life) activists responded to threats against clinics (and practitioners) in their own right. For an excellent analysis, see Carol Mason (2002) *Killing for Life: The Apocalyptic Narrative of Pro-Life Politics.*

5   We note the few occasions when we use a pseudonym to protect the confidentiality of an interviewee.

6   The term "pedagogy" refers to theories about teaching and learning; "feminist pedagogy" has been the preferred term in women's studies.

7   This slogan was used as part of a popular advertising campaign for Virginia Slims cigarettes. It involved targeting the generation of young women who were influenced by the second wave of the women's liberation movement. While the goal of the original marketing campaign was to encourage women to associate smoking with emancipation, we've decided to reclaim the message and use it for our own goals.

8   This figure is based on a National Center for Education Statistics (NCES) 2003 report on post-secondary faculty at degree-granting institutions (see www.nwsa.org/projects/mapping.php).

9   See Wendy Kolmar and Frances Bartkowski (2010) *Feminist Theory: A Reader*, 3rd Edition, Columbus, OH: McGraw Hill.

10 See Mary Daly (1993) *Beyond God the Father: Toward a Philosophy of Women's Liberation and Christ*, Boston: Beacon Press. Carol Christ (Ed.) (1992) *Womanspirit Rising: A Feminist Reader in Religion*, New York: HarperOne.

11 Praxis has its roots in ancient philosophy and the writings of Aristotle. Later it was associated with nineteenth-century Marxist thought, as well as with twentieth-century neo-Marxist writers such as Georg Lukács and Paulo Freire.

12 Some of the major feminist theoretical perspectives include: liberal (oppression is largely based on structural inequality), radical (oppression is rooted in patriarchy), Marxist/socialist (oppression can be linked with economic systems). For excellent references, see Rosemarie Putnam Tong (2008) *Feminist Thought: A More Comprehensive Reader*, New York: Westview Press; and Kolmar and Bartkowski's (2010) *Feminist Theory: A Reader*. These texts not only provide an overview of the major perspectives, but give examples of key feminist writings that exemplify the perspectives.

13 Here is a sampling of organizations in professional disciplines that promote gender equity:

> Feminist Philosophers: http://feministphilosophers.wordpress.com/
> Western Association of Women Historians: www.wawh.org/
> Association of Women in Psychology: www.awpsych.org/
> Organization of Women Architects: www.owa-usa.org/
> Women in Science and Engineering (various websites):
> http://cs-www.cs.yale.edu/homes/tap/sci-women-groups.html

14 This can be especially true for students attending research-intensive universities.

15 The use of the word "female" is intentional here.

16 E. Koyama (2003) "Transfeminist Manifesto," in R. Dicker and A. Piepmeier (Eds.) *Catching a Wave: Reclaiming Feminism for the 21st Century*, Boston: Northeastern University Press.

17 Unfortunately, we did not inquire on the survey as to whether students declared their major/minor/concentration prior to attending college or university, after their first women's and gender studies course, or during their matriculation process.

18 Women's centers are found on college campuses and universities, and are institutional units designed to promote the empowerment of women faculty, administrators, staff, and students through programming that seeks to raise awareness about issues of inequality.

19 See the work of Australian women's studies researcher MaryAnn Dever (2004); *Ms.* magazine's ongoing collecting of responses by women's and gender studies graduates to the question: "What has women's studies meant to your life? And what are you currently doing with your women's studies degree?" (available at www.msmagazine. com); Barbara Luebke and Mary Reilly's (1995) *Women's Studies Graduates: The First Pioneers*, New York: Teachers College Press; and vignettes from various women's studies students presented in the various editions of *Women, Image and Realities: A Multicultural Anthology* by Amy Kesselman, Lily D. McNair and Nancy Schniedewind (Columbus, OH: McGraw Hill).

20 The Women's Studies department at Minnesota State University, Mankato, is situated in the College of Social and Behavioral Sciences.

21 Adrienne Rich (1979) "Claiming an Education," reprinted in S. Shaw and J. Lee (Eds.) (2009) *Women's Voices, Feminist Visions: Classic and Contemporary Readings*, 4th edn, New York: McGraw-Hill.

22 For more information on the programs we highlight in this section see:

> Macquarie University: www.iws.mq.edu.au
> Spelman College: www.spelman.edu/academics/programs/women/index.shtml
> Swarthmore College: www.swarthmore.edu/x19973.xml
> University of Capetown, Middle Campus, South Africa:
> www.agi.ac.za/academic/undergraduate
> University of Maryland, College Park: www.womensstudies.umd.edu
> UNC, Chapel Hill: www.unc.edu/depts/wmst
> University of California, Santa Barbara: www.womst.ucsb.edu

23 This constitutes a partial list of such programs:

> Washington University's Women's, Gender and Sexuality Studies:
> http://ascc.artsci.wustl.edu/~women/wgs_undergrad.htm
> CSU Long Beach: www.csulb.edu/colleges/cla/departments/wgss
> Swarthmore College: www.swarthmore.edu/x19973.xml
> University of Kansas: www.womensstudies.ku.edu
> University of Cincinnati: www.artsci.uc.edu/womens_studies
> University of Minnesota: http://gwss.umn.edu
> Wesleyan College: www.wesleyan.edu/fgss
> New York University: http://genderandsexuality.as.nyu.edu/page/undergraduate

24 Pivotal texts and activists include Sojourner Truth (1851) "Ain't I a Woman"; bell hooks (1984) *Feminist Theory: From Margin to Center*; Rita Mae Brown's activism as a response to "the lavender menace" (purging of lesbians from NOW); the inspiring statement of the Combahee River Collective (1977); and Gloria Anzaldua (1987) *Borderlands*. These have challenged women's studies to listen to the voices of its marginalized members and to place their perspectives where they belong—in the center of theory, scholarship, and activism.

25 Some departments and programs do not have this requirement and instead work to develop course content that engages students with these issues in every class. Other departments and programs seek to do this, but also feel that it is important to provide classes that specifically focus on race, nationality, ethnicity, and other dimensions of social identity in upper-division courses.

26 See O. Brafman and R. Beckstrom (2006) *The Starfish and the Spider: The Unstoppable Power of Leaderless Organizations*, New York: Portfolio Hardcover.

27 New Leadership refers to leadership programs originally developed by the Center for American Women and Politics at Rutgers University in 1981. Typically, these programs feature a week-long residential experience in which college students and female activists in the community gain knowledge, experience, and mentoring in order to further their empowerment goals. See http://wrin.unlv.edu/new, http://appserv.mnstate.edu/whitede/conference/index.htm, or www.mankatoywca.org/womensleadership.php for more information.

28 See http://womenscenter.unlv.edu.

29 "Tip Drill" (2003) is a video that depicts several misogynist and demeaning images of women, including a man holding a credit card and simulating sliding it through the back of a woman's thong.

30 Later in this chapter, we discuss stereotypes and assumptions about women's and gender studies and students who choose this as their major.

31 This name is a pseudonym.

32 We will discuss the role of politics in the next section.

33 This was an actual comment that was said to our research assistant, Sarah "Tucker" Jenkins.

34 We are indebted to Christal Lustig for this insight.

35 Susan Faludi (1992) was one of the first authors to examine the various social forces that converged in attacking feminism and women's studies in *Backlash: The Undeclared War Against American Women*, Norwell, MA: Anchor.

36 See, for example, www.speech-topics-help.com/elevator-speech.html.

37 The closest kind of refrigerator magnet kit that might be suitable is one by Jessica Valenti, author of *Full Frontal Feminism*. We've heard that this kit exists but have not been able to locate one.

38 We have developed this list after looking at a wide array of assessment reports on the field of women's studies (see Levin 2007).

39 To protect the anonymity of survey respondents, we have chosen to remove identifying cities, names of local or state organizations, etc.

40 On December 6, 1989, Mark Lapine shot fourteen women in an engineering school in Montreal. He did this because he believed that women were overtaking men in engineering. This incident became known as the "Montreal Massacre" and had a

defining effect on generating national attention on gendered violence. Peter was in his last year of high school when this event happened, and by the time he got to university, he, along with many other students, found themselves primed to take on issues of sexual violence on campuses.

41 Ladyfest started in 2000 in Olympia, Washington. It is a community-based, not-for-profit global music and arts festival for female artists that features bands, musical groups, performance artists, authors, spoken word and visual artists, and workshops; it is organized by volunteers. All the proceeds are donated, and the Ladyfest events that have happened around the world are independently organized (see http://ladyfestten.com).

42 Proposition 8 (or the California Marriage Protection Act) was a ballot proposition and constitutional amendment passed in the November 2008, state election. The measure added a new provision, to the California Constitution, which provides that "only marriage between a man and a woman is valid or recognized in California" (see www.courtinfo.ca.gov/courts/supreme/highprofile/prop8.htm).

43 It is now increasingly common that high school students begin one business before they graduate.

REFERENCES

Aaron, J. and Walby, S. (Eds.). (1991). *Out of the Margins: Women's Studies in the Nineties*. Bristol, PA: Falmer Press.

American Association of University Women Educational Foundation. (2006). *Drawing the Line: Sexual Harassment on Campus*. Washington, DC: AAUW.

AmeriCorps. (2010). "Segal AmeriCorps Education Award." Retrieved August 1, 2010, from www.americorps.gov/for_organizations/manage/commcenter_archive.asp.

Andreeva, N. (2009). "HBO Signing Up for Women's Studies," *Reuters*, April 15, 2009. Retrieved November 13, 2009, from www.reuters.com/article/televisionNews/idUSTRE53E11720090415.

Anzaldua, G. (1987). *Borderlands: The New Mestiza/La Frontera*, 1st edn. San Francisco: Aunt Lute Books.

Aranti, L. (2009). "A New Crop of Farmers," *The Washington Post*, June 28, 2009. Retrieved June 28, 2009, from www.washingtonpost.com/wpdyn/content/article/2009/06/27/AR2009062702386.html.

Baxandall, R. and Gordon, L. (Eds.). (2001). *Dear Sisters: Dispatches from the Women's Liberation Movements*. New York: Basic Books.

Berger, M. (1998). "Workable Sisterhood: A Study of the Political Participation of Stigmatized Women with HIV/AIDS," unpublished dissertation, the University of Michigan.

——. (2004). *Workable Sisterhood: The Political Journey of Stigmatized Women with HIV/AIDS*. Princeton, NJ: Princeton University Press.

Berger, M. and Guidroz, K. (Eds.). (2009). *The Intersectional Approach: Transforming the Academy through Race, Class, and Gender*. Chapel Hill, NC: The University of North Carolina Press.

Bolles, R. (2010). *What Color is Your Parachute? 2010. A Practical Manual for Job-Hunters and Career Changers*. Berkeley, CA: Ten Speed Press.

266

Boston Women's Health Collective and Norsigian, J. (2005). *Our Bodies, Ourselves: A New Edition for a New Era*, 4th edn. Oneonta, NY: Touchstone Press.

Bourgeois, T. (2007). *Her Corner Office: A Guide to Help Women Find a Place and a Voice in Corporate America*. 2nd edn. Dallas: Dallas Books.

Boxer, M. J. (2001). *When Women Ask the Questions: Creating Women's Studies in America*. Baltimore: The Johns Hopkins University Press.

Brafman, O. and Beckstrom, R. (2006). *The Starfish and the Spider: The Unstoppable Power of Leaderless Organizations*. New York: Portfolio Hardcover.

Braithwaite, A., Heald, S., Luhmann, S. and Rosenberg, S. (2005). *Troubling Women's Studies: Pasts, Presents, and Possibilities*. Toronto: Sumach Press.

Bravo, E. (2007). *Taking on the Big Boys: or Why Feminism is Good for Families, Business, and the Nation*. New York: The Feminist Press at CUNY.

Brooks, K. (2009). *You Majored in What? Mapping your Path from Chaos to Career*. New York: Viking.

Buckingham, M., and Clifton, D. (2001). *Now, Discover your Strengths*. New York: The Free Press.

Bureau of Labor Statistics, US Department of Labor. (2008). "Number of Jobs Held, Labor Market Activity, and Earnings Growth among the Youngest Baby Boomers: Results from a Longitudinal Survey." Retrieved August 1, 2010, from www.bls.gov/news.release/pdf/nlsoy.pdf.

——. (2009). "College Enrollment and Work Activity of 2008 High School Graduates," Bureau of Labor Statistics news release. Retrieved February 26, 2010, from www.bls.gov/news.release/hsgec.nr0.htm.

——. (2010). "Occupational Outlook Handbook, 2010–11 Edition, Job Opportunities in the Armed Forces." Retrieved August 1, 2010, from www.bls.gov/oco/ocos249.htm.

Business and Professional Women's Foundation. (2007). "101 Facts on the Status of Working Women." Retrieved August 1, 2010, from www.bpwusa.org/files/public/101FactsOct07.pdf.

Byrd, P. R., Cole, J. and Guy-Sheftall, B. (Eds.). (2009). *I Am Your Sister: Collected and Unpublished Writings of Audre Lorde*. Oxford: Oxford University Press.

Cameron, J. (2002). *The Artist's Way: A Spiritual Path to Higher Creativity*. New York: Tarcher.

Carter, J. (2007). *Double Outsiders: How Women of Color Can Succeed in Corporate America*. St. Paul, MN: JIST Books.

Chicago Women in Trades. (2010). "Women in Skilled Trades Project." Retrieved August 1, 2010, from www.chicagowomenintrades.org/artman/publish/article_252.shtml.

Christ, C. (Ed.). (1992). *Womanspirit Rising: A Feminist Reader in Religion*. New York: HarperOne.

Cobble, D. (2007). *The Sex of Class: Women Transforming Labor*. Ithaca, NY: Cornell University Press.

Code of Federal Regulations. (1980). Title 29: Section 1604.11a. 45 Federal Register 74677, November 10, 1980.

Collins, P. (1990). *Black Feminist Thought: Knowledge, Consciousness, and the Politics of Empowerment*. Boston: Unwin Hyman.

Collins, P. Hill. (1993). "Toward a New Vision: Race, Class, and Gender as Categories of Analysis and Connection," in T. Ore (Ed.) (2008) *The Social Construction of Difference and Inequality*, 4th edn. Columbus, OH: McGraw-Hill.

Combahee River Collective. (1977). *Combahee River Collective Statement*. Boston: The Combahee River Collective.

Connell, R. W. and Messerschmidt, J. (2005). "Hegemonic Masculinity," *Gender and Society*, 19: 6, pp. 829–859.

Costa, T. (2010). *Farmer Jane: Women Changing the Way We Eat*. Layton, UT: Gibbs Smith.

Daly, M. (1993). *Beyond God the Father: Toward a Philosophy of Women's Liberation*. Boston: Beacon Press.

de Beauvoir, S. (1965). *The Second Sex*. New York: Bantam Books.

Dever, M. (2004). "Women's Studies and the Discourse of Vocationalism: Some New Perspectives," *Women's Studies International Forum*, 27: 5 & 6, pp. 475–488.

Dicker, R. and Piepmeier, A. (Eds.). (2003). *Catching a Wave: Reclaiming Feminism for the 21st Century*. Northeastern, MA: Northeastern University Press.

Doyle, S. (2010). "Career Tests—Taking a Career Test." Retrieved August 1, 2010, from http://jobsearch.about.com/od/careertests/a/careertests.htm.

Faludi, S. (1992). *Backlash: The Undeclared War Against American Women*. Norwell, MA: Anchor.

Fausto-Sterling, A. (1993). "The Five Sexes: Why Male and Female Are Not Enough," *The Sciences*, March/April, pp. 20–24.

Firestone, S. and Koedt, A. (Eds.) (1970) *Notes from the Second Year: Women's Liberation: Major Writings of the Radical Feminists*. Shulamith Firestone and Anne Koedt.

Freedman, E. (2002). *No Turning Back: The History of Feminism and the Future of Women*. New York: Ballantine Books.

Freeman, J. (1968). "The BITCH Manifesto," in S. Firestone and A. Koedt (Eds.) (1970) *Notes from the Second Year: Women's Liberation: Major Writings of the Radical Feminists*. Shulamith Firestone and Anne Koedt.

——. (1970). "The Tyranny of Structurelessness," in R. Baxandall and L. Gordon (Eds.) (2001) *Dear Sisters: Dispatches from the Women's Liberation Movements*. New York: Basic Books.

——. (1976). "TRASHING: The Dark Side of Sisterhood," *Ms.*, April, pp. 49–51, 92–98.

——. (1994). *Women: A Feminist Perspective*. Columbus: McGraw-Hill.

——. (1996). "We've Come a Long Way . . .?" *PS: Political Science and Politics*, 2: pp. 182–183.

Friedan, B. (1963). *The Feminine Mystique*. New York: W. W. Norton and Company.

Friere, P. (2001). *Pedagogy of the Oppressed*. New York: Continuum.

Frye, M. (1983). *The Politics of Reality*. Trumansburg, NY: The Crossing Press.

Garrett, C. D. and Rogers, M. (2002). *Who's Afraid of Women's Studies?* Lanham, MD: AltaMira Press.

Goffman, I. (1959). *Presentation of Self in Everyday Life*. New York: Doubleday.

Greenhouse, S. (2010). "The Unpaid Intern, Legal or Not," *New York Times*, April 2, 2010. Retrieved August 2, 2010, from www.nytimes.com/2010/04/03/business/03intern.html#.

Guy-Sheftall, B. (2009). "Forty Years of Women's Studies," *Ms.*, Spring, pp. 56–57.

Hesse-Biber, S. N. and Leavy, P. L. (2007). *Feminist Research Practice: A Primer*. Thousand Oaks, CA: SAGE.

HigherEdJobs.com. (2010). "Administrative Positions." Retrieved August 1, 2010, from www.higheredjobs.com/admin.

Hochschild, A. (1979). "Emotion Work, Feeling Rules, and Social Structure," *American Journal of Sociology*, 85, pp. 551–575.

———. (1983). *The Managed Heart: Commercialization of Human Feeling*. Berkeley, CA: University of California Press.

Hollibaugh, A. (2000). *My Dangerous Desires: A Queer Girl Dreaming Herself Home*. Durham, NC: Duke University Press.

hooks, b. (1981). *Ain't I a Woman: Black Women and Feminism*. Cambridge, MA: South End Press.

———. (1984). *Feminist Theory: From Margin to Center*. Cambridge, MA: South End Press.

———. (1992) *Black Looks: Race and Representation*. Cambridge, MA: South End Press.

———. (1994). *Outlaw Culture: Resisting Representations*. New York: Routledge.

———. (2000). *Feminism is for Everybody: Passionate Politics*. Boston: South End Press.

Howe, F. (Ed.). (2000). *The Politics of Women's Studies: Testimony from the Thirty Founding Mothers*. New York: The Feminist Press.

Hunte, D. (1991). "Women's Studies as a Growth Process," in A. Kesselman, L. D. McNair and N. Schniedewind (Eds.) (2008) *Women: Images and Realities: A Multicultural Anthology*, 4th edn. New York: McGraw Hill.

Kantrowitz, M. (publisher). (2010). "The Smart Student Guide to Financial Aid," FinAid Page, LLC. Retrieved February 26, 2010, from www.finaid.org/loans/.

Kesselman, A., McNair, L., and Schniedwind, N. (2008). *Women Images and Realities: A Multicultural Anthology*, 4th edn. Columbus: McGraw Hill.

Kimmel, M. (1994). "Masculinity as Homophobia: Fear, Shame, and Silence in the Construction of Gender Identity," in Paula Rothenberg (Ed.) (2003) *Race, Class, and Gender in the United States: An Integrated Study*, 6th edn. New York: Worth Publishers.

———. (1996). "Men and Women's Studies: Premises, Perils, and Promise" in N. Hewitt, J. O'Barr, and N. Rousebaugh (Eds.) (1996) *Talking Gender: Public Images, Personal Images, and Political Critiques*. Chapel Hill, NC: University of North Carolina Press.

Kimmich, A. (2009). "Undergraduate Programs," *Ms.*, Spring, p. 62.

Kolmar, W. and Bartkowski, F. (2010). *Feminist Theory: A Reader*, 3rd edn. Columbus, OH: McGraw Hill.

Koyama, E. (2003). "Transfeminist Manifesto," in R. Dicker and A. Piepmeier (Eds.) (2003) *Catching a Wave: Reclaiming Feminism for the 21st Century*. Boston: Northeastern University Press.

Levin, A. (2007). "Questions for a New Century: Women's Studies and Integrative Learning," *A Report from the National Women's Studies Association*. College Park, MD: NWSA.

Lorber, J. (1994). *Paradoxes of Gender*. New Haven, CT: Yale University Press.

Lorde, A. (1978). *The Black Unicorn*. New York: Norton.

———. (1982). *Zami: A New Spelling of My Name*. Trumansburg, NY: Crossing Press.

———. (1984). *Sister Outsider*. Trumansburg, NY: Crossing Press.

Luebke, B. and Reilly, M. (1995). *Women's Studies Graduates: The First Generation*. New York: Teachers College Press.

Magezis, J. (1997). *Women's Studies (Teach Yourself)*. Columbus, OH: McGraw-Hill.

Martin, E. C & Sullivan, J. C. (Ed.). (2010). *Click: When We Knew We Were Feminists*. Berkeley, CA: Seal Press.

Mason, C. (2002). *Killing for Life: The Apocalyptic Narrative of Pro-Life Politics*. Cornell, NY: Cornell University Press.

McCaughey, M. (2009). "Sticks and Stones," *Ms.*, Spring, p. 70.

McIntosh, P. (1988). "White Privilege and Male Privilege: A Personal Account of Coming to See Correspondences through Work in Women's Studies," Working Paper #189. Wellesley, MA: Wellesley College Center for Research on Women.

Messer-Davidow, E. (2002). *Disciplining Feminism: From Social Activism to Academic Discourse*. Durham, NC: Duke University Press.

Messner, M. A., Sabo, D. F. (1994). *Sex, Violence, and Power in Sports: Rethinking Masculinity*. Trumansburg: NY: Crossing Press.

Meyers, N. (director). (2003). *Something's Gotta Give* [motion picture]. Columbia Pictures Corporation.

Minnesota State University, Mankato. (2008). "Advising, General Education & Cultural Diversity," in *Undergraduate Bulletin 2008–2009*. Mankato: Minnesota State University. Retrieved November 15, 2009, from www.mnsu.edu/supersite/academics/bulletins/undergraduate/2008-2009/generalinfo/generaleduandhonors.pdf.

National Center for Education Statistics. (2007). "Digest of Education Statistics (Annual Report)." Washington, DC. Retrieved September 14, 2009, from http://nces.ed.gov/das/.

National Science Foundation, Division of Science Resources Statistics. (2009). "Doctorate Recipients from US Universities: Summary Report 2007–08. Special Report NSF 10–309." Arlington, VA: NSF. Retrieved August 1, 2010, from www.nsf.gov/statistics/nsf10309.

National Women's Studies Association. (2007). "Mapping Women's and Gender Studies Data Collection: Executive Summary." College Park, MD: NWSA. Retrieved August 1, 2010, from www.nwsa.org/projects/mapping.php.

Nelly. (2003). *Tip Drill* [music video].

Nichols, M. (director). (2003). *Angels in America* [motion picture]. Avenue Pictures Productions.

Økland, J. (2010). "How it happened that a country's public debate was focused on gender studies for months on end," May 10, 2010. Retrieved September 30, 2010, from www.gender.no/Open_dialogue/Gender_blog/8420.

Peacecorps. (2010). "Financial Benefits and Loan Deferment." Retrieved August 1, 2010, from www.peacecorps.gov/index.cfm?shell=learn.whyvol.finben.

Pipher, M. (2006). *Writing to Change the World*. New York: Riverhead Trade.

Radeloff, C. (2004). "Vectors, Polluters, and Murderers: HIV Testing toward Prostitutes and the State of Nevada," unpublished dissertation, University of Nevada, Las Vegas.

Rich, A. (1979). "Claiming an Education," in S. Shaw and J. Lee (Eds.) (2009) *Women's Voices/Feminist Visions: Classic and Contemporary Readings*, 4th edn. New York: McGraw-Hill.

Rivera, C. (2006). "A Women's Studies Graduate Goes to Africa," in A. Kesselman, L. D. McNair, and N. Schniedewind (2008) *Women: Images and Realities: A Multicultural Anthology*, 4th edn. New York: McGraw Hill.

Rosen, R. (2006). *The World Split Open: How the Modern Women's Movement Changed America*. New York: Penguin Press.

Roy, J. (2009). "Community College Programs," *Ms.*, Spring, p. 62.

Schneider, C. (2009). "Forward," in E. L. Dey et al. *Civic Responsibility: What Is the Campus Climate for Learning?* Washington, DC: Association of American Colleges.

Scott, J. W. (Ed.). (2008). *Women's Studies on the Edge*. Durham, NC: Duke University Press.

Segal, P. (director). (2000). *Nutty Professor II: The Klumps* [motion picture]. Universal Pictures.

Shaw, S., and Lee, J. (2009). *Women's Voices 4th edn. Feminist Visions: Classic and Contemporary Readings*. Columbus, OH: McGraw-Hill.

Shilts, R. (2007). *And the Band Played On: People, Politics, and the AIDS Epidemic, 20th Anniversary Edition*. New York: St. Martin's Griffin.

Shrewsbury, C. (1993). "What is Feminist Pedagogy?" *Women's Studies Quarterly* 21.3–4, pp. 8–16.

Silius, H. (2005). "The Professionalization of Women's Studies Students in Europe: Expectations and Experiences." in G. Griffin (Ed.) (2005) *Doing Women's Studies: Employment Opportunities, Personal Impacts, and Social Consequences*. London: Zed Books.

Stevenson, A., Elliot, J. and Jones, R. (Eds.). (2002). *The Oxford Color English Dictionary*, 2nd edn. Oxford: Oxford University Press.

Stewart, N. A. (2007). "Transform the World: What You Can Do With a Degree in Women's Studies," *Ms.*, Spring, pp. 65–66.

Sontag, S. (2001). *Illness as Metaphor and AIDS and Its Metaphors*. New York: Picador.

Thompson, S. (2002). "Becoming a Feminist Physician," in A., Kesselman, L. D. McNair, and N. Schniedewind (Eds.) (2008) *Women: Images and Realities: A Multicultural Anthology*, 4th edn. New York: McGraw Hill.

Tong, R. P. (2008). *Feminist Thought: A More Comprehensive Reader*. New York: Westview Press.

The University of Arkansas Career Development Center. (2008). "Externships/Job Shadowing." Retrieved August 1, 2010, from http://career.uark.edu/Students/Externships.aspx.

US Department of Education, National Center for Education Statistics. (2007). "Integrated Postsecondary Education Data System (IPEDS)." Retrieved November 10, 2009, from http://nces.ed.gov/ipeds/.

Valenti, J. (2007). *Full Frontal Feminism: A Young Woman's Guide to Why Feminism Matters*. Emeryville, CA: Seal Press.

Walker, T. (2000). "A Feminist Challenge to Community Service: A Call to Politicize Service Learning," in B. J. Balliet and K. Hefferman (Eds.) (2000) *The Practice of Change: Concepts and Models for Service-Learning in Women's Studies*. Washington, DC: American Association for Higher Education.

Weigman, R. (Ed.). (2002). *Women's Studies on Its Own: A Next Wave Reader in Institutional Change*. Durham, NC: Duke University Press.

West, C. and Zimmerman, D. (1987). "Doing Gender," *Gender and Society* 1: 125–151.

White, E. (2003). *Fast Girls: Teenage Tribes and the Myth of the Slut*. Berkley, CA: Berkley Trade.

Wilson, K. (2006). *Hip Tranquil Chick: A Guide to Life On and Off the Yoga Mat*. Novato, CA: New World Library.

——. (2010) *Tranquilsta: Mastering the Art of Enlightened Work and Mindful Play*. Novato, CA: New World Library.

INDEX